VERONICA FRANCO IN DIALOGUE

MARILYN MIGIEL

Veronica Franco in Dialogue

UNIVERSITY OF TORONTO PRESS
Toronto Buffalo London

Toronto Buffalo London
utorontopress.com

ISBN 978-1-4875-4258-0 (cloth)
ISBN 978-1-4875-4259-7 (EPUB)
ISBN 978-1-4875-4260-3 (PDF)

Library and Archives Canada Cataloguing in Publication

Title: Veronica Franco in dialogue / Marilyn Migiel.
Names: Migiel, Marilyn, 1954– author.
Series: Toronto Italian studies.
Description: Series statement: Toronto Italian studies | Includes bibliographical references and index.
Identifiers: Canadiana (print) 2021037800X | Canadiana (ebook) 20210378077 | ISBN 9781487542580 (cloth) | ISBN 9781487542597 (EPUB) | ISBN 9781487542603 (PDF)
Subjects: LCSH: Franco, Veronica, 1546–1591 – Criticism and interpretation.
Classification: LCC PQ4623.F6 Z65 2022 | DDC 851/.4–dc23

We wish to acknowledge the land on which the University of Toronto Press operates. This land is the traditional territory of the Wendat, the Anishnaabeg, the Haudenosaunee, the Métis, and the Mississaugas of the Credit First Nation.

University of Toronto Press acknowledges the financial support of the Government of Canada, the Canada Council for the Arts, and the Ontario Arts Council, an agency of the Government of Ontario, for its publishing activities.

Canada Council for the Arts
Conseil des Arts du Canada

Funded by the Government of Canada
Financé par le gouvernement du Canada

Canada

To William J. Kennedy, scholar, teacher, and colleague extraordinaire

Contents

Acknowledgments

In reflecting on the people who have made it possible for a book like *Veronica Franco in Dialogue* to come into existence, I have realized that a principal debt of gratitude goes to all the scholars who with their textual readings, historical research, and translations have expanded the field of Italian studies so that it includes many more women writers of the early modern period than it did when I first began my scholarly career. It is deeply satisfying to see that focusing on women writers is no longer an undertaking that places one at the margins of the profession.

I have been fortunate, in the course of writing this book, to receive generous commentary from friends, colleagues, and students. Special thanks go to the participants of our writing group: Kathleen Perry Long, Irene Eibenstein-Alvisi, Giulia Andreoni, Julia Karczewski, Riccardo Samà, and Magdala Jeudy. William J. Kennedy and Hannah Chapelle Wojciehowski provided important feedback on grant applications that helped me clarify the stakes of the project. Konrad Eisenbichler, Margaret Rosenthal, Michael Sherberg, and Janet Smarr offered helpful suggestions following my presentations at scholarly conferences. Reading Veronica Franco's poetry with students at Cornell University and Bucknell University and in Telluride Association Summer Programs always proved invigorating.

The two scholars who provided anonymous readers' reports to the University of Toronto Press offered invaluable comments that helped me strengthen the argumentation and the writing. Angela Wingfield's expert copy-editing was invaluable, especially because it saved me from some inadvertent errors. To Suzanne Rancourt I express my thanks for her having solicited such helpful readers' reports and for her having proposed the strikingly elegant image on the book jacket.

Thomas Gordon of the University of Manchester very kindly supplied information about the copy of Veronica Franco's *Terze rime* found in the John Rylands Library.

I gratefully acknowledge permission to reprint material that I published previously. Chapter 1 and a portion of the introduction are drawn from a revised version of my "Veronica Franco's Gendered Strategies of Persuasion: *Terze rime* 1 and 2" (© 2016 Johns Hopkins University Press). This article first appeared in *MLN* 131, no. 1 (January 2016): 58–73. The reading of *Terze rime* 13 in chapter 7 is a revised version of my analysis of that poem published in "Gender Studies and the Italian Renaissance," in *Interpreting the Italian Renaissance: Literary Perspectives*, edited by Antonio Toscano (Stony Brook, NY: Forum Italicum, 1991), 29–41.

The Italian text of Veronica Franco's *Terze rime* is quoted by permission of Ugo Mursia Editore, S.r.l. from Veronica Franco, *Rime*, edited by Stefano Bianchi, © 1995 Ugo Mursia Editore S.r.l. English translations of the same are quoted by permission of the University of Chicago Press from *Poems and Selected Letters* by Veronica Franco, edited and translated by Ann Rosalind Jones and Margaret F. Rosenthal, © 1998 The University of Chicago.

Veronica Franco in Dialogue is dedicated to William J. Kennedy, Avalon Foundation Professor Emeritus in the Humanities at Cornell University. Over the course of his distinguished career, in his impeccable scholarship and his inspired teaching, Bill has modelled for us how to read literary texts with precision and care and how to write about them in ways that will engage others effectively. A consummate gentleman as well as a consummate scholar, Bill has also modelled for us how to support others so that they can do their best work. Dedicating this book to him is a way to thank him not only for everything he has done for me but also for everything he has done to ensure that Renaissance studies continues to flourish.

Note on the Text and Translations of Veronica Franco's *Terze rime* (*Poems in Terza Rima*)

For the Italian text and the English translation of Veronica Franco's *Terze rime (Poems in Terza Rima*, 1575), I rely on *Poems and Selected Letters*, by Veronica Franco, edited and translated by Ann Rosalind Jones and Margaret F. Rosenthal (Chicago: University of Chicago Press, 1998). I document in footnotes the instances where I have modified Jones and Rosenthal's translation. I also indicate the instances in which I substitute my own translation for that of Jones and Rosenthal.

While it has been customary to use the Italian term *capitolo* (plural *capitoli*) when writing about Franco's poems in terza rima, I have opted to remain in English and speak about them as "poems." In citing passages of the poems, I give the poem number followed by the line numbers (e.g., 1.121–6 to indicate lines 121 through 126 in the first poem).

VERONICA FRANCO IN DIALOGUE

Introduction: What Do We See in Veronica Franco?

Twenty to thirty years ago, Veronica Franco (1546–91), courtesan and writer in sixteenth-century Venice, was a central figure in North American scholarship that focused on women's and gender studies in the Italian Renaissance.[1] Franco was also the subject of a 1992 theatre piece authored by the prominent Italian feminist writer Dacia Maraini – *Veronica, meretrice e scrittora* (*Veronica, Prostitute and Writress*) – and a popular 1998 film directed by Marshall Herskovitz, *Dangerous Beauty*.[2] In the last twenty years, however, as more works by other early modern women writers have been made available, and as scholars have dedicated their energies to these other women, Franco has received relatively little attention.[3]

1 Notable contributions include Rosenthal's prizewinning book, *The Honest Courtesan*; Jones and Margaret Rosenthal's translation of Franco's *Poems and Selected Letters*, ed. and trans. Ann Jones and Rosenthal; and the following scholarly essays: Jones, "City Women and Their Audiences; Adler, "Veronica Franco's Petrarchan *Terze Rime*"; Bassanese, "Private Lives and Public Lies"; Jones, "Eros Equalized"; Jones, "Designing Women"; Migiel, "Gender Studies and the Italian Renaissance"; Phillippy, "*Altera Dido*"; and Migiel, "Veronica Franco (1546–1591)."

2 Maraini, *Veronica, meretrice e scrittora*, published in English as *Veronica Franco: Courtesan and Poet*, trans. Campbell and Sbrocchi; *Dangerous Beauty*, dir. Marshall Herskovitz. As the title of the published English translation of Maraini's play does not capture the meaning of "meretrice" and the invented word "scrittora," I have translated the title as "Veronica, Prostitute and Writress."

3 Notable contributions to scholarship on Veronica Franco in the first two decades of the twenty-first century include Bassanese, "Veronica Franco's Poetics of Redemption"; Jaffe, with Colombardo, "Veronica Franca (1546–1591): The Unhappy Courtesan"; Robin, "Courtesans, Celebrity, and Print Culture"; Eibenstein-Alvisi, "Dialoguing with the Past"; Bassanese, "Defining Spaces: Venice in the Poetry of Gaspara Stampa and Veronica Franco"; Crivelli, "'A un luogo stesso per molte vie

With this book, *Veronica Franco in Dialogue*, I aim to bring Franco back into our discussions of Renaissance women writers. The study includes the first fourteen poems (out of twenty-five poems) in *Terze rime* (*Poems in Terza Rima*), which was published under her name in 1575. These poems feature her back-and-forth exchanges with an unknown male author, to whom poems 1, 4, 6, 7, 9, 11, and 14 are ascribed; the unknown male author might be a single male, multiple males, or possibly even a creation of Franco herself. I choose to focus on these fourteen poems because I maintain that in order to understand better what Franco is doing in the poetic collection for which she is best known, we need to understand the poems under the signature of the unknown male author and we need to understand how Franco constructs her identity as author, lover, and sex worker in relation to him.

My substantive analyses of these fourteen poems, the majority of which have never been studied in depth, are used to consider our ideological investments in the stories we tell about early modern women authors and their cultural production. In the battle of the sexes that we witness in Franco's work, readers have been predisposed to see her as unqualifiedly victorious: a courtesan who embraced and celebrated her sexuality; an important intellectual and cultural presence in sixteenth-century Venice; and an outspoken champion of women and their worth.

I believe that our dwindling scholarly interest in Franco is related to our initial embrace of her as a proto-feminist icon. In the 1980s and 1990s, as women scholars in North America sought to have their own value recognized in the academy and in society at large, Veronica Franco stood as an understandably attractive model. Women scholars demonstrated how limited was the view of Veronica Franco as "merely a sexual commodity rather than as a writer who participated in important intellectual coteries in Venice and who published her works."[4] They highlighted Franco's singularity as a courtesan who embraced and celebrated her sexuality and defended herself and her profession.[5] They reaffirmed her as a champion for women, emphasizing her pro-woman views; this emerges with particular insistence in Ann Rosalind Jones and Margaret Rosenthal's introduction to their translation of Franco's poems and letters, published in 1998. Noting that Franco "presents

vassi'"; Wojciehowski, "Veronica Franco vs. Maffio Venier"; Ray, "The Courtesan's Voice"; Quaintance, "Women Writers between Men."

4 Rosenthal, *The Honest Courtesan*, 10.

5 Fiora Bassanese writes, "Franco, unlike other women writers of her century, openly acknowledges her sexuality. Indeed, capitolo 16 operates as a defense of her profession" ("Veronica Franco," 778).

protofeminist arguments in sometimes oblique, sometimes openly defiant language," Jones and Rosenthal assert that not only did she defend herself from attacks by a male poet, "in a genuinely feminist mode, she also wrote to protect fellow courtesans against mistreatment by men and to criticise the subordination of women in general."[6] In summing up her achievements, they write: "Franco's *Letters* and *Poems* dramatize her search for autonomy and her solidarity with women at the same time that they record her skillful courtship of the male-dominated cultural elite on whom she depended for security and fame."[7]

One senses that women scholars were trying to understand what made Franco's kind of writing possible, for if we could do that, perhaps we could understand better how to move forward in the struggle for women's rights and equality. Consider the conclusion to Ann Rosalind Jones's *The Currency of Eros: Women's Love Lyric in Europe, 1540–1620*, published in 1990.[8] Invoking Franco's surname, which means both "frank" and "free," and comparing Franco to Louise Labé to whom similar qualities were attributed, Jones highlights frankness and freedom in these poets' writing and sees their frank speech as a "consequence of the relative autonomy available to them in the societies they inhabited."[9] She draws attention to how these women poets "claimed the same right to fame as their male contemporaries," how they "appropriated old and new arguments to defend women," and how they "wrote about sexual pleasure as sexual pleasure."[10] In the very last sentence of her book she proclaims: "The enfranchised cities of Lyon and Venice certainly contributed to Labé's and Franco's oppositional feminism and their challenging reinscription of sixteenth-century languages of love."[11] In writing this conclusion, Jones outlines an ideological and political program for her contemporaries: given that individual and public spheres are deeply intertwined, we must, in order to have enfranchised women, have enfranchised social environments.

In her introduction to *The Honest Courtesan: Veronica Franco, Citizen and Writer in Sixteenth-Century Venice*, published in 1992, Rosenthal describes what drew her to Franco and, in so doing, provides a succinct

---

6 Jones and Rosenthal, "Introduction: The Honored Courtesan," in Franco, *Poems and Selected Letters*, 1–2.

7 Jones and Rosenthal, 21.

8 *The Currency of Eros* was published by Indiana University Press, recognized at the time as a premier press for women's and gender studies.

9 Jones, *The Currency of Eros*, 199.

10 Jones, 199–200.

11 Jones, 200.

portrait that captures nicely the strong appeal that Franco exercises on readers:

> When I first read Veronica Franco's poems and letters many years ago, I was struck, as I still am, by her forthright polemical stance. She writes passionately in support of women unable to defend themselves. She writes with conviction about social and literary inequalities. Deploying an eroticized language in her epistolary verses, Franco calls attention to the performative, seductive nature of all poetic contests – courtesanry, like courtiership, relies on debate, contest, and competition. It is Franco's insight into the power conflicts between men and women, and her awareness of the threat she posed to her male contemporaries, who were also aspiring writers, that makes her literary works and her interaction with Venetian intellectuals so forceful and so extraordinarily modern. Franco is dramatic in her indignation – comic, coy, and vehement in her repudiation of social injustices. She adopts the epistolary form in all of its literary manifestations in the Renaissance – as poetic debate, familiar letter, verse epistle, elegy – to engage in a conversation with her male contemporaries.[12]

This is a powerful statement about Veronica Franco as champion – for women, for justice, and for truth. It is also a powerful statement about Franco's range as a writer and intellectual. That power is embedded in the words that carry this passage. Franco writes "passionately" and "with conviction"; she has "insight" and "awareness"; her works are "forceful"; her indignation is "dramatic"; her command of the epistolary form is extensive, as indicated by the list of genres ("poetic debate, familiar letter, verse epistle, elegy"), and similarly extensive is her command of emotion, since she is "comic, coy, and vehement" in her struggle for justice.

The more we invest in a notion of Veronica Franco as feminist icon, however, the more it appears that ambivalence and uncertainty must be kept at bay. To put Franco's victory into question has become tantamount to putting the feminist project into question. But if the project of reading Veronica Franco is essentially to protect her as a feminist icon, it is understandable that the project can become rote and mechanical. The poems about which we choose to speak become more restricted because they are required to contain the messages readers want to reinforce, and even the specific passages about which readers choose to speak become more restricted. This threatens to diminish our readings.

12 Rosenthal, *The Honest Courtesan*, 10.

Consider what we have seen happen with scholarship on other sixteenth-century authors such as Vittoria Colonna and Gaspara Stampa. While Colonna and Stampa seemed at first to contribute only minimally to our understanding of women's fight for equality, vigorous scholarly activity has allowed us to revise and expand our understanding of them and their work, to tell their stories in new and exciting ways.[13]

The kind of language now used to highlight the accomplishments of some other women writers who have captured our attention in recent years is telling. I shall offer two examples, one regarding Vittoria Colonna and the other regarding Gaspara Stampa.

In her *New York Times* book review of Ramie Targoff's *Renaissance Woman: The Life of Vittoria Colonna* (2018), Sarah Dunant calls Vittoria Colonna "a surprisingly engaging character."[14] She explains: "What could have been the story of a religious good girl becomes instead the study of a passionate, complex woman with formidable poetic talents: someone who, while embedded in her own age, emerges as a thinker and seeker in tune with a modern audience. Vittoria Colonna has always deserved to be better known. Ramie Targoff's fine book will surely make that happen."[15] Targoff, in the concluding paragraph of her biography, reflects on Colonna's distinctive qualities:

> It is hard to say what exactly made Vittoria the remarkable person she was, or what single feature was most responsible for her fame. From the perspective of Italian literary history, she has the obvious distinction of being the first woman ever to see a book of her own poems in print. But the simple designation she is given on the card next to her portrait – "poetess and friend to Michelangelo" – does not begin, as I hope this book has shown, to capture her. Who was Vittoria Colonna? A religious pioneer who embraced Protestant ideas at the very moment when the Catholic

---

13 The number of scholarly articles, books, and dissertations on sixteenth-century Italian women writers is growing all the time, and particularly remarkable has been the expansion of scholarship on Gaspara Stampa and Vittoria Colonna. The collected essays in *Rethinking Gaspara Stampa in the Canon of Renaissance Poetry*, ed. Falkeid and Feng, constitute a major contribution to Stampa studies. Ramie Targoff's biography of Vittoria Colonna, published by a leading U.S. trade press, stands as a monumental contribution to the field; see her *Renaissance Woman: The Life of Vittoria Colonna*. For summaries of the state of scholarship on Vittoria Colonna, see Brundin, "Vittoria Colonna," and *A Companion to Vittoria Colonna*, ed. Brundin, Crivelli, and Sapegno.

14 Dunant, "Who Was Vittoria Colonna?" A version of this article appeared in print in the Sunday Book Review, *New York Times*, 3 June 2018, p. 53, with the headline "Free Verse."

15 Dunant, "Who Was Vittoria Colonna?"

> Church came closest to a reformation of its own; a canny and strategic diplomat who negotiated on behalf of her family with emperors and popes; an important critic and friend of the greatest writers and artists of her time; a spiritual inspiration to many of those around her, who regarded both her sonnets and her company as uplifting to their souls; a role model for women throughout Italy and the continent, whose example emboldened endless numbers of women both to write and to publish their own works. Vittoria was, in short, at the very heart of what we celebrate when we think about sixteenth-century Italy. Once her story has been told, it is impossible to imagine the Renaissance without her.[16]

Durant's and Targoff's rhetorical choices give us clues about what we find compelling. The Renaissance woman writer, while "embedded in her own age" and therefore representative of it, needs to be "in tune with a modern audience." She must be exemplary in a way that we find palatable: "a religious pioneer" (and note that her embrace of Protestant ideas remains under the protected umbrella of Catholic reforms), "a canny and strategic diplomat" (with a specification that this is "on behalf of her family," thus dispelling notions about self-interestedness), a cultural figure who moves in the circles of the "greatest writers and artists" (and who is not just a friend to them but also a critic), and finally, "a role model for women" (not just in a circumscribed local environment but "throughout Italy and the continent").

In 2015, Unn Falkeid and Aileen Feng published an edited collection of ten essays on the poet and musician Gaspara Stampa, *Rethinking Gaspara Stampa in the Canon of Renaissance Poetry*, offering "new avenues of investigation for Stampa criticism, those that would position her within the larger cultural movements of not only early modern Italy, but continental Europe as well."[17] They draw attention to how Stampa "was in dialogue with the various cultural movements that have come to define the Renaissance," how she "has consistently been defined as part of a virtual community of women writers," and how she is an "exemplum of [...] female cultural leadership."[18]

The two instances of scholarship on Colonna and Stampa cited here rely on an operational script that worked to bring Veronica Franco to the fore, but without charging the women writers with being defenders of a feminist project. In contrast, holding firm to a view of Franco as

16 Targoff, *Renaissance Woman*, 289.

17 Falkeid and Feng, introduction to *Rethinking Gaspara Stampa in the Canon of Renaissance Poetry*, 9.

18 Falkeid and Feng, 8–9.

strong, forthright, determined, and independent has led us to underrate any moments in her poetry that might call this view into question.

I do not intend to argue that we should completely undo the perception of Franco as a champion of herself, of courtesans, and of women in general. The fact is that contemporary readers tend to respond to Franco's outspoken polemicism and her embrace of sexuality with vigorous approval. Numerous weblogs stand as evidence of this, as do the reactions of students in our classrooms, where I have seen how reading Veronica Franco has led certain of the students, particularly the shyer women, to feel empowered.[19]

Still, it is imperative that we capture women writers in all their complexity and that, even when we find them inspiring, we permit them to express not only those views that we want to privilege in a particular moment but also the views that they, in their historical moment, chose to express. This is especially important when we deal with questions about their identity and sexuality. In the case of Veronica Franco, we have an opportunity to grapple with questions about the politics of sexuality that continue to beset us: What stories are we choosing to tell about an early modern courtesan who has considerable cultural capital? Are these stories of autonomy and self-determination? Are they stories of compromise and negotiation? Could they be both? And what place do we assign to less palatable elements such as fear, regret, insecurity, and violence?

Furthermore, it is instructive to consider the place that Veronica Franco has thus far been assigned in the intellectual history of women. While granting that Franco merits some attention for her literary contributions, scholars who have written such histories in the last thirty years have chosen to give more prominence to other women writers of the Renaissance and early modern period. In this arena the contributions of the intellectual historian Margaret King and of the literary scholar Virginia Cox are particularly germane.

19 In a recent seminar I taught on Italian Renaissance literature, women students highlighted Franco's willingness to take on controversial topics and admired her courage in speaking out against people who thought ill of her. One student was particularly struck by Franco's use of bodily imagery to show that women have power; in a final reflection on the course she wrote: "Above all, this course taught me not only that women had a Renaissance but also that during the Renaissance there was a space for the female body that was not just its typically sexualized one. I learned that the bodies of Renaissance women – and my own female body in this modern time – are sites of power" (my English translation of the student's Italian).

In *Women of the Renaissance* (1992), Margaret King places Veronica Franco among the "great female poets of the sixteenth century."[20] For King, Franco merits attention for the way that she dealt with love and loss of love, and for the way that her profession and her cultural practices put her at risk of male aggression. King relegates Franco to secondary status, however, because King is keen to provide a narrative about how women can escape male control and aggression. Thus, following her comments on Franco, King turns to what she calls the "*grandes dames* among women poets," Vittoria Colonna, Veronica Gambara, and Marguerite de Navarre, in order to highlight them as women who "while still immersed in the thematics of love, are better able to distance themselves from male aggression."[21] King then closes her narrative by turning to writers "who began for the first time to probe in a critical and comprehensive mode the predicament of female existence in a male society."[22] She showcases three women authors hailing from different national traditions: the fifteenth-century Frenchwoman Christine de Pizan, "the first woman of the Western tradition to live by the power of her pen"; the sixteenth-century Venetian woman Moderata Fonte, who, like Christine de Pizan, imagined "a space for womankind apart from the world of men"; and the seventeenth-century Englishwoman Mary Astell, who "describe[d] the architecture of a female community secluded from men for refuge and strength."[23]

In *Women's Writing in Italy, 1400–1650*, published in 2008, Virginia Cox maintains that Franco's *Terze rime* were "[i]mportant in terms of quality but negligible in terms of profile (it was published semi-clandestinely in Venice and in a very limited print-run)."[24] While Cox acknowledges that in the period 1560–80 Franco was the lone woman poet "capable of emulating the achievements of the past generation," she cuts Franco off at the knees in the same sentence by labelling her "a purely local, Venetian phenomenon."[25] Cox remains more committed to asserting the primacy of Veronica Gambara and Vittoria Colonna, women poets whose poetic accomplishments were widely praised during their lifetimes, including in the very widely read *Orlando Furioso* (1532) by Ludovico Ariosto. Cox sums up: "To an extent to which we need to

20 King, *Women of the Renaissance*, 215.

21 King, 218. King consistently uses Marguerite de Navarre's birth name, i.e., Marguerite d'Angouleme, but this departs from typical scholarly practice.

22 King, 219.

23 King, 219, 228, 232.

24 Cox, *Women's Writing in Italy, 1400–1650*, 122.

25 Cox, 122.

remind ourselves today, Gambara and Colonna were the unquestioned giants within the panorama of Cinquecento women's writing, utterly dwarfing figures who stand large in the female critical canon, such as Gaspara Stampa and Veronica Franco."[26]

These two endeavours – one a history of women in Renaissance Europe, the other a literary historical account of women's writing in the early modern period – depend on organizing women writers in a hierarchy of achievement. Which women writers achieved greater independence from men, portrayed women exercising their autonomy in a separate space, and argued for women's independence from men? Which women were the "giants" in the literary scene of their time, had the greatest impact across the Italian peninsula, and garnered the most enthusiastic accolades, most especially from their male contemporaries? In both of these endeavours, Franco is necessarily a "lesser" figure because her work as a courtesan made her dependent on men, and writing as a courtesan made her dependent on the good will of powerful men like Domenico Venier, a Venetian aristocrat who ran a renowned and influential literary salon that she frequented. In addition, Franco's writings were unlikely to be published except semi-clandestinely; consequently, her literary reputation outside Venice and the Veneto was not going to be as widespread as the literary reputation of noblewomen like Gambara and Colonna.

The intellectual histories of women that Margaret King and Virginia Cox have published are indisputably magisterial; they offer useful lenses for understanding early modern women and their cultural production. It is imperative, however, that we ask if the criteria they apply for evaluating and ranking women writers are the criteria we believe to be the most valid. How do we decide that a given woman writer is more or less meritorious than another? (For that matter, how do we decide that a given woman writer is more or less meritorious than a male writer?) What criteria do we use when we rank women writers as having greater or less impact?

Indeed, what we see from these magisterial histories of women's writing is that they privilege women writers whose class status, or whose ability to rise above the social class into which they were born, gave them distinct advantages both in the world of letters and in the world at large. Furthermore, Cox's evaluation appears to require that to be truly acclaimed, an early modern woman's writings need to be applauded by contemporary luminaries (who of course were men).

26 Cox, 64.

In contrast, the scholars and readers who have constructed the female critical canon in which Veronica Franco and Gaspara Stampa loom large recognize that a woman writer's worth does not always emerge clearly in her own time, especially because women's achievements have been heavily conditioned by their class and economic status.

I myself remain more interested in understanding how Veronica Franco's poetry works than in promoting her as a proto-feminist standard bearer or in advocating for her to occupy a higher position in women's intellectual history. I have maintained and will continue to maintain that literary works do not always function as reliable anchors for political and ideological agendas.[27] Only if I were writing an intellectual history of women poets that used as its primary criterion the intellectual and aesthetic achievements of their poetry would I seek to determine Franco's place in such a history. Personally, I find Franco's poetry more engaging than that of other early modern Italian women poets. That may well be because she privileges the *capitolo* in terza rima, which offers a more extended narrative energy. Moreover, I maintain that we should be wary of overzealous attempts to assert Franco's influence and worth that are based on questionable textual readings and slim biographical information.[28]

Before providing an overview of my arguments about the dialogic poems, I should like to offer several clarifying observations about the known exemplars of the *Terze rime*, about the poems attributed to an unknown male author, and about my decision to analyse only the

27 See Migiel, "The Untidy Business of Gender Studies," 217–33.

28 In trying to underscore that Franco meets the bar that scholars like King and Cox set for special achievement in the intellectual history of women, readers may be tempted to make claims about Franco that are not fully sound. In discussing the Venetian literary salon culture in which Franco participated, for example, Diana Robin claims that Franco ran a salon out of her own home; her characterization of Franco as an active organizer of the Venetian literary scene (rather than solely a participant in Domenico Venier's literary salon) is based on her misreading of a line in letter 17 of Franco's *Lettere familiari a diversi* (Familiar letters to various people). Robin mistakenly believes that when Franco refers to the "teatro della publica concorrenza" (theatre of public competition), she is describing a literary salon run out of Franco's own home (Robin, "Courtesans, Celebrity, and Print Culture," 39). The phrase from letter 17 can be found in Franco, *Lettere*, ed. Bianchi, 59; for the English translation, see Franco, *Poems and Selected Letters*, ed. and trans. Jones and Rosenthal, 34. Robin also claims that Venier's salon was "the principal stage for [Franco's] own performances" (Robin, "Courtesans, Celebrity, and Print Culture," 43); there is no historical evidence to back this up, however, because the salons, known as *ridotti*, were private and we have sparse information about them.

fourteen dialogic poems without addressing the eleven poems under Franco's signature that follow.

There is no autograph manuscript of Franco's *Terze rime*. Franco published her twenty-five-poem collection with the title *Terze rime al Serenissimo Signor Duca di Mantova et di Monferrato*. Since the publication was semi-clandestine and without permission, the volume bears no place of publication, no publisher, and no date; it is believed to have been published in Venice, either in 1575 (the year that matches the 15 November 1575 date on Franco's accompanying dedicatory letter) or, according to Benedetto Croce, in 1576.[29] Some of the 1575 exemplars show Marco Venier as the author of the first poem; others attribute the first poem to an unknown male author.

In the scholarship there is considerable confusion about how many copies of the 1575 *Terze rime* exist. By my count, there are nine extant copies. Two of these copies (i.e., the ones in the Biblioteca Nazionale Centrale in Florence and in the Biblioteca Civica in Padua) show Marco Venier as author of the first poem.[30] Five copies (i.e., the ones in the Biblioteca Marciana, the Biblioteca del Museo Correr, the British Library, the University of Pennsylvania Library, and the John Rylands Library at the University of Manchester) attribute the first poem to the unknown male author. As many libraries have been closed during the COVID-19 pandemic that has raged in the past year and a half, it has not been possible to see (or even to gain further information about) the copies in the Bibliothèque nationale de France or in the Bibliothèque Mazarine, so I am unable to say who appears as the author of the first poem in those volumes.

If I count nine surviving copies, how is it that some scholars tend to speak of three (or fewer) surviving copies? The number three (and the discordant views about whether copies showing Marco Venier as author of the first poem have survived into our time) appears to be the result of a "game of telephone." As the case is instructive about some of the pitfalls of scholarship, I shall provide my best surmise of what has happened.

In his 1913 edition of Veronica Franco's poetry, Abdelkader Salza writes that there are very few surviving copies of the *Terze rime*. He mentions the three copies that Emmanuele Antonio Cicogna was aware

29 Croce, "Veronica Franco," xxvi, xxxi.

30 The call number of the copy in the Biblioteca Nazionale Centrale in Florence is RIN.F.251, and of the copy in the Biblioteca Civica di Padova is CF.0599. The Milton S. Eisenhower Library at Johns Hopkins University has a photocopy of the *Terze rime* owned by the Biblioteca Nazionale Centrale in Florence.

of in 1842: one that had belonged to Apostolo Zeno, in the Biblioteca Marciana in Venice; one that had belonged to Marco Foscarini; and one belonging to Count Pietro Leopoldo Ferri. Cicogna had recorded that the copies belonging to Foscarini and Ferri showed Marco Venier as the author of the first poem; the copy in the Biblioteca Marciana showed that poem to be by an unknown male author.[31] Salza does not say there are only three copies, but these are the only three copies he mentions. He does not say which of them he has consulted, but when he edits the first poem, he attributes authorship to Marco Venier, just as the 1575 copies belonging to Foscarini and Ferri do.[32] When Margaret Rosenthal published her extensive research on Veronica Franco's *Terze rime* in a *Renaissance Quarterly* essay in 1989 (reproduced later in her 1992 monograph), she referred to the passage in which Salza cited Cicogna's knowledge of three copies of the *Terze rime*; she added that "two of them (now lost) registered Marco Venier as the author of the first *capitolo*."[33] In 1990, Ann Rosalind Jones, relying on Salza's bibliographical details, asserted that Marco Venier's "name was torn out of one of the three surviving copies of the collection."[34] This representation seems a tad dramatic, as the operative hypothesis is that the print run of the edition attributing the first poem to Marco Venier was suppressed, with subsequent editions attributing the poem to an unknown male author (*incerto autore*). Although Jones cites Rosenthal's work, it is not clear whether she was aware of Rosenthal's assertion that there was a lone surviving copy of the *Terze rime*, one that attributed the first poem to an unknown male author.[35] Based on what I knew from Rosenthal's 1989 essay, I went to Venice in 1992 to consult what I believed to be the sole surviving copy of the *Terze rime*, housed in the Biblioteca Marciana. Following my research, I published a bio-bibliographical essay on Veronica Franco in 1994, from which I quote:

> There is a danger of interpreting Salza to mean that we now have only a single surviving copy of the *Terze rime*, one that attributes the first poem to

31 See Stampa and Franco, *Rime*, ed. Salza, 381.

32 Salza has authorship as "Del Magnifico Messer Marco Veniero alla signora Veronica Franca"; the 1575 edition that attributes the first poem to Marco Venier has "Del Mag.co M. Marco Veniero alla S. Veronica Franca."

33 See Rosenthal, "Veronica Franco's *Terze Rime*," 229n. See also Rosenthal, *The Honest Courtesan*, 278n.

34 Jones, *The Currency of Eros*, 180; see also her reference to Salza on 219n.

35 Jones, 180, 219n.

an *incerto autore*. Some scholars also believe, incorrectly, that the Biblioteca Marciana owns the sole surviving copy of the *Lettere familiari*.

I would like to dispel these mistaken beliefs before they spread to later works about Veronica Franco. First, although copies of the *Terze rime* and *Lettere familiari* are indeed quite rare, there are more copies beyond the one in the Biblioteca Marciana in Venice. (I have seen three other copies of the *Terze rime*, although some of the original pages at the end of the copy in the University of Pennsylvania Library are missing and have been substituted by pages with handwritten transcription. As for the *Lettere familiari*, there is a complete copy in the University of Pennsylvania library, as well as the copy in the Biblioteca Marciana.) The copy of the *Terze rime* currently found in the Biblioteca Marciana is no longer the one with Apostolo Zeno's *ex libris*, to which Salza referred in 1913. The Marciana discovered in 1922 that this book was missing; another copy was purchased in 1935. And contrary to what scholars believe, the edition showing Marco Venier as the author of the first poem of the *Terze rime* is not lost. I have found one such edition in the Biblioteca Nazionale Centrale in Florence (Consultazione Rinascimento F.251).[36]

In his 1995 edition of Franco's *Terze rime*, Stefano Bianchi mentions two editions of the *Terze rime*, a copy in Florence that shows Marco Venier as author of the first poem and a copy in the Biblioteca Marciana in Venice that attributes the first poem to an unknown male author.[37] In his 2013 monograph on Gaspara Stampa and Veronica Franco, Bianchi documents the existence of a second exemplar of the *Terze rime* that shows Marco Venier as author of the first poem; this exemplar, he explains, is housed in the Biblioteca Civica in Padua and was owned by Count Pietro Leopoldo Ferri.[38] Bianchi thus accounts for three copies (although of course it is conceivable that he may know of other exemplars since he never says there are only three copies). Despite my documenting in 1994 that I had seen four copies (a fact that Jones and Rosenthal cite in their 1998 translation of Franco's poems),[39] some scholars remain fixed on the number three. In 2002, Irma Jaffe wrote, "We know of only three copies of the book that have survived, and Marco's name is omitted in

36 Migiel, "Veronica Franco (1546–1591)," 142.
37 Franco, *Rime*, ed. Bianchi, 41.
38 Bianchi, *La scrittura poetica femminile nel Cinquecento veneto*, 84.
39 Jones and Rosenthal, introduction to *Poems and Selected Letters*, by Franco, 21n.

the third copy."[40] Wendy Sloan, in her entry on Veronica Franco for the *The Mezzo Cammin Women Poets Timeline Project*, makes a similar statement about three copies, suggesting that she has overlooked the information about four copies in Jones and Rosenthal's introduction and is instead following Jaffe.[41]

If in 1994 I knew at least four copies of the *Terze rime* existed, how is it that I now believe that there are at least nine? It is for the following reasons: Bianchi, in 2013, recorded the existence of the copy in the Biblioteca Civica in Padua;[42] on 3 August 2016, Google completed the digitization of a copy housed in the British Library;[43] and after discovering Google's digitized copy, I searched select online library catalogues and found evidence of copies of the *Terze rime* in the library at the University of Manchester, in the Bibliothèque nationale de France, and in the Bibliothèque Mazarine. This leads me to believe that there might be other copies of the *Terze rime* about which we do not yet know.

My reader might be puzzled. After all, how much does the exact number of copies matter? It certainly matters that we know that two surviving copies show Marco Venier as the author of the first poem and that we have at least five (i.e., more than one or two) copies that attribute the first poem to the unknown male author. But my point goes beyond this. It is crucial that we think carefully about how we use previous scholarship when we transmit information about authors and texts. While we all do our best to represent complex matters accurately, information can be misinterpreted, ambiguities can be amplified, fact-checking can be challenging, and it seems that especially when information is supplied in footnotes, it may be overlooked.

If there can be tangled questions about the existence of physical objects like the 1575 exemplars of Franco's *Terze rime*, consider what happens when conjectures are involved, as is the case in the scholarly discussions about the identity of the unknown male author.

---

40 Jaffe, "Veronica Franca (1546–1591)," 347. Jaffe provides no documentation to support this.

41 See Sloan, "Veronica Franco," accessed 14 July 2020. She writes: "Marco Venier's name appears on the opening *capitolo* (Capitolo 1) in two of the three surviving copies of Franco's *Terze rime*, but it is omitted from the third, in which all of the male poets are named only as 'incerto autore' ('uncertain author')." Sloan's essay is undated, but a look at her bibliography indicates that the essay had to be written in or after 2013. I found it through a reference on a Women in History blog page dated 25 December 2018, http://womenofhistory.blogspot.com/2018/12/did-you-know-that-leading-16th-century.html.

42 Bianchi, *La scrittura poetica femminile nel Cinquecento veneto*, 84.

43 Available as an e-book at https://play.google.com.

Currently there are three theories about the *incerto autore*. In modern times they are registered as follows in Italian scholarship: In his 1913 edition of the *Terze rime*, Salza noted that according to Marco Foscarini, the poems not written by Franco were by various male authors, and that according to Giovanni Degli Agostini (with whom Emmanuele Antonio Cicogna agreed), these poems were all by Marco Venier; Salza judged Degli Agostini's hypothesis less probable.[44] In 1986, Alvise Zorzi advanced the hypothesis that Franco herself was the author of all the poems attributed to a man. In his 1995 edition of the *Terze rime*, Bianchi dismissed Zorzi's hypothesis as untenable, on the grounds that the poems attributed to an unknown male author are superficial and dilettantish.[45]

In North American scholarship, Rosenthal's comments about the authorship of poems 1, 4, 6, 7, 9, 11, and 14 have carried significant weight, given that she has written the most extensive monograph on Franco. In *The Honest Courtesan* she asserts that Marco Venier is "most likely the author of all of the poems now labeled by the *incerto autore*."[46] In subsequent publications, however, whether the 1998 edition and translation of Franco's *Poems and Selected Letters* or her Veronica Franco Project published on the web by the University of Southern California, Rosenthal never says anything about whether Marco Venier could be the author of all the poems attributed to the unknown male author.[47] As for the theory that Franco might herself have written the poems attributed to a man, Rosenthal dismisses this in *The Honest Courtesan* and never addresses the issue subsequently.[48] Other scholars' views appear to depend on whether they support Rosenthal's earlier belief that Marco Venier was behind the mask of the unknown male author – a belief consonant with that of Degli Agostini and Cicogna – or they support her later less committal accounts.[49]

---

44 Stampa e Franco, *Rime*, ed. Salza, 381–2.

45 Zorzi, *Cortigiana veneziana*, 119. Bianchi's comment appears in Franco, *Rime*, ed. Bianchi, 41.

46 Rosenthal, *The Honest Courtesan*, 155.

47 See Franco, *Poems and Selected Letters*, ed. Jones and Rosenthal, 13–7; and "Veronica Franco: Poems and Letters," *Veronica Franco Project*, https://dornsife.usc.edu/veronica-franco/the-woman/.

48 See Rosenthal, *The Honest Courtesan*, 155, where she comments on and dismisses a theory, advanced by a "number of critics" (whom she does not identify), that Franco was the author of all sides of a staged "three-way poetic debate" in which the participants were Franco herself, a male author writing in Italian (i.e., Marco Venier and/or the unknown male author), and a male author writing in Venetian dialect who produced a series of satirical poems attacking Franco.

49 Noting that there are "many questions that cannot be answered with the available information," Irma Jaffe believes that it is "plausible in light of what [Franco] herself

While I myself currently believe that the poems by the "unknown male author" are authored not by Franco but by multiple male authors, I am open to changing my mind if research shows otherwise. If these poems are authored by Franco, they are different enough in approach and in style to look as if they are by multiple male authors. For the purposes of my argument in this book, however, determining the exact provenance of these poems by the unknown male author is not relevant. What is important to me is that for the first fourteen poems of her *Terze rime* Veronica Franco chose to stage a dialogue with multiple male voices, that she determined that the male-authored poems should appear in a given order, and that, with a single exception (i.e., the initial printing in which Marco Venier appears as author of the first poem), she chose not to name any man who was her interlocutor in the dialogic poems.

When I first conceived of this project two decades ago, I planned for it to provide readings of each and every poem in the collection. In the last six years, however, as I worked on the Franco project in earnest, I realized that to provide detailed close readings of all twenty-five poems would require some six hundred or more manuscript pages that likely would not be finished until 2024. I then decided to restrict the focus of the project in order to write a book that would not be excessively long and costly and would also make earlier completion feasible.

Of course, every decision to anthologize by focusing on select parts of a work produces a somewhat different story about what the author of the work has achieved. This holds for my research on Veronica Franco in this book – where the anthologization is patently obvious – and it is true of other studies of Franco that do not typically foreground the ways in which their selection of material has helped to shape their conclusions. My editorial decision to focus on a clearly defined subset of Franco's poems, driven by economic and time constraints, allows us to identify distinct concerns that emerge in Franco's poetic exchanges with male voices, and it allows us to compare Franco's rhetorical strategies with those of her male interlocutors.

In the seven chapters of this book I investigate the way in which Franco and the unknown male author use literary allusions, rhyme, metre,

has written in the *capitoli* and her letters" that Marco Venier is the author of all the poems attributed to the unknown male author (*Shining Eyes, Cruel Fortunes*, 347–8). Jaffe does, however, also suggest that poem 6 could have been written either by Marco Venier or by Domenico Venier (361). Courtney Quaintance states that Marco "may well be the author" of the seven poems attributed to an unknown male author; see her "Poems in Terza Rima by Veronica Franco," accessed 14 July 2020. Wendy Sloan says that these poems "were written either by Marco Venier […] or by unidentified male poets" (see her "Veronica Franco," accessed 14 July 2020).

and sound texture to craft their messages. The study considers what Franco achieves by her ordering of the poetic statements and responses, and explores questions such as the following: How does Franco use her dialogue with the unknown male author to construct her identity? What strategies does she adopt as she responds to the unknown male author's entreaties, criticisms, and threats? What strategies does she use in disagreeing with him and criticizing him? When she occupies apparently contradictory positions – expressing moral superiority on the one hand and complicity on the other, celebrating erotic aggression at the same time that she deflects and defers aggression, assigning praise and blame while simultaneously blurring agency – what does she gain from this oscillation?

As I see it, Franco uses the first three poems under her signature (poems 2, 3, and 5) to define who she is and what she values: her respect for virtue and valour, her way of responding to male aggression, her ability to feel and express pain, her connectedness, her desire to adhere to reason, and her ability to admit when she has been on the wrong path. She uses the next three poems under her signature (poems 8, 10, and 12) to illustrate how she responds to men who plead for her love, whether they complain of her cruelty (as in poems 7 and 9) or whether they shower her with praise and adulation (as in poem 11). Poem 13, "Non più parole, ai fatti, in campo a l'armi" ("No more words! To deeds, to the battlefield, to arms!"), has typically been read as an example of Franco's passionate polemicism; it features her challenging an unknown man to a duel, threatening him with mutilation and death, and then using double entendres to transform the violent encounter into a bedroom scene of rough sex. I show instead how this poem, which Franco places at the centre of her *Terze rime*, expresses profound ambivalence about speaking and writing, and I reflect on why other readers have dismissed as unimportant and uninteresting the response of the unknown male author in poem 14.

The story I tell about Veronica Franco's *Terze rime* accounts for the moments of ambivalence, uncertainty, and precariousness in her poetry that other readers have tended to elide. I fully subscribe to what Barbara Johnson eloquently proclaims as the mission of those of us who teach literature: "Teaching literature is teaching how to read. How to notice things in a text that a speed-reading culture is trained to disregard, overcome, edit out, or explain away; how to read what the language is doing, not guess what the author was thinking; how to take in evidence from a page, not seek a reality to substitute for it."[50]

50 Johnson, "Teaching Deconstructively," 140.

The titles of the seven chapters signal the main questions that emerge with each pair of poems. Chapter 1, "Gendered Strategies of Persuasion," reflects on how we construct and understand language usage to be inflected along gender lines as "female" or "feminine" on the one hand, and "male" or "masculine" on the other. I explore Franco's presentation of a strategy (implicitly defined as a female strategy) of managing aggression, responding to it, using it when necessary, and redirecting it. Chapter 2, "Poetic Identity and Community," considers how Franco crafts a poetic identity within a community of voices, a community that the unknown male author in poem 4 attempts to reduce to a one-on-one love relationship. Chapter 3, "Repenting as a Courtesan," speaks to how poem 5 is unconventional as a statement of repentance for love based on sensual attraction, since Franco remains firmly within a secular framework while hinting at spiritual values that transcend it. Furthermore, both poem 5 and the unknown male author's response to it in poem 6 reconfigure notions of frailty and power so that what emerges is a potentially equitable exchange between a woman and a man. Chapter 4 ("Complaining and Cognitive Reframing"), chapter 5 ("Seductive Insinuation and Obliquely Frank Refusal") and chapter 6 ("Verona, Venezia, Veronica") examine the rhetorical strategies that Franco uses to reject men who want her to love them and who beg her to return to them. Responding to the man who complains of her harshness in poem 7, she expands the discussion, offering a broader perspective on people suffering from unrequited love. To the man who tries in poem 9 to bend Franco to his will by insinuating himself into Franco's interior space and by demanding that she function as witness to his being, Franco adopts an attitude of oblique frankness that allows her to present any disapproval as benevolent. To the man who seeks to gain her favour by offering hyperbolic praise of her and of the city of Verona, Franco utilizes forms of direct criticism that she does not apply anywhere else in the *Terze rime*. Chapter 7, "Attacks and Concessions under Erasure," shows how Franco, in poem 13, deflects and defers violent aggression at the same time that she celebrates it; then it considers how, when the unknown male author responds to this threat of aggression in poem 14, he contemporaneously concedes and withholds power. In the conclusion I outline next steps for research.

As will become clear in the course of my analyses, I respectfully take my distance from the theory advanced by Rosenthal that we can identify a "core of the *Terze rime*" constituted by seven poems (e.g., the exchanges in dialogic poems 1–2, 11–12, 13–14, and Veronica Franco's response in poem 16 to Maffio Venier's scurrilous and satirical verses about her that circulated in manuscript).[51] According to Rosenthal's narrative, Veronica Franco engages principally with Marco Venier, even when he is masked as the unknown male author; Franco comes to believe that Marco Venier is responsible for the scurrilous verses and speaks out forcefully against him in poem 13, challenging him to a duel; Marco Venier, apparently unaware of the verses attacking Franco, cannot respond efficaciously in poem 14; and finally, in poem 16, Franco brings the polemical exchange to a close by "perform[ing] a critical reading of her adversary's vituperative poem."[52] With poem 16, Rosenthal claims, "we have come full circle. We have witnessed the unfolding of a poetic *tenzone* performed as a battle of wits, and as a comic struggle deformed by mistaken identities."

In contrast, in Franco's *Terze rime* I see the potential for multiple narratives to emerge in tension with each other, depending on which poems we may identify as particularly salient at a given moment. For these more complex stories to emerge, however, we need to suspend the impulse to train an especially strong light on select poems or on select parts of poems that support a privileged core narrative, while downplaying parts of the *Terze rime* that might call that narrative into question. With the analysis of the dialogic poems that follows, I invite the reader to listen for the stories about Franco and her male interlocutors that have not previously resounded.

---

51 Rosenthal advances this theory first in "Veronica Franco's *Terze Rime*," 231, and repeats it in *The Honest Courtesan*, 160. The theory informs Jones and Rosenthal's discussion of the "story of Franco as a poet" that they present in their introduction to Franco, *Poems and Selected Letters*, 14–19.

52 Rosenthal, *The Honest Courtesan*, 190.

1 Gendered Strategies of Persuasion: *Terze rime* 1 and 2

How do we construct and understand language usage to be inflected along gender lines as female or feminine on the one hand, and male or masculine on the other? In this chapter I examine the first male-female exchange in the *Terze rime* in order to show how Veronica Franco distinguishes her own rhetoric (presumably gendered female) from the rhetoric of a male interlocutor. Rather than focusing on questions of embodiedness, intellectual valour, and equality – questions that have been explored in the artistic endeavours dedicated to Veronica Franco and in much of the previous scholarship about her – I propose to explore Franco's presentation of a strategy (implicitly defined as a *female* strategy) of managing aggression, responding to it, using it when necessary, and redirecting it.[1]

The male-authored "S'io vi amo al par de la mia propria vita" ("If I love you as much as my own life") is followed by Franco's response, "S'esser del vostro amor potessi certa" ("If I could be certain of your love"). Among scholars there is a tacit understanding that this first male-female exchange provides a template for understanding how Franco positions herself with respect to male interlocutors. The man's poem stands, ostensibly, as his declaration of love; we hear about the man's suffering in love, his faithfulness, Veronica Franco's cruelty, the pity she should show him, and his longing for her. In her response

1 Commenting on my analyses of Veronica Franco's poetry and analyses made by Irene Eibenstein-Alvisi, Dolora (now Hannah) Chapelle Wojciehowski has pointed out that Eibenstein-Alvisi and I "contend that the literary evidence of the *Terze Rime* reveals a more precarious and violent existence for the courtesan poet than that which is usually celebrated by critics and historians" ("Veronica Franco vs. Maffio Venier," 368). The present chapter continues to explore the rhetoric that Franco would have used to respond to violence and aggression.

Franco argues the difference between potentially misleading appearances and true love, which reveals itself in deeds and not just words; she expresses regret both because he feels pain and because he impedes her desire to respond to true love; she tells him the conditions under which she will return his love, emphasizing the importance of virtuous deeds; she ends by reaffirming that she longs to have reason to love him; and she reiterates that the decision is his. In responding to the male author of the poem that she places first in her own collection, Franco defines her own approach to love, sexuality, excellence, successful attainments, and the literary tradition.

Following her analysis of these two poems, Margaret Rosenthal sums up: "By redefining the Petrarchan muse as poetic collaborator rather than disembodied and silent addressee, Franco decenters the lyrical love tradition which commonly uses the woman simply as literary currency. However, she also manipulates the courtly and erotic elements of the poetic system represented in the *incerto autore*'s verses in order to promote herself as intellectual and erotic *virtuosa*."[2] The commentary is representative for its emphasis on the woman's *embodiedness* (she is no longer simply a "Petrarchan muse"), on her *voice* (she is no longer silent), and on her *intellectual virtuosity* (she is not just a sexual object; she has brains too). Here Veronica Franco, faced with the prospect of being made a "literary object" – a woman encoded as just another addressee of tiresome literary commonplaces – responds by reaffirming her presence, her agency, her literary worth, and her ability to define herself.

I would not go so far as to say that we should not admire such a spirited voice. Nevertheless, let us explore aspects of Franco's poems that attenuate the celebratory claims set forth by readers who emphasize Franco's self-affirmation. Given that I have a different perception of the male and female desires expressed in these first poems, I read the project of the *Terze rime* differently: not as a heroic self-celebration and an affirmation of personal agency but as a tempered reflection on how to manage aggression.

In the opening poem of the *Terze rime*, I see a male interlocutor who, in attempting to persuade Franco to submit to him sexually, oscillates between declarations of love on the one hand and controlling and threatening assertions on the other. Why, I must perforce ask myself, do I see aggression when other readers appear inclined to emphasize rough-and-tumble sexuality? Is my response justified by the text?

2 Rosenthal, *The Honest Courtesan*, 186.

Which type of response is more justified by the text? Or are both readings equally justified?

For me, the key lines appear toward the end of the first poem, when the male poet imagines his hands on Veronica Franco and follows up with an imagined encounter in a bed:

> Prenderei con le mani il forbito oro
> de le trecce, tirando de l'offesa,
> pian piano, in mia vendetta il fin tesoro.
> Quando giacete ne le piume stesa,
> che soave assalirvi! e in quella guisa
> levarvi ogni riparo, ogni difesa! (1.121–6)

> (I would take in my hands the burnished gold
> of your tresses, pulling that fine treasure,
> gently, in revenge for your offense.
> When you lie stretched out upon the pillows
> how sweet to fall upon you! and in that way
> to strip you of any retreat or defense!)

Everything depends on how we imagine this, based on the textual clues that we are provided and based on the tone with which we read these verses. This passage is at the very least ambiguous, situated someplace between playful and violent aggression. Yet the translators encourage us to read this as *playful* aggression. Rather than rendering the verb "assalirvi" in line 125 as "to assail you" or "to assault you" or "to attack you" – translations that work off an English cognate – they translate this as "to fall upon you." The English translation thus purges the sense of active violence with intent to injure, substituting instead the idea that the male poet might not even be responsible for his action. Although it seems unlikely that one could attack someone without the intention to do so, it is possible to fall upon someone else without *really* intending to do harm.

The translators thus follow the lead of the male poet, whose poetic language is very rhetorically sophisticated, designed to pull toward minimization of any attack. The male poet represents the woman as lying down, and therefore vulnerable, but we are invited to see her not simply in a bed but rather in a kind of feathery fluffiness, "ne le piume," which the translators render here as "upon the pillows" and which we could also describe as "in a featherbed." This provides a context that seems non-threatening. The adverbs "pian piano" (used to describe the "gentle" pulling of the hair) and "soave" (used to describe the "sweet" mode of assault) encourage us to see the act as tenderly passionate. In the moment of the assault the poet compliments the woman, describing her hair as a "fine treasure" and "burnished gold" (forbito oro; no doubt a reference to the "forbito oro" of Laura's hair in Petrarch's famous canzone "Chiare fresche et dolci acque").[3] In this specific context, the use of a Petrarchan phrase should be read not only as an attempt to codify the woman as object but also as an attempt to reinforce the sense that the male poet could not possibly be levelling a real attack on the woman; if there is an aggressor in Petrarch's poetry, it will be the woman, or Love, not the male poet.

I might be willing to concede that this passage is an example of playful aggression, but for the fact that I read it in the context of other more insidious indications that the male poet is seeking to establish control. Note, for example, how the male poet establishes that there will be punishment for non-compliance with his desire; the woman will lose her beauty over time unless she refuses to be cruel:

> Pria che de' be' crin l'òr si faccia argento,
> da custodir è quel che poi si perde,
> chi 'l lascia in man del tempo, in un momento:
> e se bene sète d'età fresca e verde,
> nulla degli anni è più veloce cosa,
> sì ch'a tenervi dietro il pensier perde;
> e mentre di qua giù nessun ben posa,
> nasce e spar la beltà più che baleno,
> non che qual nata e secca a un tempo rosa.
> Ma poi chi la pietà chiude nel seno,
> col merto de la fama sua ravviva
> le chiome bionde e 'l viso almo e sereno.
> Dunque, per farvi al mondo eterna e diva,
> amica di pietà verso chi v'ama,
> siate di crudeltà nemica e schiva. (1.28–42)

> (Before the gold of your lovely hair turns silver
> you must take good care of what is lost
> in a single moment, once left in the hands of time;
> and though you're now in a fresh and flowering age,
> nothing flies past so swiftly as the years,
> which outstrip even thought;

3 Francesco Petrarca, "Chiare fresche et dolci acque," poem 126 in *Petrarch's Lyric Poems*, trans. and ed. Durling. The reference to the "forbito oro" of Laura's hair is at line 48.

and while here on earth no good thing lasts,
beauty is born and vanishes quick as a flash,
like the rose that blooms and withers all at once.
But whoever harbors pity in her breast
by virtue of her fame brings back to life
her golden locks and her kind and serene face.
So, to become eternal and divine on earth,
be hostile and averse to cruelty,
a friend to pity for the man who loves you.)

The male poet insists on defining and delimiting the possibilities among which Veronica Franco might choose. His poem is about trying to *make sure* – not offering her the option but trying to *make sure* – that she chooses Venus over Apollo, sexual love over poetry and intellectual activity. He insists that she look upon him and that she turn her body toward him: "Ma guardatemi" (But behold my heart; 1.49); "volgete a me pietosamente gli occhi" (turn your eyes toward me pitifully; 1.55); "stendete a me la bella e bianca mano" (reach out to me your fair white hand; 1.58). When, if ever, does Franco insist imperiously that a male gaze upon her? When does she ever demand the submission of his body? (As we will see shortly, she will not use these imperative forms.)

There is a brief moment when it seems that the male poet's control might be relaxed. He writes: "La penna e 'l foglio in man *prendete* intanto, / e *scrivete* soavi e grate rime, / ch'ai poeti maggior tolgono il vanto" (1.76–8; emphasis mine). Are the verbs "prendete" and "scrivete" to be understood as imperatives, so that we should translate these lines (as Jones and Rosenthal do) as: "*Take* pen and paper in hand, then / and *write* pleasant and graceful rhymes, / which strip the glory from the greatest poets" (1.76–8; emphasis mine)? If so, whose authority – his, hers, or theirs – do we see these imperatives reinforcing? Or might we instead read these verbs as indicatives, so that we would have to translate as: "You do take paper and pen in hand, then; / you do write pleasant and graceful rhymes / which strip the glory from the greatest poets"? On the one hand, the indicatives offer reaffirmation of what seems obvious to readers who know that Veronica Franco writes; on the other, they are more generous than imperatives in that they involve a compliment for work well done rather than a command to do such work.

Curiously, however, once the male poet permits the woman's hand to hold a pen and once he entertains the possibility that she would move in the company of great poets, he also sets about delimiting the possibilities that writing would offer her:

O bella man, che con bell'arte esprime
sì leggiadri concetti, e le sue forme
dentro 'l mio cor felicemente imprime!
De l'antico valor segnando l'orme
questa ne va sì candida e gentile,
svegliando la virtù dove più dorme;
né pur rinova il gloriöso stile
del poetar sì celebre trascorso,
che non ebbe fin qui par né simíle;
ma de le menti afflitte alto soccorso
è quella man ne l'amorosa cura,
che quivi ha 'l suo rifugio e 'l suo ricorso. (1.79–90)

(Oh, lovely hand, which with lovely art
expresses such winning conceits, and happily
imprints its shape upon my heart!
Following the footsteps of ancient valor,
it moves along, so pure and gentle, awakening
virtue where it sleeps so deeply;
not only does it revive the splendid style
of the celebrated poetry of the past,
which so far has had no like or equal;
but to suffering minds, that hand
is a great help in the suffering of love,
for here it finds its shelter and relief.)

In lines 79–81 the male poet clearly invokes the Petrarchan topos of *la bella mano*, thanks to the prominent placement of this phrase at the very beginning of the tercet. The principal source of such poetry in praise of the woman's hand is sonnet 199 of Petrarch's *Rerum vulgarium fragmenta* (*Rvf*):

O bella man, che mi destringi 'l core
e 'n poco spazio la mia vita chiudi,
man ov' ogni arte et tutti loro studi
poser Natura e 'l Ciel per farsi onore,

di cinque perle oriental colore,
et sol ne le mie piaghe acerbi et crudi,
diti schietti soavi: a tempo ignudi
consente or voi, per arricchirme Amore.

Candido leggiadretto et caro guanto
che copria netto avorio et fresche rose:
chi vide al mondo mai sì dolci spoglie?

Così avess' io del bel velo altrettanto!
O incostanzia de l'umane cose,
pur questo è furto, et vien chi me ne spoglie.[4]

(O beautiful hand that grasps my heart and encloses in a little space all my life, hand where Nature and Heaven have put all their art and all their care to do themselves honor,

neat soft fingers, the color of five oriental pearls, and only bitter and cruel to wound me: to make me rich, Love now opportunely consents that you be naked.

White, light and dear glove, that covered clear ivory and fresh roses: who ever saw in the world such sweet spoils?

Would I had again as much of that lovely veil! Oh the inconstancy of human life! Even this is a theft, and one is coming who will deprive me of it.)

In Petrarch's sonnet 199, the hand stands in, *pars pro toto*, for the woman who is beautiful but unkind. The hand grips the poet's heart so forcefully that his life is at risk; the fingers wound him bitterly and cruelly. The actively cruel and offensive nature of the hand is highlighted in the critical commentaries. Thus, James Mirollo notes that "it is clear that we have an example here of the hand as an active and cruel agent as well as a static and materialized beautiful object of contemplation,"[5] Gerhard Regn describes the hand as "offensive […] symboliz[ing] a love relationship that frustrates the lover,"[6] and the Petrarch Reading Group at the University of Oxford tells us that "direct contact with the lady is presented as destructive and invasive."[7] While both within Petrarch's *Rvf* and more widely within the romance tradition there is an awareness that Love and the lady possess curative as well as destructive

4 For the Italian text and the English translation, see Petrarca, *Petrarch's Lyric Poems*, trans. and ed. Durling.
5 Mirollo, "In Praise of *La bella mano*," 34.
6 Regn, "Eros and Eschatology," 100.
7 "Canzoniere 199," *Petrarchreadinggroupoxford*, accessed 31 May 2019.

powers, the poet of sonnet 199 does not explicitly draw our attention to the hand's ability to heal.[8]

When the male poet of *Terze rime* 1 marshals the Petrarchan topos of *la bella mano*, however, he offers a compensatory fantasy. All traces of cruelty and violence disappear; the writing hand still has a direct relationship with the poet's heart, but now the hand felicitously "imprints its shape" (le sue forme [...] imprime; 1.80–1) within his heart. If we are minimally attentive to the erotic energy of the passage, we will notice that the male poet is evidently redirecting the writing hand to a place where he most wants it to rest; there, the hand, "awakening a dormant power" (svegliando la virtù dove più dorme; 1.84) and engaging in "loving attentive care" (amorosa cura; 1.89), may no longer be writing.

If the male poet describes the woman's hand as engaged in amorous, laudable, and caring activity, and if violence is here kept at bay, how then does it happen that the spectre of aggression will work its way back into the poem subsequently? Everything here turns on the male poet's desire for union and unicity. Union and unicity are not easily achieved, however. And why is that? It is because the male poet perceives Franco as double. For him, there are two Veronicas, the cruel one and the merciful one, the one who writes and the one who cedes to her lover, the one who gains fame through her verses and the one who gains fame by preserving her beauty from being damaged by her cruelty. She is thus both "integral" and "potentially duplicitous." Playing on Veronica Franco's first name, and implicitly invoking the idea that "names are the consequence of the things they name" (*nomina sunt consequentia rerum*),[9] the male poet describes the woman's beauty as "vera e unica" (true and unique; 1.115). In the very next lines, however, at the same time, he implies that there could be a fundamental rift between reality and appearance: the woman is "di costumi adorna e di virtude / con senil senno in giovenil etade" (adorned with refined manners and

8 For a discussion of scenarios of wounding and concomitant possibilities of healing, see Sturm-Maddox, *Petrarch's Laurels*, 91–100.

9 In the Italian literary tradition the idea that names are revelatory of the way things are certainly brings to mind Dante's statement in the *Vita nuova* 6 (XIII) 4 that "lo nome d'Amore è sì dolce a udire, che impossibile mi pare che la sua propria operazione sia nelle più cose altro che dolce, con ciò sia cosa che li nomi seguitino le nominate cose, sì come è scritto: 'Nomina sunt consequentia rerum.'" (The name of Love is so sweet to hear that it seems impossible to me that the effect itself should be in most things other than sweet, since, as has often been said, names are the consequences of the things they name: *Nomina sunt consequentia rerum*). See Alighieri, *Vita nova*, ed. Gorni; the English translation is from Alighieri, *Dante's Vita Nuova, New Edition*, trans. Musa, 123.

virtue / with the wisdom of elders at a young age; 1.116–17).[10] The alternation of unicity and duplicity in the woman alone seems to guarantee that violation and violence are part of the ecstatic experience for this male poet, since, as I see it, the erotic energy of the poem is directed at breaking through this doubleness in order to get to ecstatic union.

The poem's eroticism also nestles in the tension between the transcendent and the earthly. The male poet twice exclaims on the beauties of paradise, each time straining for transcendence but very possibly still grounded in the experience of the here, the now, and the materially carnal: "Oh beltà d'ogni essempio altro divisa, / di cui l'anima in farsi umil soggetta, / stando lieta qua giù s'imparadisa!" (Oh, beauty quite apart from any other, / through which the soul, in making itself a humble subject, / happily imparadises itself here on earth!; 1.61–3, translation mine);[11] and later, "Oh che grato e felice paradiso, / dal goder le bellezze in voi sì rade / non si trovar giamai, donna, diviso" (Oh, what a cherished and joyful paradise / never to be parted from enjoying, / lady, your singular charms; 1.112–14, translation mine). As the lines describe union with the woman's paradisiacal beauty, the pairing in rhyme position of "divisa" (apart) and "s'imparadisa" (imparadises), and of "paradiso" (paradise) and "diviso" (parted), reminds us that this union might be tenuous. Using a Dantesque hapax legomenon, "s'imparadisa," the male poet reaches toward the experience described by Dante in *Paradiso* 28.1–3, "'ncontro a la vita presente / d'i miseri mortali aperse 'l vero / quella che 'mparadisa la mia mente" (she who imparadises my mind revealed the truth against the present life of wretched mortals").[12] Whether or not we see the male poet of the *Terze rime* as successful in his achievement of paradise will depend on how we understand the woman's beauty and the paradise it offers and whether it is distinguishable from the life of mere mortals.

Given the presence of doubleness and division as a thematic issue, no one will be surprised to find out that double entendres run rampant in this poem. Eroticism surges forward in the male poet's desperate cry early on in the poem – "perch'almen con la morte quelle pene / ch'io soffro per amarvi, non troncate?" (why do you not at least end with

10 Here I have substituted my own translation for that of Jones and Rosenthal since their translation ("improved with fine manners and skill / with mature wisdom in your early youth") de-emphasizes the tension between reality and appearance that I see introduced in the adjective *adorna*, which I have translated as "adorned."

11 Here I take "soggetta" to be the feminine form of the masculine noun "soggetto" (subject).

12 Dante Alighieri, *Paradiso*, ed. Chiavacci Leonardi. The English translation is mine.

death / this pain I endure for love of you?; 1.5–6) – since quite beneath the obvious pangs of suffering ("quelle pene"), the reader is sure to be aware of the swollen male member ("il pene"). The poem strains toward satisfying this erotic urge. This produces more representations of sexualized tension. Once again there will be attention to pain, which allows the double entendre on "pene": "il mio soverchio duolo, / e come in lui convien ch'ognor trabbocchi / di pene cinto da infinito stuolo" (my crushing pain, / and how at every moment it must overflow, / bound to an infinite throng of woes; 1.52–4). Subsequently, as I have noted, the sexual energy is mobilized by the hand that moves "sì candida e gentile, / svegliando la virtù dove più dorme" (so pure and gentle, awakening / virtue where it sleeps most deeply; 1.83–4). The current of sexual energy is also, I believe, at the heart of a series of words repeated in the rhyme scheme, either as identical rhymes or as equivocal rhymes: "si perde," "perde" (1.29, 1.33); "brama," "brama" (1.43, 1.45); "vaga," "vaga" (1.101, 1.105); "opre," "s'opre" (1.130, 1.133). These rhymes create the sense that one is repeatedly bumping up against something – a sense that is reinforced thematically by the male poet's claim to want to despoil Franco of every defence, every haven.

Veronica Franco's response (poem 2) relies on strategies that, at least in their formal and structural elements, often appear similar to those we have seen the male poet employ. I would caution, however, that we remain alert to fundamental differences in rhetorical effect.

Like the male poet who represents Franco as both singular and double, Franco identifies the male poet as occupying a potential divide. But here we see the installation of alternate pairings: words and deeds, appearances and reality, uncertainty and certainty. Driving home her point about the tenuous connection between words and deeds, or appearances and realities, she makes frequent recourse to hypotheticals. Rendered with imperfect subjunctives and conditionals, these hypotheticals mark her poem as occupying a tentative, contingent, provisionary, less than fully predictable space. There are eight imperfect subjunctives in a 190-line poem, four of them in the first nine lines, which then establish the tone for the rest of the poem. By way of comparison, the imperfect subjunctive appears three times in poem 1, written under a male signature. There the two imperfect subjunctives that appear approximately a quarter of the way into the poem are crushed into certainty:

> Oh, se vedeste in me l'ardente brama
> c'ho di servir voi sola a tutte l'ore,
> con quel pensier ch'ognor vi chiede e brama;

se mi vedeste in mezzo 'l petto il core,
a me son certo che null'altro amante
pareggereste nel portarvi amore! (1.43–8)

(Oh, if you were to see my fiery longing
to serve only you at every hour of the day,
and my thought, which always seeks and longs for you,
if you were to see my heart deep in my breast,
I know that you could compare no other lover
to me for the love he feels toward you.)

The third and final imperfect subjunctive serves ominously to reinforce the poet's desire that the woman submit to him:

E così 'l vanto avete tra le belle
di dotta, e tra le dotte di bellezza,
e d'ambo superate e queste e quelle;
e mentre l'uno e l'altro in voi s'apprezza,
d'ambo sarebbe l'onor vostro in tutto,
se la beltà non guastasse l'asprezza. (1.133–8)

(And so among beauties you are famous for your learning,
and among learned women you are known for your beauty,
and in both you excel one group and the other;
and while each of these qualities wins you admiration,
the honor for both would be yours altogether,
if only your harshness did not spoil your beauty.)

Like her male interlocutor, Veronica Franco looks to the future both to predict and to promise, as in the lines "io son per camminar col vostro piede, / ed amerovvi indubitatamente, / sì com'al vostro merito richiede" (I am ready to walk in step with you, / and I will love you beyond any doubt, / just as your merit requires I should; 2.67–9). The male poet spoke of exchange: he had offered his faith, and he had received no compensation in return, so he looks to the future to define a Franco who will deliver on the goods. Franco's poem is also about exchange. Repeatedly, she sets up the equation "if you were to do *x*, I would do *y*," which, in the future tense, is rendered as "I will do *x* if you do *y*." Franco's proposal is about correspondence, about her own willingness to be open to connection. It is also about merging and dissolving boundaries: under propitious conditions she will walk by his side, feeling what he feels, susceptible to the flames of Love as he is (see 2.70–5). It is about a mutuality and reciprocality that is born in the doubling of experiences. In short, Franco's response is about connection in a way that the first poem, authored by a man, is not. The male poet seeks to bring Franco into line with him, to make her compensate him, to batter her defences, making her compensate him, making her drop her defences, making her give in. The second poem is about bringing two people into line with each other, offering reciprocal exchanges, paying back a deposit (2.35–56), generously paying back a loan with interest (2.82–90).

Franco offers her interlocutor a chance to respond and to define things as he might see them:

Vi par che buono il mio discorso sia,
o ch'io m'inganni pur per aventura,
non bene esperta de la dritta via? (2.61–3)

(Does what I say seem good to you,
or do you think I am perchance mistaken,
incapable of staying on the right path?) (translation mine)[13]

And again, more explicitly, she offers him the choice:

Io bramo aver cagion vera d'amarvi,
e questa ne l'arbitrio vostro è posta,
sì che in ciò non potete lamentarvi. (2.136–8)

(I myself long to have real reason to love you,
and this is left to you to decide,
so that you cannot complain.)[14]

And yet again, in her conclusion, she redoubles her exhortation to free choice, echoing her earlier language in 2.136–8:

Aver cagion d'amarvi io bramo forte:
prendete quel partito che vi piace,
poi che in vostro voler tutta è la sorte. (2.187–9)

13 I have substituted my own translation for that of Jones and Rosenthal, who offer the following: "Does what I say seem right to you, / or do you instead perhaps think I am wrong, / lacking experience to choose the right path?" (2.61–3).

14 I have substituted my own translation for that of Jones and Rosenthal, which is: "I long to have a real reason to love you / and I leave it up to you to decide, / so that you have no right to complain" (2.136–8).

(I yearn to have cause to love you:
Take the side that you like,
For everything depends on your will.) (translation mine)[15]

Crucial to the rhetorical strategies of poem 2 are the persistent wordplays that redirect into more clearly positive territory the energy forwarded by the male interlocutor. The identical and equivocal rhymes recede, however. The lone equivocal rhyme to appear in this poem trains our attention on the compliments and praise ("lodi," "lodi"; 2.56–8) that Franco would prefer to displace. Moreover, with her wordplay, Franco tries to dislodge the male poet's wordplay, which had been directed at a phallic eroticism. Her own wordplay is based not on the double senses of single words but on paronomasia, where sparks are generated when two very similar words or concepts try to merge: "ne l'amar le mie voglie cortesi / si studian d'esser *caute*, se non *caste*" (when I love, my courteous desires, / if not *chaste*, are decidedly *chary*; 2.86–7, emphasis mine); "Dal *merto* la *mercé* non fia discosta" (There'll be no gap between *merit* and *reward*; 2.139, emphasis mine). This is not to say that Franco shies away from acceptance of this phallic eroticism or from the metaphorical language used to render it. It is clear from the following lines that she does not:

S'avete del mio amor l'alma conquisa
procurate d'avermi in dolce modo
via più che la mia penna non divisa.
Il valor vostro è quel tenace nodo
che me vi può tirar nel grembo, unita
via più ch'affisso in fermo legno chiodo:
farvi signor vi può de la mia vita,
che tanto amar mostrate, la virtute,
che 'n voi per gran miracolo s'addita. (2.172–80)

(If your soul is vanquished by love for me,
arrange to have me in far sweeter fashion
than anything my pen can declare.
Your valor is the steadfast knot
that can pull me to your lap,
joined to you more tightly than a nail in hard wood;

15 Jones and Rosenthal's translation reads: "I yearn and long to have a good reason / to love you: decide what you think best, / for every outcome depends on your will" (2.187–9).

your skill can make you master of my life,
for which you show so much love –
that skill that miraculously stands out in you.)[16]

Here, what seems especially striking is the blurring of eroticized subjectivities. Franco's pen, powerfully trained on imaginative transport, yields to the male poet. As the moment of psychic coupling gives way to imagined physical coupling, it is no longer clear who is in possession of the phallus: for if the male poet has the "valor" that is a "steadfast knot" (tenace nodo) that draws Franco to his bosom or "lap" (grembo), it is no longer so clear who is the male active presence and who is the female static presence – who is the nail and who the hard wood.

Redirecting the male poet's energies also involves rechannelling references to Dante's experience. As I noted previously, the male poet, desirous of bliss with his lady, marshals language sure to recall Dante's *Paradiso*; he uses this to gesture toward erotic bliss here on earth. Marshalling the moral import of Dante's message, Franco focuses on leaving false appearances behind (2.24), choosing the right path or "dritta via" (2.63), and moving from the centre to the circumference, which is part of gaining translunar understanding (see 2.123, which echoes language from the Heaven of the Sun in *Paradiso* 14.1). Franco gestures toward a paradisiacal state but resolutely does not name it, even though she has the opportunity to do so as she twice reproduces the male poet's rhyme sequence. In 1.59–63 the male poet rhymed "guisa," "divisa," and "s'imparadisa"; in 1.110–14, he rhymed "viso," "paradiso," and "diviso." In the initial tercets of her poem Veronica Franco seems to be tracking the male poet's lead when she reproduces his rhymes on "guisa" and "divisa" (2.5 and 2.7), but then she refuses his rhyme on "s'imparadisa" and instead offers "derisa" (2.9). Toward the end of the poem she again links up "guisa" and "divisa," this time offering a rhyme sequence of "guisa," "conquisa," and "divisa" (2.170–4).

Franco lays out a strategy of persuasion that depends not on a kind of control and threats of violence (which are especially evident in the first poem), but on identification among speakers and on free choice of a higher good. By foregrounding her response to violence and control in a poem in which she signals her readiness to make herself available

16 The grammatical subject of 2.178–80 is "virtute" (2.179), which Jones and Rosenthal translate as "skill" (2.178, 2.180), a choice that is in keeping with the erotic nature of the passage. It seems likely, however, that Franco is marshalling the semantic richness of *virtute*, since it can mean "virtue, "virtuousness, "excellence," and "manliness," as well as "skill."

to a man under the right conditions, she sets a bottom line. She avoids responding in a way that would warrant her being denounced as a cruel, heartless woman. While her parting remark "Altro non voglio dir: restate in pace" (I have no more to say; go in peace; 2.190) could veer toward "I wish to say only this: rest in peace" – a comment that might not be too far from "My last words are: drop dead" – any hint of mordancy likely dissolves as the previous 189 lines set the tone for the poem. If we are inclined to hear Franco sending a message of "go in peace" rather than "rest in peace," it is because she succeeds in casting herself as above acerbic cruelty.

2 Poetic Identity and Community: *Terze rime* 3 and 4

In poem 3, "Questa la tua fedel Franca ti scrive" ("This your faithful Franca writes you"), Veronica Franco laments her absence from Venice and a lover who is still there, and, in poem 4, "A voi la colpa, a me, donna, s'ascrive" ("To you, lady, belongs the blame"), an unknown male author responds, using the same rhyme scheme that Franco uses in poem 3. Margaret Rosenthal reads poem 3 as "an intimate, personal confession of love and desire" and "an introduction to a love story that culminates in capitolo 20,"[1] and Sara Maria Adler sees it as "correcting the tradition of the absent lady typically considered cruel because of her silence and indifference."[2] I maintain that poem 3 should be seen as a poetic manifesto, a statement about the terms of Franco's poetic identity. Highlighting the moments in which Franco casts herself as Orpheus-like, I shall argue that Franco acknowledges the alienation that comes with being a masterful poet on the model of Orpheus while also emphasizing the community and connections that would temper this alienation. Turning to poem 4, I shall analyse the strategies that the unknown male author adopts to restrict the relationship between him and Franco so that a more expansive community can be restricted to an exclusive community of two.

---

1 Rosenthal, *The Honest Courtesan*, 220. Rosenthal's reading remains consistent with the summary label that Abdelkader Salza applies: "Lontana dall'amante, soffre e piange, e sospira Venezia. Dove appena sarà tornata, a lui che l'attende darà, in amorosa lotta, dolce ristoro delle noie passate" (Far from her lover, she suffers and weeps, and longs for Venice. Just as soon as she returns there, she will, in amorous combat, give sweet reparation for past troubles to him who awaits her). See Stampa and Franco, *Rime*, ed. Salza; the English translation is mine.

2 Adler, "Veronica Franco's Petrarchan *Terze Rime*," 217.

In poem 3, more than in any other of her dialogic poems, Franco foregrounds her literary forebears, principally Ovid, Petrarch, and Ariosto. In the opening line, "Questa la tua fedel Franca ti scrive" (This your faithful Franca writes you; 3.1), she recalls the opening of Ovid's *Heroides*, where Penelope writes, "Haec tua Penelope lento tibi mittit, Ulixe" (These words your Penelope sends to you, O Ulysses, slow of return that you are").[3] In 3.16–27 she describes how Echo, Procne, and Philomela second her laments. While the Ovidian references draw attention to writing, speaking, singing, and lamenting, Petrarch is mobilized mainly for his vocabulary to describe the sufferings of love. Adler, who describes Franco as "Petrarchanly pretentious as she elaborates on her misery," points out that if poem 3 were isolated from its context, it "would be indistinguishable from many other Petrarchan poems of longing."[4] Furthermore, in recounting her suffering at having left her lover in Venice, Franco recalls an elegiac poem in *terza rima* entitled "Meritamente ora punir mi veggio" (I now see myself justly punished), in which Ludovico Ariosto tells of his distressing separation from his beloved Alessandra Benucci after he had to leave Ferrara for Garfagnana.[5]

Previous scholarship has emphasized how Franco carves out a different identity, both as a woman and a lover, while refashioning the roles that women occupy in Ovid's *Heroides* and Petrarch's *Rerum vulgarium fragmenta*. She suffers in love not because she is abandoned but because she has elected to leave the place where her heart resides; it is she who laments the fact that she has left her city and, with it, her lover; and it is she who – even before a man pleads with her in poem 4 to return to him – reaffirms her faithfulness and says that she hopes to be reunited with the man she loves. Not content to be written about by another, she takes the initiative to express herself in writing. She is not a cruel lady but a woman who expresses care and concern for her lover, a woman who intends to fulfill his desires. As Adler notes, "Veronica's role is that of a new Laura, who interrupts the conventional Petrarchan monologue with her laments and her initiatives."[6]

---

3 The Latin text and English translation are taken from Ovid, *Heroides and Amores*, trans. Showerman. Rosenthal notes that the first tercet of poem 3 recalls several opening lines of the *Heroides* and therefore establishes a clear Ovidian genealogy that will extend later to poems 17 and 20, which similarly call attention to their status as epistolary missives; see Rosenthal, *The Honest Courtesan*, 218–21.

4 Adler, "Veronica Franco's Petrarchan *Terze Rime*," 216.

5 See capitolo 3 in Ludovico Ariosto, *Opere minori*, ed. Segre; the English translation is mine.

6 Adler, "Veronica Franco's Petrarchan *Terze Rime*," 217.

As I see it, however, this poem is not primarily concerned with the kind of *woman* and the kind of *lover* Veronica Franco will be. Furthermore, it is not simply sending the message that she is a poet, rather than a woman whose voice is silenced. The poem sends a message about the *kind of poet* Franco wishes to be. As Franco bemoans her separation from her lover, she fashions herself as an Orphic poet. Here are the crucial verses:

Oimè, ch'io 'l dico, e 'l dirò sempre mai,
che 'l viver senza voi m'è crudel morte,
e i piaceri mi son tormenti e guai.
Spesso, chiamando il caro nome forte,
Eco, mossa a pietà del mio lamento,
con voci tronche mi rispose e corte;
talor fermossi a mezzo corso intento
il sole e 'l cielo, e s'è la terra ancora
piegata al mio sì flebile concento;
de le loro spelunche uscite fuora
piansero fin le tigri del mio pianto,
e del martir che m'ancide e m'accora;
e Progne e Filomena il triste canto
accompagnaron de le mie parole,
facendomi tenor dì e notte intanto.
Le fresche rose, i gigli e le vïole
arse ha 'l vento de' caldi miei sospiri,
e impallidir pietoso ho visto il sole;
nel mover gli occhi in lagrimosi giri
fermarsi i fiumi, e 'l mar depose l'ire
per la dolce pietà de' miei martiri.
Oh quante volte le mie pene dire
l'aura e le mobil foglie ad ascoltare
si fermâr queste e lasciò quella d'ire!
E finalmente non m'avien passare
per luogo ov'io non veggia apertamente
del mio duol fin le pietre lagrimare. (3.13–39)

(Alas, I say now and will always say
that life is cruel death to me without you,
and pleasures to me are torments and woes.
Often, as I cried aloud that dear name,
Echo, touched with pity by my lament,
answered me with brief and broken calls.

At times in mid-course the sun and the sky
stood still, intent, and even the earth
bent down to hear my pitiful tones.
Coming out of their secret lairs,
even tigers wept at my weeping
and the mortal pain that stabs my heart.
And Procne and Philomela joined in
with my sad melody and words,
singing in harmony both day and night.
The cool roses, lilies and violets
were burnt by the wind of my hot sighs,
and I saw the sun turn pale with pity.
Moving their eyes in tearful swirls,
the rivers stood still, and the sea quelled its rage
through tender pity for my suffering.
Oh, how many times the trembling leaves
stood still and the breeze ceased to blow,
in order to listen to my bitter pain.
And finally, never could I make my way
through any place where I did not see
even stones weep openly for my grief.)

Franco's voice, like that of Orpheus, is capable of making the natural world respond in remarkable ways. The sun and the heavens stop mid-course (3.19–20). The earth bends (3.21). Tigers emerge from their lairs to weep at her weeping (3.22–4). The sun turns pale; the waters, the foliage, and the breeze stand immobile (3.28–36). Stones weep openly (3.37–9).

Being like Orpheus, however, also means to be threatened with loss, isolation, renunciation of sexuality, and dismemberment. Orpheus shows us both the power of the master and the impotence of the master. He loses his beloved in this world and then loses her a second time in Hades. This experience brings him to speak only to the inanimate world and to beasts and, moreover, to spurn sexuality (or at least to spurn heterosexuality). Having spurned women, he becomes the victim of an assault by the Bacchants and is dismembered.

If Veronica Franco's attitude in poem 3 is that of an Orphic poet, why hasn't this been noticed previously? I would suggest that the claim to be like Orpheus is not immediately evident because, despite the marked situational resemblances, there are no strong verbal echoes of passages in which Virgil and Ovid relate Orpheus's story.[7] Furthermore, in describing how she moves in a natural landscape as if she is Orpheus, Franco states that she is accompanied by Echo (who, according to Ovid, wasted away for love but lives on through her voice) and by the singing of Procne and Philomela (who, according to Ovid, were transformed into a swallow and a nightingale), logical companions for a grieving Franco.[8] Echo responds to her compassionately (3.17–18), and Procne and Philomela sing in harmony with her (3.25–7). These mythological figures from Ovid's *Metamorphoses* appear to have been chosen in order to create a female community that supports Franco as she expresses her sorrow at being separated from her lover. Undoubtedly important as well is the fact that in the *Metamorphoses* these figures must contend with the loss of their ability to communicate effectively with language. Echo, deprived by Juno of her ability to generate speech independently, can speak only when she echoes the last words she has heard from another who addresses her; after Tereus raped Philomela and cut out her tongue so that she could not reveal what he had done, Philomela wove a tapestry that revealed his heinous deed; and upon seeing the tapestry, Philomela's sister, Procne, finds no words capable of expressing what she feels.

---

7 A thrice-repeated name of a loved person, for example, would ensure recall of the well-known passage in Virgil's *Georgics* where Orpheus's severed head calls out Eurydice's name twice and her name is then echoed by the river banks (*Georgics* 4.523–7). Dante offers us an example of what such a recall might look like when in *Purgatorio* 30.49–51 he mourns the loss of Virgil by repeating Virgil's name three times, just as Eurydice's name is repeated three times in the *Georgics*.

If there is any recall of the Latin passages, it is with Franco's description of her song as "flebile concento" (pitiful tones; 3.21). Here she appears to be picking up on the word "flebile" (pitiful, mournful) that Ovid uses insistently as he describes Orpheus's lyre and his head, separated from his body, as they continue in mournful lament: "membra iacent diversa locis, caput, Hebre, lyramque / excipis: et (mirum!) medio dum labitur amne, / *flebile* nescio quid queritur lyra, *flebile* lingua / murmurat exanimis, respondent *flebile* ripae." (The poet's limbs lay scattered all around; but his head and lyre, O Hebrus, thou didst receive, and [a marvel!] while they floated in mid-stream the lyre gave forth some *mournful* notes, *mournfully* the lifeless tongue murmured, *mournfully* the banks replied; *Metamorphoses* 11.50–4, emphasis mine.) Importantly, however, if Franco is recalling this passage from the *Metamorphoses*, she reduces the thrice-repeated "flebile" to a single instance, weakening the Orphic presence. (The Latin text and English translation are taken from Ovid, *Metamorphoses*, trans. Miller.)

8 For the story of Echo, see Ovid, *Metamorphoses* 3.339–401, and, for the story of Philomela and Procne, see Ovid, *Metamorphoses* 6.401–674.

Why might Franco embrace an Orphic stance and simultaneously draw a veil over it? I believe it is because she uses poem 3 to acknowledge the alienation that comes with being a masterful poet on the model of Orpheus and to emphasize the community and connections that would temper this alienation. She tells two stories about identity. On the one hand, she constructs a narrative that we can read as affirming a stable integrated identity and active sexual connection to a specific male individual. That is the narrative that has been reaffirmed by previous scholarship, which highlights Franco's absolute integrity, her faithfulness, and her repudiation of any sort of duplicitousness.[9] But when we look more closely, we see that the poem also enacts a kind of dismemberment and fragmentation as it undercuts notions of a stable core identity, whether for the poet herself or for her addressee.

Questions about identity emerge as the poem opens:

> Questa la tua fedel Franca ti scrive,
> dolce, gentil, suo valoroso amante;
> la qual, lunge da te, misera vive.
> Non così tosto, oimè, volsi le piante
> da la donzella d'Adria, ove 'l mio core
> abita, ch'io mutai voglia e sembiante:
> perduto de la vita ogni vigore,
> pallida e lagrimosa ne l'aspetto,
> mi fei grave soggiorno di dolore;
> e, di languir lo spirito costretto,
> de lo sparger gravosi afflitti lai,
> e del pianger sol trassi alto diletto.
> Oimè, ch'io 'l dico e 'l dirò sempre mai,
> Che 'l viver senza voi m'è crudel morte,
> e i piaceri mi son tormenti e guai. (3.1–15)

> (This your faithful Franca writes you,
> her tender, well-bred, and gallant lover,
> she who lives unhappily far from you.
> No sooner, alas, had I turned my steps
> from the maiden of Adria, where my heart dwells,
> than I was transformed in will and appearance:

9 See Rosenthal, *The Honest Courtesan*, 218–24.

my life bereft of any strength,
with my face turned pale and bathed in tears,
I passed a time weighed down with grief;
and, with my spirit forced to languish,
my only real pleasure came from reciting
heavy, pain-filled lays and from weeping.
Alas, I say now and will always say
that life is cruel death to me without you,
and pleasures to me are torments and woes.)[10]

The narrating voice of the first three lines clarifies the author (Franca, which is to say Veronica Franco), the addressee (the lover), their relationship (Franco is away from him and therefore unhappy), and the way in which Franco communicates (through writing). These lines clearly invite a comparison with the opening lines of *Heroides* 1: "Haec tua Penelope lento tibi mittit Ulixe; / nil mihi rescribas attinet: ipse veni!" (Your Penelope sends this to you, dallying Ulysses; don't write back to me – come yourself!) Just as Ovid's Penelope defines herself in terms of her addressee, Ulysses, these lines show Franco defining herself in terms of her lover.[11] Even more than Penelope, she takes the opportunity early on to showcase her own positive qualities. She is not only "your Franca" but "your faithful Franca." Unlike Penelope, whose letter to Ulysses is marked, as Howard Jacobson has pointed out, by "complaints, utterances of self-pity [and] ungracious allegations," Franco showcases the positive qualities of her lover.[12] She benefits from her generous representation as well, since the first two adjectives of line 2 – "dolce, gentil" (tender, well-bred), adjectives that are unmarked as to gender – attach nicely to the Franco of the first line before we realize that they are more likely meant to qualify her clearly male "gallant lover" (valoroso amante) named at the end of line 2. The closest Franco gets to a complaint is in line 3, where it becomes clear that she lives "unhappily" (misera) because she is separated from her lover.

Since these first three lines so clearly recall the first lines of *Heroides* 1, where Penelope speaks about the missive she is sending to Ulysses,

10 I have modified Jones and Rosenthal's translation of 3.2 so as to include the possessive pronoun "her" (suo), and I have substituted "unhappily" as a translation for "misera" in 3.3.

11 For commentary on Penelope's self-configuration in *Heroides* 1, particularly in light of the Homeric subtext, see Lindheim, *Mail and Female*, 37–51, and especially 48–9.

12 Jacobson, *Ovid's Heroidos*, 250.

and since Ovid's Penelope subsequently continues to speak in her own voice, we are predisposed to assume that Veronica Franco is speaking about herself as the poem opens. Something very curious happens in the subsequent lines, however. The narrating voice of the first three lines turns out to be different from the narrating voice of the rest of the poem. In the first tercet the lover is addressed with the informal second-person singular: "la *tua* fedel Franca *ti* scrive [...] lunge da *te*, misera vive" (This *your* faithful Franca writes *you* [...] she who in misery lives far from *you*; 3.1–3, emphasis mine). Beginning with line 14, where Franco exclaims "viver senza *voi* m'è crudel morte" (that life is cruel death to me without *you*; emphasis mine), she consistently uses formal address.

Nowhere other than in poem 3 does Franco establish one form of address with a man and then switch to another within the same poetic composition.[13] Furthermore, in poem 20, where Franco explicitly recalls the opening of poem 3 as she takes up the elegiac mode once more,[14]

---

13 In ten of the thirteen poems in which Franco addresses a man, formal address predominates. She uses formal address in poems 2, 8 (where she responds to a lover who uses informal address with her), 12, 15, 16, 18, 19, 20, 23, and 24; she uses informal address in poem 10 (responding to a man who has addressed her formally), poem 13 (writing to a man who subsequently addresses her formally), and poem 17 (to communicate with a lover who has betrayed her).

14 Poem 20 opens thus:

> Questa quella Veronica vi scrive,
> che per voi, non qual già libera e franca,
> or d'infelice amor soggetta vive;
> per voi rivolta da via dritta a manca,
> uom ingrato, crudel, misera corre
> dove 'l duol cresce e la speranza manca. (20.1–6)

> (This letter is written to you by that Veronica
> who now lives neither free nor frank
> but as a slave of unrequited love.
> Turned for your sake from the right path to the wrong,
> thankless, cruel man, in misery she runs
> where sorrow grows and hope decreases.)

These lines – especially given the opening rhyme on "scrive" / "vive" and the naming of Franco as author – signal that the situation will be like that of poem 3. Then the twists follow. Not only does the narrating voice not use the informal address that was used to open poem 3, but the narrating voice has changed its tone with the addressee, who was previously a "gallant lover" and is now a "thankless, cruel man" responsible for Veronica Franco's subjection, her unhappiness, and evidently also her spiritual decline.

she maintains formal address, both in the opening section where she is spoken about in the third person as a woman who is a victim of unrequited love (20.1–12) and subsequently (20.13–268) when she describes her suffering.

Once we notice that the poem is narrated by two voices, we are positioned to explore further how Veronica Franco complicates notions of relationality. Because the opening lines state that Franco writes to "her gallant lover" (suo valoroso amante) and because these lines recall Penelope's address to Ulysses, we may mistakenly assume that Franco will continue to address the lover directly for the rest of the poem. In lamenting her departure, however, Franco states that she turned away from "the maiden of Adria, where my heart dwells" (la donzella d'Adria, ove 'l mio core / abita; 3.4–5). Consider how many mental gyrations this statement requires the reader to make. Franco turns away from the city of Venice, which is personified as a maiden, and this maiden is also a geographical space that is home to her heart. What does this heart represent? We may feel encouraged to see the heart as standing for Franco's male lover because, after all, the opening tercet has told us that Franco is deeply unhappy at being far from her lover. But we might well wonder whether Franco's primary emotional attachment is to the place rather than to a person. When Franco calls out the "dear name" (il caro nome; 3.15), and Echo answers her, what name is she calling? The only proper name offered thus far is "Adria" (3.5). Is it possible that she is calling out something other than the name of her lover?

Franco maintains the uncertainty as she delays clarifying that she is talking about separation from a man. Her hesitancy to clarify becomes starkly evident if we compare her poem with Ludovico Ariosto's poem on his separation from his beloved Alessandra Benucci. In a poem that begins "Meritamente ora punir mi veggio / del grave error che a dipartirmi feci / da la mia donna" (Now I see myself justly punished for the grave error I made in leaving behind my lady), we know by the beginning of the third verse that the poet is speaking about his relation with a woman.[15] Even in lines 40–51 of poem 3, however, Franco continues to use periphrases to describe what she has left behind, and holds back from concretizing him as a man:

> Vivo, se si può dir che quel ch'assente
> da l'anima si trova viver possa;
> vivo, ma in vita misera e dolente:

15 See capitolo 3, lines 1–3, in Ariosto, *Opere minori*; the English translation is mine.

e l'ora piango e 'l dì ch'io fui rimossa
da la mia patria e dal mio amato bene,
per cui riduco in cenere quest'ossa.
Fortunato 'l mio nido, che ritiene
quello a cui sempre torno col pensiero,
da cui lunge mi vivo in tante pene!
Ben prego il picciol dio, bendato arciero,
che m'ha ferito 'l cor, tolto la vita,
mostrargli quanto amandolo ne pèro. (3.40–51)

(I live, if a person can be said to live
who finds herself bereft of her own soul;
I live, but a life of misery and mourning,
and I lament the hour and the day
that I was taken from my home and my beloved,
for whom my bones now melt into ash.
Fortunate dwelling of mine, which still enfolds
the man to whom I always return in thought,
from whom I live at such distance and pain!
I implore the little god, blindfolded archer,
who wounded my heart and stole away my life,
to show that man how I perish for love of him.)

The English translation of this passage sometimes makes it difficult to see the delayed clarification. When Franco states, "[I]o fui rimossa / da la mia patria e dal mio amato bene," the translation has, "I was taken from my home and my beloved," but the lines could also be translated as "I was taken from my homeland and from all that I hold dear," thus making it clear that Franco is concerned about community in a wider sense ("homeland" rather than "home") and also about love of the good ("all that I hold dear" rather than a beloved individual man). Particularly interesting are the lines "Fortunato 'l mio nido, che ritiene / quello a cui sempre torno col pensiero, / da cui lunge mi vivo in tante pene!" (Fortunate dwelling of mine, which still enfolds / the man to whom I always return in thought, / from whom I live at such distance and pain!; 3.46–8.) The social space designated as a "nido" (dwelling; 3.46) could also be understood as a "nest" or "nesting space" because the "nest" is a privileged metaphor that Franco often uses to describe her home city of Venice.[16] Most perplexingly ambiguous is Franco's reference to "quello

16 In 11.104, the unknown male author asks that Franco return to the "nido" where she was born, and in her response to him Franco praises Venice as the "eterno nido" (eternal nest; 12.41) of God's faith and asks why the male poet has not praised this

a cui sempre torno col pensiero," which can be translated both as "the man to whom I always return in thought" and as "what I continue to think about." If Franco had wanted to dispel any ambiguity, she could have written "*colui* a cui sempre torno col pensiero" (emphasis mine) because "colui" could refer only to a man.[17] Only with the introduction of Cupid in 3.49–51, and the request that Cupid "show him" (mostrargli; 3.51, translation mine), does Franco begin to use language that will encourage us to think of what she left behind as a man.

Upon establishing with somewhat greater certainly that hers is a painful separation from a man she loves, Franco then backtracks in the subsequent tercets:

> Oh quanto maledico la partita
> ch'io feci, oimè, da voi, anima mia,
> bench'a la mente ognor mi sète unita,
> ma poi congiunta con la gelosia,
> che, da voi lontan, m'arde a poco a poco
> con la gelida sua fiamma atra e ria! (3.52–7)

> (Alas, how I curse my departure from you,
> although, dear soul, in all my thoughts,
> you are still tightly united with me,

"nido" (12.62). In poems 21 and 22, in which she reflects on being away from Venice, she uses "nido" to refer to the city (21.53, 22.2, 22.225). Only three times does "nido" not refer to Venice: in 13.41 where, evidently speaking about a bed, Franco speaks about the place where she experienced sexual joy; in 23.66 where she is referring to birds in a nest; and in 25.11 where she praises Fumane, the villa belonging to Marcantonio Della Torre.

17 For those curious about whether "colui" would have been the preferred demonstrative pronoun, I offer the following passage from chapter 15 of Machiavelli's *Prince*, in which Machiavelli uses both "colui" and "quello," in close proximity to each other, to refer to an individual male: "Lasciando, adunque, indrieto le cose circa uno principe imaginate, e discorrendo quelle che sono vere, dico che tutti li uomini, quando se ne parla, e massime e principi, per essere posti più alti, sono notati di alcune di queste qualità che arrecano loro o biasimo o laude. E questo è che alcuno è tenuto liberale, alcuno misero (usando uno termine toscano, perché avaro in nostra lingua è ancora *colui* che per rapina desidera di avere, misero chiamiamo noi *quello* che si astiene troppo di usare il suo)" (Putting aside, then, the imagined things concerning a prince, and taking into account those that are true, let me say that all men, when they are spoken of, and especially princes, since they are on a higher level, are judged by some of these qualities which bring them blame or praise. And this is why some are considered to be generous, others stingy [using a Tuscan word, since "avaricious" in our language is still used to refer to *one* whose desire involves robbing others; we call "stingy" *that one* who over-refrains from using what he has]). Emphases mine. See Machiavelli, *Machiavelli's The Prince*, trans. and ed. Musa, 126–7.

but joined to me by jealousy, too,
which, far from you, little by little, burns me,
with its freezing, dark, savage flame!)

As English does not have grammatical gender, it is impossible for the English translation to communicate how Franco uses grammatical gender in this passage to blur identities. When she speaks of having left behind "voi, anima mia" (you, my soul; 3.53, translation mine), we are encouraged by the context to believe that she is addressing a man she has left behind, even though she refers to him with the feminine noun "anima." Then in the following verses, however, she does something quite startling. In affirming that "a la mente ognor mi sète *unita* / ma poi *congiunta* con la gelosia" (you are still tightly *united* with me / but *joined* to me by jealousy; 3.54–5, emphasis mine), she has the feminine past participles "unita" and "congiunta" agree with the grammatically feminine "anima" (soul). What is the effect of this curious rhetorical choice, which, as far as I am able to tell, is one of a kind in the *Terze rime*? Franco continues to avoid concretizing the man as a male embodied being. She briefly floats the possibility that she might be referring not to a man but to the city of Venice, gendered feminine. Most important, she indicates that the man from whom she is separated is indeed united with her, so firmly that his male identity is subsumed into the identity of her own soul, which determines the adjectival endings.

Only in the final sixteen lines of the poem, when Franco imagines a reunion, does the figure of the lover materialize:

Le lagrime, ch'io verso, in parte il foco
spengono; e vivo sol de la speranza
di tosto rivedervi al dolce loco.
Subito giunta a la bramata stanza,
m'inchinerò con le ginocchia in terra
al mio Apollo in scïenzia ed in sembianza;
e da lui vinta in amorosa guerra,
seguiròl di timor con alma cassa
per la via del valor ond'ei non erra.
Quest'è l'amante mio, ch'ogni altro passa
in sopportar gli affanni, e in fedeltate
ogni altro più fedel dietro si lassa.
Ben vi ristorerò de le passate
noie, signor, per quanto è 'l poter mio,
giungendo a voi piacer, a me bontate,
troncando a me 'l martìr, a voi 'l desio. (3.58–73)

(The tears that I shed quench the fire, in part,
and I live only in the hope
of seeing you soon again, in that sweet place.
The moment I reach the room I have longed for,
I will bow down, my knees on the ground,
before my Apollo in knowledge and beauty.
Then vanquished by him in loving war,
I'll follow after him, my soul freed from fear,
on valor's path, from which he never strays.
This is my lover, who surpasses
every other man in enduring woes,
and whose faithfulness leaves all others behind.
I'll willingly make up to you for past suffering,
my lord, as far as my power allows,
bringing pleasure to you, good to myself,
ending my suffering and your desire.)[18]

If one focuses principally on these lines, it makes sense to treat the poem as an "an intimate, personal confession of love and desire," as Rosenthal does. These verses are seductive. Franco calls the man "my lord" (signor; 3.71) for the first time, says she will kneel before him, praises him for his intellect and valour, and affirms his sway over her as she will be "vanquished by him in loving war" (vinta da lui in amorosa guerra; 3.64). She represents the bond between the man and herself as invincible. The man's power over Franco is complete; but so is her possession of him, which she asserts by calling him "my Apollo" (il mio Apollo; 3.63) and "l'amante mio" (my lover; 3.67).

This is the only time in the *Terze rime* that Franco affirms her unabashed willingness to give pleasure to a man in an erotic encounter, so, not surprisingly, the final seven lines were singled out for reproduction on the back cover of the 1995 edition of Franco's *Rime*, published by Mursia.[19] Elsewhere Franco is more cagey. In poem 2 she made a conditional promise: "Fate che sian da me di lei vedute / quell'opre ch'io desio, che poi saranno / le mie dolcezze a pien da voi godute" (Let me see the works / I've asked for from you, / for then you'll enjoy my sweetness to the full; 2.181–3). In poem 8 she will allow for the possibility that she might love the man who has written to her but for the

18 I have modified Jones and Rosenthal's translation of 3.67–8. Where they have "This is the man I love, who surpasses / every other man in enduring pain," I have substituted "This is my lover, who surpasses / every other man in enduring woes."
19 Franco, *Rime*, ed. Bianchi.

fact that she is in love with someone else (8.110–17). In poem 13 the erotic encounter is masked behind the threats of violence. And in the monologic poems (15 to 25), while Franco does at times profess love for a man, it is to lament her unhappiness in love; there are no mentions of joyous sexual encounters.

The reading of poem 3 that I have offered here suggests that this is the first time in the *Terze rime* that Franco seeks to occupy subject positions that are in tension with each other. She is like Orpheus and not like him; she is both an active agent and a subject who is acted upon; her unhappiness is born primarily in her being away from Venice and primarily in her being away from the man she loves; she speaks primarily to the man whom she loves and primarily to a larger community that responds to her. To read the poem by looking only at the way in which it focuses on her relationship with the man she loves – a relationship in which she overturns the tropes of the abandoned heroine and the silent, cruel woman – is to ignore the way in which the poem constructs a Veronica Franco whose power comes precisely from her ability to occupy subject positions in tension or at odds with one another.

In subsequent chapters, particularly those that treat Franco's poems 8, 10, and 13, I shall comment on the way that Franco broadcasts double messages. But now I turn to poem 4, "A voi la colpa, a me, donna, s'ascrive" ("To you, lady, belongs the blame"), in which an unknown man responds, using the same rhyme scheme, to what Veronica Franco had written in poem 3. Analysing his rhetorical and linguistic strategies will allow us not only to understand his poem better but also to see more clearly other important aspects of poem 3.

The male poet comments on Franco's having left him despite his entreaties (4.1–15) and describes his response to her recognition that she has caused him pain (4.15–30). Affirming that his love is unsurpassable (4.31–42), he maintains that he does not seek a love that would bring them to full union, and he recognizes his inferiority with respect to her (4.43–60). He then invokes the power of Love, asking that Love sustain him in his distress and, if this cannot be, that pity reign (4.61–9). In the final lines he begs her not to delude him with the pretence of pity, given how much he loves her, and he begs her to return as soon as possible, as he longs to be always at her side (4.70–3).

Perhaps the most striking thing about poem 4 is the way that it repeatedly emphasizes a "you versus me" divide: comparing what is his with what is Franco's, how he has acted versus how she has acted. This is starkly evident in the opening verses:

A voi la colpa, a me, donna, s'ascrive
il danno e 'l duol di quelle pene tante
che 'l mio cor sente e 'l vostro stil descrive.
L'alto splendor di quelle luci sante
recando altrove, e 'l lor soave ardore,
ai colpi del mio amor foste un diamante.
Io vi pregai, dagli occhi il pianto fore
sparsi largo, e sospir gravi del petto:
non m'aiutò pietà, non valse amore.
Valse, via più che 'l mio, l'altrui rispetto
e benché umil mercé v'addimandai,
pur sol rimasi in solitario tetto.
D'ir altrove eleggeste, io sol restai,
com'a voi piacque ed a mia dura sorte:
sì che invidia ai più miseri portai. (4.1–15)

(To you, lady, belongs the blame,
to me that pain of all the griefs
that my heart feels and your pen describes.
Taking away the bright shine and sweet fire
of those blessed eyes, you stood hard
as a diamond against my love's charge.
I implored you, I poured out my lament
from my eyes and deep sighs from my breast;
pity was no help and love of no avail.
Your concern for another was far stronger than for me,
and though I begged you humbly for mercy,
I still remained under a lonely roof.
You chose to go elsewhere, I stayed alone,
as your will and my cruel fate decreed,
so that I envied the most wretched creatures.)

The male poet establishes an adversarial relationship with Franco, dividing up all the blame on her side and all the grief on his. The primary strategy is to split verses, so that Franco remains on one side of the caesura and the male poet on the other, as in lines 1, 3, 6, 13, and 14. The first two lines obviously recall Petrarch's address to Love in line 78 of *Rerum vulgarium fragmenta* (*Rvf*) 207: "La colpa è vostra, et mio 'l danno, e la pena" (The blame is yours, and the harm and the pain mine; my translation). But whereas Petrarch had used the possessive adjective "yours" (vostra) to place blame not only on his addressee

(Love) but on Love working in tandem with Petrarch's beloved, Laura, the male poet narrows the players involved and assigns full responsibility for his misfortune to his addressee, Veronica Franco.[20] And to add insult to injury, while his heart feels the pain, she merely writes about it.

The male poet draws attention to all he has done, how it has proved futile, and how, as a result, he is alone. Lest this escape full notice, he repeats the morpheme "sol" (alone) three times to give it special emphasis: "pur *sol* rimasi in *sol*itario tetto. / D'ir altrove eleggeste, io *sol* restai" (I still remained *alone* under a *lonely* roof. / You chose to go elsewhere, I stayed *alone*; 4.11–12, translation and emphasis mine). Furthermore, he is alone not only in the sense that Franco has left him behind; neither pity nor love is of aid to him. He has no community. His emphasis on how alone he is in his grief when she is gone stands in stark contrast to the way that Veronica Franco described her grief at being away, when, as I noted earlier, she is without human companionship but she is accompanied both by nature and by mythical personages.

Having established that the blame is Franco's and all of the grief is his, the male poet makes a partial concession in order to acknowledge, in the first if-clause of his poem, that she may feel some pain and then to conclude, based on this, that pity still lives on in her:

E s'or avvien che a voi pentita apporte
alcun dolore il mio grave tormento,
in ciò degno è ch'amando io mi conforte.
Dunque per me del tutto non è spento
quel foco di pietà, ch'ove dimora
fa d'animo gentil chiaro argomento. (4.16–21)

(And if it's now the case that my severe torment
causes you, repentant, some pain,
it is appropriate that I, loving you, take comfort from it.
So for me pity's fire is not entirely spent,
that pity which, wherever it dwells,
gives visible proof of a gentle soul.) (translation mine)

---

20 One of the anonymous readers for this book noted that Petrarch opens *Rerum vulgarium fragmenta* (*Rvf*) 207 "by addressing Amor with the informal *tu* ('a che condutto m'ài / tu 'l vedi, Amor, che tal arte m'insegni'; 207.5–6)," so that when he switches to using the second-person plural possessive pronoun "vostra," it is absolutely clear that he is referring both to Amor and to Laura.

These tercets show the male poet primarily concerned with himself. Even in conceding that his suffering may cause Franco "some pain" (alcun dolore), he still splits line 17 so that what she might feel looks negligible by comparison to his "severe torment" (grave tormento). By affirming his love for her as he justifies his own satisfaction that she may feel pain too, he encourages us not to ask whether this is the response of a truly loving person. He appears to be graciously acknowledging Veronica Franco's gentility.

In order to understand how the male poet of poem 4 is positioning himself with respect to Veronica Franco, let us consider *Rvf* 217, "Già desiai con sì giusta querela," a sonnet in which Petrarch had also written of "the flame of pity" (foco di pietà) that he hoped, by means of his laments and his poetry, to awaken in Laura's hard heart:

Già desiai con sì giusta querela
e 'n sì fervide rime farmi udire
ch' un foco di pietà fessi sentire
al duro cor ch' a mezza state gela.

et l'empia nube, che 'l rafredda et vela
rompesse a l'aura del mi' ardente dire,
o fessi quell'altrui in odio venire,
che' belli (onde mi strugge) occhi mi cela.

Or non odio per lei, per me pietate
cerco; ché quel non vo', questo non posso.
tal fu mia stella et tal mia cruda sorte.

Ma canto la divina sua beltate
che quand' i' sia di questa carne scosso
sappia 'l mondo che dolce è la mia morte.[21]

(Once I wanted to make myself heard with so just a lament and in such fervent rhymes that I would make a fire of pity felt in the hard heart that is frozen in midsummer,

and, with the wind of my hot words, break the cruel cloud that cools and veils it, or else make her hateful to others, who hides her lovely eyes with which she melts me.

21 The Italian text and English translation are taken from Petrarca, *Petrarch's Lyric Poems*, trans. and ed. Durling.

Now I no longer seek hatred for her nor pity for myself, since I do not wish the former and the latter is beyond me; such was my star and such my cruel fate!

But I sing her divine beauty, that when I have departed from this flesh the world may know that my death is sweet.)

The sonnet is neatly divided between the octave, where Petrarch speaks about what he desired in the past, and the sestet, where he addresses what his current objectives are. In its overarching statement it communicates that Petrarch previously hoped to soften Laura's stance toward him but now is content to praise her beauty rather than expecting recompense. The sonnet affirms that Petrarch has transcended not only the desire for pity but also the impulse to wish that others would hate Laura for her coldness toward him. In the final tercet Petrarch imagines that there will be satisfaction in knowing that his poetry will allow the world to know that his death is sweet.[22]

What does the author of poem 4 take from Petrarch? Like Petrarch he has previously used sighs to plea for pity; unlike Petrarch, he now uses his poetry to garner pity. Very possibly inspired by Petrarch's decision to sing the heavenly beauties of Laura, the author of poem 4 moves to praise Veronica Franco's beauty in lines 22–7. He does not speak of ever wanting others to hate Franco, but, in repeatedly blaming her for his suffering and in stating that he is content to know that she suffers, he exhibits an undercurrent of aggression that is present also in lines 7–8 of sonnet 217, when Petrarch acknowledges that he hoped others would hate Laura for her indifference.

Now Petrarch had affirmed that he did not seek either pity or hate but that he had moved beyond these to sing of Laura's godlike beauty. The male author of poem 4, even as he acknowledges Franco's beauty, has not moved to transcendence. He articulates what he seeks by first stating, like Petrarch, what he does not seek:

In voi non cerco affetto d'egual possa,
quel ch'a far di duo uno, un di duo, viene,
e duo traffigge di una sol percossa.

22 Quoting the final tercet of sonnet 217, Fred Botting and Scott Wilson write: "Death is the highest state of existence because (it is hoped) death may confer eternal life through, on the one hand, the immortality of fame and the 'laurel' of Poet, or on the other hand, 'imaginary fusion' with Laura and continuity with God" (*Bataille*, 53).

Troppo del viver mio l'ore serene
fôrano, e tanto più il mio ben intero,
quanto più raro questo amando avviene:
quanto Amor men sostien sotto 'l suo impero
che 'n duo cor sia una fiamma egual partita,
tanto più andrei de la mia sorte altero. (4.43–51)

(In you I don't seek affection equally strong,
the kind that makes one of two and two of one,
and transfixes two with a single stroke.
My life would be too full of happy hours
and my happiness too complete,
should love of such rarity happen to me.
The less often Love decrees that two hearts
under his rule should equally share
one flame, the prouder I'll be of my fate.)[23]

These are curious lines. At the same time that the male poet says that he does not expect Veronica Franco to respond with a love equal to his, he evokes a scene of union that can be read not only as a union of two souls but as a union of two bodies in simultaneous orgasm. This is the only place in his poem where he marshals erotic language. And he uses this erotic language as a springboard to enter into a more theoretical reflection on how his happiness and his satisfaction are in inverse relation to the frequency with which such love happens. He returns to comment on the relation of "two" and "one" when he highlights the "two hearts" that "equally share one flame," but by then the physically erotic charge has dissipated.

At this point, since the male author is responding with the same rhyme scheme and the same number of verses, he knows he must start wrapping up. In the next three tercets he highlights questions about relative strength of emotion and about relative worth:

Sì come troppo è la mia speme ardita,
che sì audaci pensieri al cor m'invia,
per strada dal discorso non seguìta:
da l'un canto il pensar sì com'io sia,
verso 'l vostro valor, di merto poco,
dal soverchio sperar l'alma desvia;

23 I have modified Jones and Rosenthal's translation of 4.43–5 in order to emphasize that the male poet is comparing Franco's level of affection to his own.

da l'altro Amor gentil ch'adegui invoco
la mia tanta con voi disagguaglianza,
e gridando mercé son fatto roco. (4.52–60)

(Because my hope is too daring
and it sends such bold thoughts to my heart,
on a path that discursive thinking does not follow.
on one hand, the thought of how slight is my merit,
compared to your worth, waylays my soul,
off the path of its high hope;
on the other hand, I call on gentle Love
to lessen my great inferiority to you,
and I am hoarse from calling for mercy.)[24]

Line 54 is particularly challenging. What does it mean to send bold thoughts to a heart "on a path that discursive thinking [*discorso*] does not follow"? While "discorso" can mean "speech," or perhaps even "everyday speech," which is how Jones and Rosenthal translate it, I believe that here it has a connotation that is philosophical and I have therefore translated "discorso" as "discursive thinking." (Consider the philosophical reflections, such as those of Thomas Aquinas, on whether God's knowledge is "discursive," that is, whether God thinks of one thing and then thinks of another, as opposed to seeing everything at once.)[25] The male poet is describing a struggle between non-discursive thinking that is proper to the heart and discursive thinking that is proper to the intellect. Essentially, he is saying that he cannot help but be irrational about what he wants, and then he goes on to say, in lines 55–60, that he alternates between being overwhelmed by how inferior he is to Franco and imploring Love to make him less inferior.

Elaborating on his invocation of Love, the male poet enters into territory that is worth further consideration:

24 Jones and Rosenthal's translation of 4.52–4, "Because my hope is much too daring / to send such bold thoughts to my heart / on a path untraveled by everyday speech," communicates that the poet might not be sending the bold thoughts to his heart at all or that he might be sending them with speech that is not run of the mill.

25 See Thomas Aquinas, *Summa Theologiae*, first part (prima pars), question 14, article 7, "Is the knowledge of God discursive?" This philosophical meaning of "discorso" is present also in one of the attestations of the word in the dictionary of the Accademia della Crusca: "La virtù ch'a ragion discorso ammanna," which C.H. Grandgent translates as "that power which provides discrimination [*discorso*] for reasoning"; see his "Confessio Dantis," 321.

D'Amor, ch'a nullo amato per usanza
perdona amar, dove un bel petto serra
pensier cortesi, invoco la possanza:
quella, onde 'l ciel ei sol chiude e disserra,
e, perch'a lui la terra è poco bassa,
gli spirti fuor de l'imo centro sferra,
prego che l'alma travagliata e lassa
sostenga; e, se non ciò, vaglia pietate
là dove 'l vostro orgoglio non s'abbassa. (4.61–9)

(Of Love, which by habit spares no one loved
from loving in return, wherever a fair breast
encloses courteous thoughts, I invoke the might –
that might through which he alone
shuts and opens heaven, and unleashes the spirits
from the core of the earth, which is not deep to him.
I pray him to sustain my troubled, weary soul;
and if not, then I pray that pity may reign
there where your pride refuses to bend.)

The most striking recall is in the words, "D'Amor, ch'a nullo amato per usanza / perdona amar, dove un bel petto serra / pensieri cortesi, invoco la possanza" (Of Love, which by habit spares no one loved / from loving in return [...] / I invoke the might; 4.61–3). At the end of a poem that has been largely Petrarchan in its echoes of other texts, the male poet suddenly involves Dante, as he evokes the language that the damned Francesca da Rimini uses in *Inferno* 5, the circle of the lustful, to describe Love's power over her: "Amor, che a nullo amato amar perdona, / mi prese del costui piacer sì forte / che, come vedi, ancor non m'abbandona" (Love, who permits no one who is loved not to love in return, seized me so strongly with his charm, that as you see, it remains with me still).[26] Like Francesca, the male poet seems not attuned to the way in which this view of love might not be fully legitimate.

Yet the male poet deflects any notion that this view of love might affect him. Whereas Francesca da Rimini speaks of how Love affected her, by requiring her to reciprocate Paolo's love, the male poet makes the rule about Love contingent rather than absolute. First of all, Love has this power "per usanza," which Jones and Rosenthal translate as "by habit," but which we could also translate as "customarily." Even more

26 Dante Alighieri, *Inferno*, ed. Chiavacci Leonardi. The English translation is mine.

important, Love has this power when there are "courteous thoughts in a fair breast," and, while anyone can have courteous thoughts, the "fair breast" (bel petto) is likely gendered female.

Let us also recognize that Love's mighty power is portrayed as somewhat frightening. Not only does Love alone control access to heaven, which we might take to be a figurative representation of Love's ability to bring happiness or not, but he "unleashes the spirits from the core of the earth," which sounds quite ominous. Also not reassuring is the fact that the earth is said to be "not deep" to him, which puts him into greater proximity with spirits who inhabit nether regions.

Having displayed the awful might of Love, the male poet does not, contrary to what we might expect, ask Love to wield that awful might against Veronica Franco. Rather he requests that Love sustain his "troubled, weary soul," and, as if to acknowledge that Love's might has limits, he provides an alternative, involving pity: "e, se non ciò, vaglia pietate / là dove 'l vostro orgoglio non s'abbassa" (and if not, then I pray that pity may reign / there where your pride refuses to bend; 4.68–9).

This brings the male poet to his final pleas to Veronica Franco:

> Di mercé sotto aspetto non mi date
> lusingando martìr, tanto più ch'io
> v'adoro; e quanto prima ritornate,
> ch'al lato starvi ognor bramo e desio. (4.70–3)

> (Do not make me suffer under pretended pity,
> all the more since I adore you;
> and return as soon as you possibly can,
> for I long and desire to be always at your side.)

In his parting statement the male poet places into question Veronica Franco's sincerity, suggesting that her words offer merely the semblance of pity. He, on the other hand, affirms his devotion, fidelity, and intense longing. He ends the poem with the word "desio" (I desire; 4.73). While he has been writing his poetic response in the same rhyme scheme that Veronica Franco used in poem 3, only twice does he use the exact same word that Franco uses. One of those instances is in his final rhyme on "desio" (I desire), which Franco had used when she ended her poem by saying "troncando a me 'l martír, a voi 'l desio" (ending my suffering and your desire; 3.73).[27] The repetition of "desio" functions as an olive

27 The other instance is in 3.31 and 4.31, with a rhyme on "giri," which Franco uses as a noun ("swirls") and the male poet uses as a verb ("turns"; translation mine).

branch, an offer of union and harmony – and all the more because the male poet proclaims his adoration of Franco.

Franco sets out questions about poetic identity and community, thus defining the terms of the discussion; she establishes a rhyme scheme that he accepts, and, given that she has already promised the man that she will make up for his past suffering, he comes off as carping, especially when he wishes her ill. In the court of public opinion she appears larger hearted, all the more so because she spares herself the trouble of responding to him on his terms.

3 Repenting as a Courtesan: *Terze rime* 5 and 6

In poem 5, Franco writes to an unknown man, declaring that his virtue, valour, and eloquence have freed her from loving another; she affirms that whereas she followed her senses previously, she is now guided by reason. In poem 6 the unknown male author responds, using Franco's rhyme scheme. He expresses appreciation for her commitment to virtue and writes that, although he actually lacks virtue, he, like her, has a strong desire to possess it. He expresses cautious hope that she will make her way toward him and he will be able to demonstrate to her his sincerity, affection, and loyalty. At twenty-two lines each, these two poems are the shortest of the collection.

Previous commentaries on these poems tend to place them in a biographical narrative, often to speculate on the man's identity;[1] however, a sustained close reading of them will reveal that they are a crucial moment in Franco's construction of her personal and poetic identity. I shall read poem 5 in light of several Petrarchan antecedents and demonstrate how unconventional it is as a statement of repentance for love based on sensual attraction; I shall also reflect on what Franco accomplishes by positioning this poem and the unknown man's response to it relatively early in her twenty-five-poem collection.

1 Arturo Graf reads poem 5 as addressed to the same man as in poem 4 (*Attraverso il Cinquecento*, 312–13). Irma Jaffe suggests that poem 5 could have been written after Franco's stay at Fumane, described in the final poem of the *Terze rime*, and claims that it is addressed either to Marco Venier or to Domenico Venier (*Shining Eyes, Cruel Fortune*, 361–2). In the introduction to their edition and translation of Franco's poems and letters, Ann Rosalind Jones and Margaret Rosenthal state that the unnamed man is "probably Domenico Venier" (Franco, *Poems and Selected Letters*, ed. and trans. Jones and Rosenthal, 85).

Here is poem 5 in its entirety:

Signor, la virtù vostra e 'l gran valore
e l'eloquenzia fu di tal potere,
che d'altrui man m'ha liberato il core;
il qual di breve spero ancor vedere
collocato entro 'l vostro gentil petto,
e regnar quivi, e far vostro volere.
Quel ch'amai più, più mi torna in dispetto,
né stimo più beltà caduca e frale,
e mi pento che già n'ebbi diletto.
Misera me, ch'amai ombra mortale,
ch'anzi doveva odiar, e voi amare,
pien di virtù infinita ed immortale!
Tanto numer non ha di rena il mare,
quante volte di ciò piango: ch'amando
fral beltà, virtù eterna ebbi a sprezzare.
Il mio fallo confesso sospirando,
e vi prometto e giuro da dovero
mandar per la virtù la beltà in bando.
Per la vostra virtù languisco e pèro,
disciolto 'l cor da quell'empia catena,
onde mi avolse il dio picciolo arciero:
già seguì' 'l senso, or la ragion mi mena. (5.1–22)

(Sir, your virtue and your great valor
and your eloquence had such power
that they freed my heart from another's hand;
and that heart I soon hope to see
placed within your noble breast,
and ruling there and doing your will.
What I most loved I now despise,
and I no longer value weak and frail beauty
and repent of ever having delighted in it.
Unhappy me, who loved a mortal shadow
that I should have hated and loved you instead,
endowed with infinite, undying virtue!
The sea does not have as many grains of sand
as the number of times I weep over this:
loving frail beauty, I disdained endless virtue.
Sighing, I confess my mistake,
and I promise and swear to you truly

that I'll banish beauty in favor of virtue.
I languish and die, longing for your virtue,
my heart freed from that evil chain
with which the little archer god bound me;
once I followed my senses, now reason is my guide.)

Franco organizes this poem around a series of dichotomies: present versus past; virtue versus beauty; what is undying versus what is mortal; repentance versus delight; freedom versus constraint; reason versus the senses. Although in her two previous poems she had allowed for praise of male beauty and the possibility of mutual sexual fulfilment, here she claims to reject what she valued in the past and to turn toward loftier values. By distancing herself from sensual love, Franco appears to be inserting herself into a conventional poetic conversion narrative.

Strikingly absent, however, is the kind of strict dichotomy between love and friendship that we see, for example, when Petrarch writes about his friend and patron, Cardinal Giovanni Colonna, and Laura. Sara Maria Adler, who argues that the "notion of love and friendship as complementary, rather than mutually exclusive, is […] found throughout [Franco's] *Rime*," sees poem 5 as the most striking example of this.[2] As evidence, she cites Petrarch's *Rvf* 266, "Signor mio caro, ogni pensier mi tira":

Signor mio caro, ogni pensier mi tira
devoto a veder voi cui sempre veggio;
la mia fortuna (or che mi po far peggio?)
mi tene a freno et mi travolve et gira;

poi quel dolce desio ch' Amor mi spira
menami a morte ch' i' non me n'aveggio;
et mentre i miei duo lumi indarno cheggio,
dovunque io son dì et notte si sospira.

Carità di signore, amor di donna
son le catene ove con molti affanni
legato son, perch' io stesso mi strinsi;

un lauro verde, una gentil colomna,
quindeci l'una et l'altro diciotto anni
portato ò in seno, et già mai non mi scinsi.[3]

---

2 Adler, "Veronica Franco's Petrarchan *Terze Rime*," 227.

3 The Italian text and English translation are taken from Petrarca, *Petrarch's Lyric Poems*, trans. and ed. Durling.

(My dear Lord, every thought draws me devotedly to see you whom I always see, but my fortune (what can it do to me that is worse?) keeps me reined in and wheels me and turns me about.

And then the sweet desire that Love inspires in me leads me to death so gradually that I am not aware of it, and while I call out in vain for my two lights, wherever I am there is sighing day and night.

Devotion to my lord, love of my lady are the chains where with much labor I am bound, and I myself took them on!

A green Laurel, a noble Column, the latter for fifteen, the former for eighteen years, I have carried in my breast and have never put from me.)

Before considering how Franco engages with Petrarch's notions of friendship and love, we should pause over *Rvf* 266 in order to understand it better. Is Petrarch's poem "structured by the relation of antithesis between what his friend represents to him and what Laura represents," as Adler claims, or does it show, as Aileen Feng argues, a "conflation of the identities of the 'Colonna patron' and the beloved"?[4] In my view, both things are going on in *Rvf* 266, and we therefore need a more sophisticated language to describe its complexities. In fact, readings of this Petrarchan sonnet provide excellent examples of why we always need to be extremely careful when we characterize what Petrarch is doing. When we read Petrarch in order to assert that later poets "subvert the master's plan," we may be tempted to make the master's plan look more stable than it is.

There are some profoundly destabilizing moves in *Rvf* 266, and a comparison of readings and translations makes this starkly evident. Consider line 6, "et mentre i miei duo lumi indarno cheggio" (and while I call out in vain for my two lights). It appears that most readers see the "two lights" as a reference to Laura's eyes, likely because the verse in question appears in a quatrain that begins with a reference to the desire that leads the poet to death, and ends with a reference to his sighs.[5] Feng acknowledges that typically Petrarch figures the two lights as Laura's eyes, but in this case she reads the verse as referring to

4 Adler, "Veronica Franco's Petrarchan *Terze Rime*," 226; Feng, *Writing Beloveds*, 40–2.

5 See the Oregon Petrarch Open Book, "Paraphrase: Poem Number: 266," https://petrarch.uoregon.edu/paraphrases/7625, which renders "the two eyes" (i duo lumi) as "her eyes" (i suoi occhi). See also the paraphrase in Italian found on the website of *HUK Parafrasi e commenti*.

Giovanni Colonna's eyes.[6] Alessandro Vellutello sees the two lights as referring to Colonna on the one hand and to Laura on the other; Mark Musa also reads the two lights as Colonna and Laura.[7]

Consider also line 9, "Carità di signore, amor di donna." It is ambiguous enough to permit us to project our own views of the nature of the emotional ties that bind Petrarch. Here I would argue that Petrarch establishes a potential tension between charitable, selfless love ("carità") and a love associated with a woman ("amor di donna"). While readers consistently accept that "amor di donna" refers to Petrarch's love for Laura, they are less in agreement about what "Carità di signore" means. Is this about Petrarch's "devotion" to or "fondness" for Giovanni Colonna?[8] Or does it refer to Colonna's "benevolence" toward Petrarch?[9] Petrarch casts mystery on the emotional bond between himself and Giovanni Colonna, allowing for a potential two-way charitable tie. If that mystery slides into "amor di donna" as well, we might see the expression of Petrarch's desire: if this refers to his love for Laura, might it also not refer to a wished-for situation in which Laura would love him?

How does Veronica Franco refashion elements from *Rvf* 266? She avoids the metaphysical language, the abstractions, and the move toward the universal that Petrarch adopts when he figures his friend as a "noble column" and Laura as the "green laurel."[10] Throughout she affirms her rectitude, not merely by her praise of virtue and her promise to adhere to virtue in the future, but also in subtler ways that draw attention to her nobler impulses. For her, love is not a way to exercise a kind of reassuring possession of the beloved, as it is for Petrarch who says he carries Colonna and Laura within his breast. Instead, she hopes that her heart, a symbol of her love that has been freed from her previous love interest's hand, will take its place in the noble breast of the male addressee of the poem. Whereas Petrarch is overcome by

6 Feng, *Writing Beloveds*, 41.

7 See Vellutello, *Il Petrarca con l'espositione d'Alessandro Vellutello*, 71r, and Musa's note to line 7 of poem 266, in Petrarca, *Petrarch: The Canzoniere*, 706.

8 Robert Durling (*Petrarch's Lyric Poems*), translates this line as "Devotion to my lord, love of my lady." Mark Musa (*Petrarch: The Canzoniere*) translates it as "Devotion to a lord, love of a lady." A.S. Kline translates it as "Fondness for my lord, love of my lady"; see Petrarca, *The Complete Canzoniere*, trans. Kline.

9 The Oregon Petrarch Open Book renders the phrase as "Benevolenza dal mio signore" (Benevolence from my lord; "Paraphrase: Poem Number: 266"), https://petrarch.uoregon.edu.

10 For a reading of *Rvf* 266 that highlights the relation of the universal and the metaphysical versus the particular, the physical, and the immanent, see Barolini, "Petrarch as the Metaphysical Poet Who Is Not Dante," 219–21.

sighs in his longing for his "two lights," Franco sighs as she repents her past error. Whereas Petrarch's love for Laura brings him toward death, Franco languishes and comes near death on account of the man's virtue. Petrarch affirms that he himself is responsible for the chains that continue to bind him; Franco says she was chained by Cupid but that she is now free of those chains.

Notably, in poem 5, Veronica Franco adopts language that portrays her addressee as god-like and that portrays herself as reformed sinner. She begins by addressing him as "Signor" (5.1), which Jones and Rosenthal translate as "Sir" but which could also be translated as "Lord." His virtue, valour, and eloquence are exceptionally powerful (5.1–3); his virtue, mentioned five times, is described as infinite and endless (5.12, 5.15); and, depending on how we read line 12, she might even be referring to him, rather than his virtue, as immortal. She speaks of her repentance in line 9 and confesses her error in line 16, and promises reparation in lines 16–17. Indeed, were it not for the fact that an unknown male author responds in poem 6, using the same rhyme scheme as that of poem 5, one might conclude that in poem 5 Franco could be addressing God himself rather than a virtuous mortal. She allows for uncertainty throughout her entire poem. Petrarch, however, allows that the opening of *Rvf* 266, "Signor mio caro, ogni pensier mi tira / devoto a veder voi" (My dear Lord, every thought draws me devoted to see you), might initially make one think that the addressee is God, but he undercuts that possibility immediately when he completes the second line by saying "cui sempre veggio" (whom I always see). As is attested both in John 1:18 and in I John 4:12, "Deum nemo vidit umquam" (No one has ever seen God).[11]

Franco's addressee in poem 5 is neither clearly identified as God nor identified as mortal. Of course, if Franco wanted us to identify her addressee as God, she could have made that patently evident. That is what Gaspara Stampa does when she addresses God in sonnet 275 (304):

> Di queste tenebrose, e fiere voglie
> Ch'io drizzai ad amar cosa mortale,
> Seguendo il van disio fallace e frale,
> Che sì rio frutto di sue opre coglie,
> S'avien, che la tua gratia non mi spoglie,
> Poi chè per me la mia forza non vale,

11 *Biblia sacra iuxta vulgatam versionem*, ed. Weber; the English translation is mine.

Temo, che l'aversario empio infernale
Non riporti di me lamate spoglie.
  Dolce Signor, che sei venuto in terra,
Et hai presa, per me terrena vesta
Per combatter', e vincer questa guerra,
  Dammi lo scudo di tua gratia, e desta
In me virtù, sì ch'io getti per terra
Ogni affetto terren, che mi molesta.[12]

  (These wild and shadowy longings
that I directed toward loving a mortal thing,
pursuing vain desire, deceptive and frail,
that gathers from its works such evil fruit –
  if it happens that your grace does not despoil
me of all this (for my own strength is not enough),
I fear the impish adversary from hell
will carry off with him my beloved spoils.
  Sweet Lord, for me you came down to earth
and took on an earthly garment
so you could fight and win this war.
  Give me the shield of your grace, awaken
in my virtue, so I may throw to earth
every mortal affection that molests me.)

In the first quatrain Stampa identifies her desire for a mortal thing and still allows for the possibility that her addressee is human; then in the second quatrain, with the reference to her limited power, to the grace she needs, and to the threat posed to her by the devil, it becomes far more likely that her addressee is God. Any doubt is dispelled in the first tercet, when, in referencing the mystery of the Incarnation, she makes it clear that her addressee is Christ. The second tercet is a prayer for the grace and strength to overcome earthly affective ties. The overall message of the sonnet is that Stampa definitively wishes to turn toward God and away from the earthly longings that could make her victim of the infernal adversary.

When Petrarch addresses God in *Rvf* 365, "I' vo piangendo i miei passati tempi," the penultimate poem and last sonnet in the *Rvf*, it is somewhat less clear that he has turned away definitively from earthly

12 The Italian text and English translation are taken from Stampa, *The Complete Poems*, ed. Tower and Tylus.

things, and it is likely the reason that Veronica Franco engages with this Petrarchan sonnet in her poem 5.

Here is the Italian text of *Rvf* 365, with two English translations, the first by Robert Durling and the second by Mark Musa:

I' vo piangendo i miei passati tempi
i quai posi in amar cosa mortale
senza levarmi a volo, abbiend'io l'ale,
per dar forse di me non bassi esempi.

Tu che vedi i miei mali indegni et empi,
Re del Cielo, invisibile, immortale,
soccorri a l'alma disviata et frale,
e 'l suo defetto di tua grazia adempi,

sì che, s' io vissi in guerra et in tempesta,
mora in pace et in porto; et se la stanza
fu vana, almen sia la partita honesta.

A quel poco di viver che m'avanza
et al morir degni esser tua man presta:
tu sai ben che 'n altrui non ò speranza.[13]

(I go weeping for my past time, which I spent in loving a mortal thing without lifting myself in flight, though I had wings to make of myself perhaps not a base example.

You who see all my unworthy and wicked sufferings, invisible, immortal King of Heaven: help my strayed frail soul and fill out with your grace all that she lacks,

so that, though I have lived in war and in storm, I may die in peace and in port, and if my sojourn has been vain, my departure at least may be virtuous.

To what little life remains to me and to my dying deign to be present: You know well that I have no hope in anyone else.) (Durling)[14]

---

13 Petrarca, *Petrarch's Lyric Poems*, trans. and ed. Durling, 575.
14 Petrarca, 574.

(I go my way lamenting those past times
I spent in loving something which was mortal
instead of soaring high, since I had wings
that might have taken me to higher levels.

You who see all my shameful, wicked errors,
King of all Heaven, invisible, immortal,
help this frail soul of mine for she has strayed,
and all her emptiness fill up with grace,

so that, having once lived in storms, at war,
I may now die in peace, in port; and if my stay
was vain, at least let my departure count.

Over the little life that still remains to me,
and at my death, deign that your hand be present:
You know You are the only hope I have.) (Musa)[15]

I have provided two English translations in order to demonstrate that *Rvf* 365 exhibits a tension between penitence for having loved a mortal thing and what one scholar has called "a residual justification of the love for Laura."[16] Readers who want to see Petrarch's turn away from mortal things as complete are wont to emphasize the echoes of *Rvf* 264, "I' vo pensando, et nel penser m'assale," the canzone that opens part 2 of the *Rvf* and identifies the spiritual predicament that will presumably be resolved in *Rvf* 366, the final poem of the collection in which Petrarch commends himself to the Virgin Mary. Particularly relevant are lines 99–103 from *Rvf* 264:

Ché mortal cosa amar con tanta fede
quanto a Dio sol per debito convensi
più si disdice a chi più pregio brama.
Et questo ad alta voce anco richiama
la ragione sviata dietro ai sensi.[17]

(For the more one desires honor, the more one is forbidden to love a mortal thing with the faith that belongs to God alone. And this with a loud voice calls back my reason, which wanders after my senses.)

15 Petrarca, *Petrarch: The Canzoniere*, trans. Musa.
16 See Foster, "Beatrice or Medusa," 54.
17 Petrarca, *Petrarch's Lyric Poems*, trans. and ed. Durling.

Readers wishing to see a complete penitential resolution will also likely highlight Petrarch's commendation of himself to God in the final tercet, which echoes a collect from the Roman mass (third Sunday after Epiphany):

> Omnipotens sempiterne deus infirmitatem nostram propitius respice atque ad protegendum nos dexteram tuae maiestatis extende.[18]
>
> (Almighty everlasting God, look mercifully upon our weakness, and, in order to protect us, stretch out the right hand of your majesty.)

Does *Rvf* 365, which ends with a request for God's aid and protection, document an unwavering repentance for past sins? Mark Musa's translation suggests that it does; Robert Durling's translation places the repentance and conversion in some doubt. Musa, on the one hand, translates the "mali indegni e empi" of line 5 as "shameful, wicked errors"; Durling, on the other hand, has Petrarch still focused on his own pain, as he offers that these are "unworthy and wicked sufferings." The tension between these two readings was evident already in Giosuè Carducci and Severino Ferrari's commentary, where, evidently concerned that readers could be tempted to interpret "mali" as "sufferings," they take care to undermine such a reading:

> La voce **mali** non significa patimenti, ma errori e peccati; e le due che seguono, **indegni et empi**, non risguardano la persona del p. quasi che indebitamente egli sofferisca alcuna miseria, ma risguardano la materia stessa dei peccati e l'oggetto contra cui empiamente e indegnamente sono commessi, ch'è Dio.[19]
>
> ("Mali" does not mean "sufferings" but "errors and sins." And "indegni" and "empi" do not refer to the person of the poet as if he wrongfully suffers misery – they refer to the sins themselves and the object against which they are wickedly and shamefully committed, i.e., God.)

---

18 *CURSUS: An Online Resource of Medieval Liturgical Texts*, http://www.cursus.org.uk.

19 Petrarca, *Le rime di Francesco Petrarca di su gli originali*, 510; the English translation is mine. Carducci and Ferrari end their commentary with the note "(T)," by which initial they refer to Alessandro Tassoni's commentary, *Considerazioni sopra le rime del Petrarca d'Alessandro Tassoni* (Modena, Italy: Giulian Cassiani, 1611). I remain puzzled by this. Granted, I have not been able to see the 1611 edition of the *Considerazioni*, but the 1609 edition in the Cornell University Petrarch Collection that I have consulted (which was also published in Modena by Giulian Cassiani) contains no such passage.

Musa tries to shore up the turn toward God by having Petrarch state that he laments having loved a mortal thing "instead of soaring high." But Musa forces "senza levarmi a volo" when he translates it thus. "Senza" clearly means "without," not "instead," and Durling correctly translates the verse as "without lifting myself in flight."

It is important that we understand *Rvf* 365 as not a full justification of the love for Laura but rather, as Foster has defined it, a *residual* justification. Since, as Aldo Bernardo has pointed out, this residual justification "emerged much more clearly in the original order of the *Canzoniere* before Petrarch decided to reorder the last thirty poems,"[20] it appears that Petrarch attenuated the justification, leaving a pull toward mortal thoughts even as he affirmed his turn toward God.

With this more nuanced understanding of Petrarch's sonnet, let us return to Veronica Franco. Comparing Franco's poem 5 to Petrarch's *Rvf* 365 allows us to see more clearly how Franco reconfigures notions of frailty and power. She draws on Petrarch's rhyme of "mortale" / "l'ale" / "immortale" / "frale" (mortal / wing / immortal / frail) with her own rhyme of "frale" / "mortale" / "immortale" (frail / mortal / immortal), but, while Petrarch highlights his own weakness as he writes of his "frail soul" (alma frale), Franco shifts the adjective "frail" away from herself, attaching it to the "weak and frail beauty" (beltà caduca e frale; 5.8) of the man she previously loved; she underscores this some lines later by again defining that beauty as "frail" (fral beltà; 5.15). Like Petrarch, she confesses that she was wrong to have loved a mortal thing, but, unlike him, she does not rely on a dichotomy of mortal being versus immortal being (i.e., Laura versus God). Rather, drawing a dichotomy of mortal qualities versus immortal qualities (i.e., beauty versus virtue), which allows her to affirm her addressee's power, she asserts that he is "pien di virtù infinita e immortale" (endowed with infinite, undying virtue). If we believe her to be addressing a human male, her syntactic placement of "immortale" (undying, immortal) is cleverly ambiguous, as it could allow for a reading that teases us with the thought that the man himself is "endowed with infinite virtue, and immortal." Petrarch's appeal to God is marked by imperatives and an exhortative that remind us that God, his only hope, has yet to provide relief for him: "soccorri a l'alma disvïata et frale, / e 'l suo defecto di tua gratia adempi [...] / A quel poco di viver che m'avanza / et al morir, degni esser Tua man presta." (Help this frail soul of mine for she has strayed, / and all her

20 Bernardo, *Petrarch, Laura, and the "Triumphs,"* 159.

emptiness fill up with grace [...] / Over the little life that still remains to me, / and at my death, deign that your hand be present.) But if Petrarch awaits the strength, power, and protection of God's hand, Franco's virtuous addressee has already intervened, to liberate her heart from her previous love. And she appears confident in her hope for her heart's future. Notably, she tells her addressee that she hopes soon to see her heart "placed within your noble breast, / and ruling there and doing your will" (collocato entro 'l vostro gentil petto, / e regnar quivi, e far vostro volere; 5.5–6). Her heart takes up a position of power by "ruling there" in the noble breast, but its position of power morphs into a position of subjection because her heart will also be doing his will. With these verses Franco affirms her addressee's power but also reaffirms her own, thus fashioning a co-equal affective relationship where the power is balanced.[21]

Before considering what Franco achieves by placing this poem fifth in her *Terze rime*, let us briefly consider her male addressee's response in poem 6:

Contrari son tra lor ragion e amore,
e chi 'n amor aspetta antivedere,
di senso è privo e di ragion è fuore.
Tanto più in prezzo è da doversi avere
vostro discorso, in cui avete eletto
voler in stima la virtù tenere;
e bench'io di lei sia privo in effetto,
con voi di possederla il desio vale,
sì che del buon voler premio n'aspetto:
e se 'l timor de l'esser mio m'assale,
poi mi fa contra i merti miei sperare,
ché s'elegge per ben un minor male.
Io non mi vanto per virtù d'andare
a segno che, l'amor vostro acquistando,
mi possa in tanto grado collocare;
ma so ch'un'alma valorosa, quando
trova uom che 'l falso aborre e segue il vero,
a lui si va con diletto accostando:
e tanto più se dentro a un cor sincero

21 Adler, "Veronica Franco's Petrarchan *Terze Rime*," 227, describes this as "the affectionate intimacy characteristic of the love between a man and a woman"; I emphasize the power equilibrium because even in intimacy there could conceivably be an imbalance of power.

d'alta fé trova affezzion ripiena,
come nel mio, ch'un dì mostrarvi spero,
se 'l non poter le voglie non m'affrena. (6.1–22)

(Reason and love are contrary to each other,
and whoever expects to predict love's course
is bereft of wit and deprived of reason.
So there is all the more cause to value
your declaration, in which you've resolved
to hold virtue in highest esteem,
and though, in truth, I lack that quality,
my desire to possess it, with you, is strong enough
that I expect a reward for my good will:
and, if fear of what I am assails me,
it makes me hope, too, in spite of my merits,
that it may be a blessing to choose a lesser evil.
I do not claim that I could attain,
by winning your love, sufficient virtue
to rise to such a lofty goal,
but I do know that a gallant soul,
finding a man who hates lies and follows truth,
makes her way toward him with delight:
and all the more if in a heart that's sincere
she finds affection, full of truest faith,
as in mine, which I hope to show you one day,
if powerlessness does not rein in my desires.)[22]

Compared to the other poems attributed to an unknown male author, poem 6 is unusual in a number of ways. It marks the first time in the *Terze rime* that a poet does not use the opening tercet to address the poem's recipient.[23] Instead, the male poet begins with an abstract

22 I have modified Jones and Rosenthal's translation of "e se 'l timor de l'esser mio m'assale, / poi mi fa contra i merti miei sperare" (6.10–11), by substituting "and, if fear of what I am assails me, / it makes me hope, too, in spite of my merits" for their "and, if fear of my true self assails me, / it makes me hope, too, in spite of my few merits."

23 Compare the opening tercets of previous poems: "S'io v'amo al par de la mia propria vita / donna crudel, e voi perché non date / in tanto amor al mio tormento aita? (If I love you as much as my own life, / cruel lady, why do you offer no relief for my suffering in such great love?; 1.1–3); "S'esser del vostro amor potessi certa / per quel che mostran le parole e 'l volto, / che spesso tengon varia alma coperta" (If I could be certain of your love, / from what your words and face display, / which often

philosophical pronouncement that reason and love are contrary to each other. Stating that reason and love are in tension threatens to blow open the potential contradiction at the heart of Franco's poem 5. If indeed reason and love are at cross purposes, can she declare her intention to love a man of virtue and at the same time assert, as she did in the final line of her poem, that reason is her guide? But the male poet avoids going there. In the second tercet he addresses Franco and swivels into a *captatio benevolentiae* to appreciate what she has said:

> Tanto più in prezzo è da doversi avere
> vostro discorso, in cui avete eletto
> voler in stima la virtù tenere. (6.4–6)

> (What you say is to be all the more appreciated
> as you have chosen to want
> to hold virtue in high esteem.) (translation mine)[24]

These verses are oddly cagey. The connection with the preceding tercet is not clear, and it is also not clear from what the male poet says that he fully believes that Franco has "resolved / to hold virtue in highest esteem." Is "choosing to want to hold virtue in high esteem" the same as "choosing to hold virtue in high esteem"? Partly by delaying the lines that respond specifically to what Franco has written, and partly by being exceptionally precise about what she appears to have promised, the male poet manages to express appreciation for Franco's stated embrace of virtue while simultaneously creating some doubt about whether we will always do what we say we will do, particularly when love is involved.

Furthermore, poem 6 marks the only time in the *Terze rime* that a male poet focuses on his insufficiency and inadequacy. In response to Franco's attribution of virtue to him, he claims that he lacks that

---

conceal a changing mind; 2.1–3); "Questa la tua fedel Franca ti scrive, / dolce, gentil, suo valoroso amante / la qual lunge da te, misera vive" (This your faithful Franca writes you, / tender, well-bred, and gallant lover, / she who in misery lives far away from you; 3.1–3); "A voi la colpa, a me, donna, s'ascrive / il danno, e 'l duol di quelle pene tante, / che 'l mio cor sente, e 'l vostro stil descrive" (To you, lady, belongs the blame, / to me the pain of all the griefs / that my heart feels and your pen describes; 4.1–3); "Signor, la virtù vostra e 'l gran valore / e l'eloquenzia fu di tal potere, / che d'altrui man m'ha liberato il core" (Sir, your virtue and your great valor / and your eloquence had such power / that they freed my heart from another's hand; 5.1–3).

24 Jones and Rosenthal's translation reads, "So there is all the more cause to value / your declaration, in which you've resolved / to hold virtue in highest esteem."

quality (6.7), that he is fearful of what he is (6.10), that his merits are few (6.11), and that he has been chosen as the lesser evil (6.12). He does not "claim [... to] attain [...] / sufficient virtue" (Io non mi vanto per virtù d'andare / a segno; 6.13–14); and in choosing the verb "vantarsi" (to boast) to deny his claim, he underscores his modesty, since the verses could also be rendered as "*I do not boast* that I could attain [...] / sufficient virtue." In the final line he floats the possibility of powerlessless ("'l non poter"; 6.22) that could rein in his desires. Even in describing his good qualities, the male poet is guarded. He does not say that he himself is committed to the truth; rather, he describes how the gallant soul will seek out a "man who hates lies and follows truth" (uom che 'l falso aborre e segue il vero; 6.17), especially if he has "a heart that's sincere / [...] full of truest faith" (un cor sincero / d'alta fé [...] affezzion ripiena; 6.19–20). Only after having established an externalized scene, does the male poet then reveal that his heart is like that sincere heart full of truest faith, and only then does he reveal that he wishes someday to show his heart to Franco.

Unlike other unknown male voices included in the *Terze rime*, this unknown man remains cagey about the nature of his own desires. At the end of his poem, when he states that he hopes to show Franco his heart, he affirms his identity, his commitment to the truth, and his rejection of falsehood – but at a moment that he hopes will happen in the future. To allow her to see his heart suggests a potential psychological intimacy. Does it also suggest physical intimacy? It is difficult to say. Still, consider that earlier in the poem, this man broaches the subject of what he expects. Speaking about virtue, he offers a tantalizing assertion: "my desire to possess it, with you, is strong enough / that I expect a reward for my good will" (con voi di possederla il desio vale, / sì che del buon voler premio n'aspetto; 6.8–9). If we read these lines with a modicum of scepticism, we have to question whether this man, who expects a reward simply for having desired to possess virtue, meets our definition of a virtuous man. What, precisely, is the reward he wants? As a man who seeks virtue, he might be referring to the honour and appreciation that are accorded to men of virtue. But given that he is writing to Veronica Franco, one must wonder whether he is also alluding to the kinds of sexual favours that an honest courtesan could grant to a favoured client. If that is the case, we would have to wonder not only whether he is truly virtuous but also whether the final verse of the poem, which acknowledges the risk that powerlessness could rein in his desires, is an acknowledgment of possible impotence.

I began this chapter by proposing sustained textual analysis as a corrective to the tendency to read poems 5 and 6 for the information they can give us about a biographical narrative. Sustained textual analysis allows us to understand the depth of Franco's poetic engagement and highlights how she drew from the poetic tradition in order to craft her personal and poetic identity.

Nevertheless, given that Veronica Franco was highly skilled at crafting her image for public consumption, we should not entirely dismiss biographical considerations. Rather, we should consider how Franco dangles them before the reader.

In the first three poems under her signature in the *Terze rime*, Franco reveals a diverse self: open to being courted under the right conditions (poem 2), capable of feeling deep grief when separated from a beloved man and the city of Venice (poem 3), willing to acknowledge wrongdoing and committed to reason and virtue (poem 5). She also implicitly reaffirms the ways in which she establishes certain rules by which her male interlocuters must play. Not only does she reserve the right to determine the terms of a man's interaction with her (poem 2), but in poems 3 and 5 she establishes the rhyme schemes that her male respondents will adopt in poems 4 and 6.

The first three poems authored by men also represent diverse personalities and approaches. Poem 1, written by a would-be lover, and poem 4, written by a current love interest, attempt to cast Franco in the mould of the cruel woman. As I have shown in chapter 1, the author of poem 1 alternates between declarations of love and assertions of control and threat. As I have shown in chapter 2, the author of poem 4 takes an adversarial approach, emphasizing the differences between himself and Franco; although her poem 3 stands as testimony to community – be that the community of the city of Venice, the community of mythological figures, or the community offered by nature – the author of poem 4 speaks only of himself and Franco. Taken together, poems 1 and 4 speak to men's desire to circumscribe Franco's activity so that she focuses on them and their fulfilment. The male voice of poem 6, however, completely without arrogance, expresses appreciation for Franco's stated commitment to virtue.

Why might Franco not reveal the identities of the authors of poems 1, 4, and 6, choosing instead to feature each of them as an "incerto autore" (unknown author)? While the attribution of the first poem to Marco Venier could certainly serve as a kind of stamp of approval, encouraging an audience to see the poetic collection as worthy, the concealment of the identities of the male authors allows all readers to speculate on the identities of the authors of poems 1, 4, and 6, and to allow male readers to imagine themselves as the would-be objects of Veronica Franco's benevolent attention. (When male readers arrive at poems 7 through

12, they will be able to imagine themselves as the would-be objects of her rejection, and when they find poem 13, they can imagine how they would react to her challenge to a duel that could take place in a bed.)

With poem 5, Franco achieves the greatest leverage, and she does this by elevating her male interlocutor. So compelling is the rhetoric of praise in poem 5 that this poem could then be selected for inclusion in an anthology of women's poetry prepared for a nineteenth-century bride (though granted, to make the poem more fitting for a virginal bride, the last line, which reads "già seguì' 'l senso, or la ragion mi mena" (once I followed my senses, now reason is my guide) was modified to read "Voi solo guardo, or la ragion mi mena" (I gaze on you alone, now reason is my guide).[25] Without naming Domenico Venier, one of the most powerful literati in sixteenth-century Venice, Franco suggests with her praise of her addressee's supreme virtue in poem 5 that she could be addressing this luminary, who was widely extolled both for his poetic talents and for his moral uprightness.[26] (Given that Domenico Venier was severely debilitated by chronic gout, this hypothesis then receives further confirmation with the unknown male author's reference, in the final line of poem 6, to possible limitations on his abilities.)[27]

Poems 5 and 6 serve as a guide to how an honest courtesan can repent for past shortcomings and affirm virtue: choose an addressee that allows for remaining within a secular framework and hint at values that supersede it; shroud the addressee's identity in mystery; reconfigure notions of frailty and power; promote a vision of equitable love that is consonant with noble friendship; recognize and allow for an expression of masculinity that appears atypical in its acknowledgment of shortcomings and in its expression of desire; and concede that, when love is involved, it is no easy matter to strive for virtue and adhere to reason. Since the two poems pivot toward virtue while also accepting human falterings, they can be positioned early in the *Terze rime* to reinforce an honest courtesan's nobility while still allowing for the expressions of sensual desire and love that we will encounter in subsequent poems of the collection.

25 See *Fiori di rimatrici italiane dal secolo XIV al XVII*, a collection that Marco Tobia assembled on the occasion of the wedding of Sofia Kohen and Angelo Modigliani. Pages are unnumbered. The volume is available as a Google e-book.

26 On Domenico Venier's reputation for virtue and moral integrity, see Quaintance, *Textual Masculinity and the Exchange of Women in Renaissance Venice*, 115–16.

27 See Jaffe, *Shining Eyes, Cruel Fortune*, 362, on the last line of poem 6: "although a certain edge of humor colors this response, suggesting Marco as its author, the last line points to Domenico, whose illness must have to some extent inhibited his relationships."

4 Complaining and Cognitive Reframing: *Terze rime* 7 and 8

In the exchanges between the unknown male authors and Veronica Franco that we find in poems 7 through 12 of the *Terze rime*, we find complaints from men who hope to gain Franco's favour. The male author of poem 7 is distressed that he does not enjoy Veronica Franco's favours at all; the male authors of poems 9 and 11 are distressed that she has absented herself. Bemoaning a cruel fate, and ascribing various degrees of responsibility for this cruelty to Franco and external forces (Love, Fate, the stars), they argue that Franco should grace them with her presence and her affection. In each of her responses (poems 8, 10, and 12), Franco defends her decision not to grant what the men ask. While it is possible, of course, that poems 7, 9, and 11 were all authored by a single man who adopts various strategies to win Franco's attention, I would maintain that Franco, by keeping the identity of the author or authors unknown, encourages us to think that she does not always grant her favours to the multiple men who seek them.

What might one say about this cluster of poems? To judge by the minimal commentary from scholars, not much. For Margaret Rosenthal, these poems bolster a biographical reading, wherein Franco and the unknown male author of poems 4, 7, 9, and 11 "operate as innocents," given that Franco, in Rosenthal's view, is convinced that the author of these four poems is responsible for satirical and defamatory poetry written in dialect about Franco.[1] Thus, Rosenthal sees poems 8, 10, and 12, written by Franco, as evidence that she "continues to mistrust her interlocutor's insistence [...] that his declarations of love are founded on virtue and devotion."[2] Patricia Phillippy, in the course of analysing

1 Rosenthal, *The Honest Courtesan*, 186.
2 Rosenthal, 186.

Veronica Franco's use of Ovid's *Heroides*, limits herself to a brief commentary on poems 7 and 8, mainly to argue that Franco's poem 8, which emphasizes a world of erotic exchange and mismatched desires, "overturns the male speaker's rhetoric [...] by refusing the charges against her (that she is cruel and immune to the effects of love)" and relies on a reading of the *Heroides* that highlights not the "exemplary natures of the heroines and their anti-heroic polemic" but rather "the dialogism of the work, especially as it appears in Ovid's double letters."[3]

Where to go from here? I would suggest that if there has been little to say about these poems in the *Terze rime*, we might consider that, similarly, previous generations of scholars had little to say about the *Heroides*, which they viewed as repetitive and monotonous. Happily, readers of Ovid have come to give him greater credit. As Laurel Fulkerson has noted in her overview of scholarship on the *Heroides*, "for now the general consensus seems to be that the monotony is precisely the point of the corpus."[4] Fulkerson's summary comment is instructive: "[W]e are encouraged to revel in the sameness of it all and also to pay particular attention to variations on the basic themes; here, as throughout the poet's work, careful reading is amply rewarded [...] The primary effect of the similarities is to encourage the reader to consider what kinds of patterns emerge throughout a reading of the corpus, and some (but not enough) interesting work has been done on the significance of the order of the poems, which seems to defy a simple pattern."[5]

In this chapter and the two chapters that follow, I focus on poems 7 through 12 to consider how Franco uses this cluster, in which three poems by an unknown male author are followed by three responses from Franco herself, to reflect on unrequited love and to expand upon themes that appeared in the first six poems of the collection. Franco has used previous poems under her signature (poems 2, 3, and 5) to define who she is and what she values: her respect for virtue and valour, her way of responding to male aggression, her ability to feel and express pain when away from Venice and from a man she loves, her connectedness, her desire to adhere to reason, and her ability to admit when she has been on the wrong path. She will use the next three poems under

3 See Phillippy, "*Altera Dido*," 11, for the one sentence she dedicates to poem 7: "[T]he male speaker echoes both his Petrarchan predecessors, in charging Franco with 'crudeltà,' and Ovid's heroines by offering, as he states it, 'le mie querele e i miei lamenti.'"

4 Fulkerson, "The *Heroides*," 80. For an extended argument regarding monotony and repetition in the *Heroides*, Fulkerson refers readers to Lindheim, *Mail and Female*.

5 Fulkerson, "The *Heroides*," 80.

her signature (poems 8, 10, and 12) to illustrate how she responds to men who plead for her love, whether they complain of her cruelty (as in poems 7 and 9) or whether they shower her with praise and adulation (as in poem 11). Overall, her responses in poems 8, 10, and 12 reveal a poet with significant rhetorical skill and technical expertise (though this is not to say, of course, that there are no missteps in her poetry). In contrast, the male-authored poems 7 and 9 are striking for their rhetorical and stylistic maladroitness, and the male-authored poem 11 stands as a hackneyed exercise in overkill.

The first pair of poems in this cluster (poems 7 and 8) allows us to see Veronica Franco's ability to respond to scattered lines of reasoning and poetry that, frankly, is not that good. Countering the complaints that the male author advances in poem 7, Franco's poem 8 is a brilliant example of what we now call cognitive reframing, a psychological technique that consists in offering an alternate perspective on experiences, situations, emotions, and ideas, and challenging negative responses to these.

It will be helpful to have an overview of the arguments that the unknown male author offers in poem 7:

7.1–15: The poet asks four questions, which could be summed up as follows: You aren't using your great beauty for love? Are you going to bring death to those who love you? What could make life worse than to have such beauty united to ill will? Why don't the Furies rise up from Hell to do harm to us?

7.16–54: He addresses Love, understood as Cupid, asserting that in beauty his lady outdoes Venus, Cupid's mother, and, in knowledge and valour, Minerva; he offers that Love will be even greater if he brings the lady under his sway; he says she has not always been so hardened.

7.55–87: He presents the lady as opening her heart to Love and then redirecting the weapons of Love in order to collect a large number of lovers and bring people to burn and waste away for love of her. He states that her singular beauty and mental ability inflame their souls with double ardour; the more they burn, the more they are joyous and blessed. He says that he too would gladly burn thus but for the fact that he is despised by the lady; no one, he claims, is more wretched than he.

7.88–102: He asserts that not only has no other living being ever been struck down by Fortune as much as he has, but his lady intent upon his ruin becomes ever more cruel; alternately accusing Love and his lady, he asks what he can do but call for death, and then he asserts that in his ravings he tries to manage, sometimes by calling out to Love for help and sometimes in other ways.

7.103–11: He addresses Fortune (lines 103–8) and then Love (109–11).

7.112–32: He presents himself as assailed by a terrible fear, which we then discover is a fear that heaven may avenge his suffering on her; he confesses that he is always weighed down by despair; he offers that he would willingly serve her later, but she torments him with harsh tyranny, and, no matter what, she becomes ever more angry and cruel.

7.133–68: Addressing the woman directly, he alternates between praising her for her beauty, her grace, her lofty manners, and her overall excellence and undercutting his praise with jabs at her pride, her cruelty, and her disdain.

7.169–81: In the final lines of the poem, he asks how it is possible that he still has hope, embeds Veronica's name in verses in which he calls upon her – "*vera, unica* al mondo eccelsa dea" (*verily unique* goddess, supreme on earth; 7.173) – and begs her not to be so cruel to him.[6]

Although scholars who summarize this 181-line poem in a sentence or two manage to present it as a coherent plea for mercy, the poem assembles a series of arguments that often feel disjointed, rambling, and tiresome.[7] At times the poem's unaesthetic stylistic features reinforce the sense of disjointedness and incoherence.

The poem begins with four questions spread out over fifteen lines and presumably addressed to a cruel lady with the respectful formal

---

6 To preserve the play on words, I have substituted my own English translation for that of Jones and Rosenthal.

7 Consider, for example, the rubric that Abdelkader Salza provides in Stampa and Franco, *Rime*, ed. Salza, 251: "Un amante, non corrisposto da Veronica, si lamenta della crudeltà di lei, e la supplica umilmente di riamarlo, invocando l'aiuto d'Amore" (A lover, spurned by Veronica, laments her cruelty, and invoking Love's help, humbly begs that she love him in return). Would that the poem were this clear! In fact, lines 1–15 do not state that the male poet complains specifically about a woman's rejection of *him*. He presents the lady's refusal of love as more general, directed at "those who love you" (chi v'ama); the harm she causes appears to be widespread, as the poet asks why, "if so much evil falls from heaven on us" (se scende a noi dal ciel cotanto male; 7.15), the Furies do not rise up from hell "to do us harm" (ai nostri danni; 7.14). The English translation suggests that readers may want a greater degree of specificity than this male poet provides. Jones and Rosenthal intervene to narrow down the lady's cruelty so that rather than being directed at "those who love you," it is directed at "a man who loves you." They render the male poet's complaint tidier and more consistent.

pronoun "voi": You aren't using your great beauty for love? Are you going to bring death to those who love you? What could make life worse than to have such beauty united to ill will? Why don't the Furies rise up from Hell to do harm to us? These four questions over fifteen lines strike me as overkill. The balance would have been better with three questions. Then, without helping the reader to make the transition, the male poet clumsily shifts focus:

> Ben sei fanciul più d'ingegno che d'anni,
> Amor, e d'occhi e d'intelletto privo,
> se 'l tuo regno abbandoni in tanti affanni. (7.16–18)

> (Love, you are indeed a child,
> more in mind than in years, without eyes or wit,
> if you leave your kingdom in such a dire state.)

As is clear in the Italian, the male poet uses informal address ("tu") in line 16 to speak to a male child ("fanciul"; 7.16), which we discover only in line 17 is Love. An English translation that would duplicate the disjointedness in Italian would read thus:

> Indeed you are a child more in mind than in years,
> Love, lacking eyes and understanding,
> if you leave your kingdom in such a dire state.

As if to try to regain a sense of harmony and balance, the male poet addresses Love, with an anaphora on "you" (te):

> Te, cui non ebbe di servir a schivo
> Giove con tutta la celeste corte,
> e ch'a Dite impiagar festi anco arrivo;
> te, del cui arco il suon vien che riporte
> spoglie d'innumerabili trofei,
> contra chi più resiste ognor più forte;
> te, cui soggetti son gli uomini e i dèi,
> non so per qual destin, fugge e disprezza,
> con la mia morte ne le man, costei. (7.19–27)

> (You, whom even Jove does not refuse to serve,
> with all the heavenly train, and who succeeded
> in inflicting wounds even on Dis;

you from whose bow must spread the fame
of numberless trophies and prizes without number,
stronger against those who most resist;
you to whom both men and gods are subject,
she flees and disdains, by a fate I know not,
with my death in her hands.)

The anaphora does offer a measure of stability, and given that the poet is addressing love, we are almost certain to recall other verses about Love or addressed to Love that rely on anaphora. Think of the much celebrated and beautiful lines pronounced by Francesca da Rimini in *Inferno* 5 and the narrator's address to Love at the end of the *Ninfale fiesolano*.[8] But the address to Love in poem 7 cited here can hardly be called mellifluous, given the heavy presence of dental consonant /t/ combined with hard /c/, both often in accented position. Moreover, the syntax is quite contorted, with the subject pronoun "she" (costei) appearing only at the very end of these nine lines, the verbs "flees and disdains" (fugge e disprezza) in the line preceding the subject, and the second-person singular object pronoun "you" (te) at the beginning of each tercet. (Since English does not distinguish between "you" as a subject pronoun and "you" as an object pronoun, the English translation does not leave us in heavy suspense about what action is being taken on Love, addressed as "you.")

The poem sports an unusual number of equivocal rhymes, that is, instances where a word rhymes with another word that has the same form but a different grammatical function and meaning. There are six in all, producing the highest percentage of equivocal rhymes in any poem in the *Terze rime*. The rhymes are on "manca" (7.7, 7.9), "vago" (7.56, 7.60), "doglia" (7.80, 7.82), "sazia" (7.107, 7.111), "turba" (7.122, 7.124), and "nome" (7.172, 7.174).

In *De vulgari eloquentia* 2.13.13, Dante identifies equivocal rhyme as one of three kinds of rhyme inappropriate for a poet writing in the high style. Labelling it "superfluous" (inutilis), he maintains that it "always seems to detract to some extent from meaning" (semper sententie quicquam derogare videtur).[9] Still, as David Robey has pointed out, "Contrary to Dante's stricture in *De vulgari eloquentia*, there are numerous (eighty-four) instances of equivocal rhyme (combining the same word forms with different meanings) in the *Commedia*, and a few

8 See *Inferno* 5.100–8, in Alighieri, *Inferno*, ed. Chiavacci Leonardi; and Giovanni Boccaccio, *Ninfale fiesolano*, ottava 468.
9 Alighieri, *De vulgari eloquentia*, ed. and trans. Botterill.

cases in the lyric poetry, in addition to the obligatory repetitions of the sestina form."[10]

Multiple studies have highlighted Dante's masterful use of equivocal rhyme,[11] with scholars dedicating special attention to understanding how Dante deploys equivocal rhymes in *Inferno* 24 and 25, dedicated to the thieves. Commenting on *Inferno* 24, the canto that harbours the greatest concentration of equivocal rhymes in *Inferno*, Joan Ferrante notes that these rhymes "are a demonstration of skill, but they can also reveal the dangers in human cleverness."[12] According to Ferrante, such rhymes, which "are in appearance the same word but with a very different meaning," portray "a deceptive identity."[13] Teodolinda Barolini focuses instead on how equivocal rhymes point toward metamorphosis. Commenting on an equivocal rhyme in the opening simile of *Inferno* 24, she writes:

> Thus, verse 13 – "veggendo 'l mondo aver cangiata faccia" (seeing the world to have changed its face [*Inf.* 24.13]) – states the theme of metamorphosis in succinct fashion. Moreover, the employment of equivocal rhymes in the simile anticipates the experience of metamorphosis. Equivocal rhymes feature rhyme-words that are the same in appearance but are not the same in substance, for the words have different meanings.
>
> The rhyme-words *faccia / faccia* in verses 11 and 13 are an example of equivocal rhyme: the two words possess the same shape – appearance – but have a different substance or meaning: in verse 11 "faccia" is the present subjunctive of *fare* (to do) while in verse 13 it is the noun "face". Dante is here broaching the issue of metamorphosis through its converse.
>
> **While equivocal rhymes have the same appearance but differing substance, metamorphosis is a transformation in which the same substance takes on a different appearance: the same substance takes on a different shape.**[14]

10 Robey, "Terza rima," 810.

11 See Baldelli, "Rima," 932; Ferrante, "A Poetics of Chaos and Harmony," 153–71; L. Tassoni, "*Aequivocatio* e statuto del senso in Dante," 131–41; Clarke, "Humility and the (P)arts of Art," 209–27.

12 Ferrante, "A Poetics of Chaos and Harmony," 163.

13 Ferrante, "Good Thieves and Bad Thieves," 86, and also Ferrante, "Canto XXIV," 318. Similarly, writing about the use of equivocal rhyme in the opening simile of *Inferno* 24, Alison Cornish states that "the use of equivocal rhyme, words that look the same but mean different things (*tempra, tempra; faccia, faccia*), is a formal reflection of the deceptive appearances central to the region of fraud" (*Reading Dante's Stars*, 55).

14 Barolini, "*Inferno* 24: Metamorphosis (Ovid)," par. 8–10.

Given that the unknown male author of poem 7 is not as technically proficient as Dante, my best surmise is that his frequent recourse to equivocal rhymes is meant to contribute to a general sense of confusion, as is also the case for the equivocal rhymes in Dante's *Inferno*.[15] Notably, the male poet also creates a tension between the suffering he experiences (which he tries to represent as infernal by evoking the image of two Furies rising up from Hell) and the happiness of other male lovers on whom Veronica Franco bestows her favours. Where the unknown male author falls short is in creating any substantive link between the formal and the thematic elements.

Poem 7 features some unusual poetic rhythms. Almost always throughout the *Terze rime*, the end of an utterance coincides with the end of a tercet. On two occasions in poem 7, the male poet has the utterance conclude one line later. The first instance of this appears along with the penultimate instance of equivocal rhyme, on "turba"/"turba" (crowd/torments) so both the delayed finish to the utterance and the equivocal rhyme communicate a sense of being off-kilter:

Ma che invece di spender signoria,
a dilettar la circostante **turba**
mi strazie sotto acerba tirannia,
questo m'affige l'animo, e mi turba. (7.121–4; emphases mine)

(But that instead of wielding her power
to delight the crowd that clusters around her,
she tears me apart under harsh tyranny –
this afflicts and torments my soul.)

The second instance of tercet overrun comes after a verse that is a head scratcher:

O donna, pregio de la nostra etate,
anzi di tutti i secoli, se 'n voi
non guastasse l'orgoglio la beltate,
onde avvien che 'l mio amor così v'annoi? (7.133–6)

15 Joan Ferrante points out that "Dante uses the equivocal rhymes differently in different canticles"; in *Inferno* they "contribute to a sense of confusion, while in *Paradiso*, and frequently in *Purgatorio* the apparently different meanings turn out, on closer study, to be related if not identical ("A Poetics of Chaos and Harmony," 162).

(Oh, lady, treasure of our age,
indeed, of all centuries, if in you
pride did not destroy your beauty,
why is it that my love vexes you so?)

Here, the male poet begins with a *captatio benevolentiae*, praising the lady for her current value that, in fact, will stand the test of time. So why add the conditional clause, "se 'n voi / non guastasse l'orgoglio la beltate" (if in you / pride did not destroy your beauty), which undercuts the praise? And why choose to formulate the Italian as "se 'n voi / non guastasse l'orgoglio la beltate" rather than "se 'n voi / l'orgoglio non guastasse la beltate," a formulation that would make the agency of pride absolutely clear? The formulation of "se 'n voi / non guastasse l'orgoglio la beltate" invites the reader to think initially that the poet is saying "if in you / beauty did not destroy pride"; obviously then the reader is set for a double take because such a reading goes absolutely counter to what the poet has just said about the woman's timeless beauty, and then the reader has to rethink the verse in order to place agency with pride.

The poet's shifts of focus are unsettling, and he uses enjambment both effectively and not. The concluding lines of the poem provide multiple examples:

E se, com'io pur volentier ragiono
de le grazie, che 'l ciel tante in voi pose
con singolar, non più veduto dono,
non mi teneste d'ogni parte ascose
quelle vostre divine e rare parti,
di che vostra persona si compose,
non fôran sì angosciosi da me sparti
sospiri, né di lagrime vedresti
avampando, cor misero, innondarti.
Ma, dond'avien che 'n me, lasso, si desti
la speme, che per prova intendo come
faccia sempre i miei dì più gravi e mesti?
E pur chiamando di mia donna il nome,
vera, unica al mondo eccelsa dea,
convien ch'a lei mi volga, e ch'io la nome.
Deh, non mi siate così iniqua e rea,
che 'l mio mal sia 'l ben vostro e che m'ancida
quella vostra beltà, che gli altri bea!
Ma quell'Amor, che v'ha tolto in sua guida,

e che tien nel cor vostro il suo bel seggio,
la crudeltà per me da voi divida;
ch'io piangendo umilmente ancor vel chieggio. (7.160–81)

(And since I speak so willingly
of the many graces granted you by heaven,
in an extraordinary gift never seen since,
if you did not hide from me on all sides
those divine and matchless limbs
of which your body is composed,
I would not have heaved such anguished sighs,
nor, unhappy heart, would you have seen
yourself, flaming, engulfed by tears.
But how does it happen that hope rises up
in me, alas, so that I feel through experience
how it makes all my days woeful and dreary?
And even as I invoke my lady's name,
verily unique goddess, supreme on earth,
I must turn to her and say her name.
Pray, be not so wicked and cruel to me
that my sorrow is your boon, and your beauty,
which blesses others, murders me!
But let Love, who has taken you for his guide,
and whose lovely throne resides in your heart,
remove, for my sake, cruelty from you;
which, humbly weeping, I also beg of you.)[16]

Most unsettling is the shift of addressee. The poet addresses the woman, using the courteous pronoun "voi," in lines 160–6, but then suddenly turns to his "unhappy heart" in lines 167–8, using the familiar second-person singular pronoun "tu": "né di lagrime *vedresti* / avampando, cor misero, *innondarti*" (nor, unhappy heart, would you have seen yourself, flaming, engulfed by tears; emphasis mine). Then in lines 169–71, when he asks a question ("But how does it happen that hope rises up?"), it is no longer even clear whom he is addressing. His heart? Himself generally? Again the woman? Following this muddle, as he begins to speak about his lady's name, it seems he might be speaking about her rather than to her (7.172), then possibly to her, if

16 I have modified Jones and Rosenthal's translation of line 173 in order to preserve the pun.

he is apostrophizing her as "verily unique goddess, supreme on earth" (7.173), but then clearly speaking about her rather than to her ("I must turn to her and say her name"; 7.174). And after clarifying that he is not speaking to her but about her, he addresses her in the final seven lines of the poem.

The Italian text is rough and bumpy. The poet begins this section with a hypothetical "E se, com'io pur volentier ragiono" (And if, since I speak so willingly; 7.160, translation mine) but does not reveal what depends on that "if" until three lines later, when he says, "non mi teneste d'ogni parte ascose" (you did not hide from me on all sides). Whereas the English translation speaks of "sides" and "limbs," the Italian offers a clumsy repetition as "parti" (limbs, or, to recognize the lack of elegance in the phrasing, parts of your body; 7.165), which echoes the "d'ogni parte" (on all sides; 7.164) of the previous line. And the three enjambments in lines 166–71 – "sparti / sospiri" (heaved / sighs); "si desti / la speme" (awakens / hope); "intendo come / faccia" (how / it makes) – combine for a not especially pleasing effect. The only one of these three enjambments that appears to be poetically driven is "si desti / la speme" (awakens / hope). But even this seems ill advised, as the male poet has just imagined what could have been if Veronica Franco had not hidden from him her "divine e rare parti," which Jones and Rosenthal translate as "divine and matchless limbs," but which we might translate as "divine and exquisite parts" in order to make clear that we might not be talking about "limbs" here but rather about parts of the body that are even more secreted from view. In this context, when line 169 ends with a question about something awakening, one might wonder whether he is about to speak about a force awakening in his own body.

To these ramblings of the unknown male author, Veronica Franco offers a coherent, carefully elaborated response in poem 8, which opens up the discussion to a larger perspective on people suffering from unrequited love. Let us begin by examining the opening six tercets:

> Ben vorrei fosse, come dite voi,
> ch'io vivessi d'Amor libera e franca,
> non còlta al laccio, o punta ai dardi suoi:
> e, se la forza in ciò d'assai mi manca
> da resister a l'armi di quel dio,
> che 'l cielo e 'l mondo e fin gli abissi stanca;
> ch'ei s'annidasse fôra 'l desir mio
> dentro 'l mio cor, in modo ch'io 'l facessi
> non repugnante a quel che più desío.

Non che sovra lui regno aver volessi,
ché folle a imaginarlo sol sarei,
non che ch'un sì gran dio regger credessi;
ma da lui conseguir in don vorrei,
che, innamorar convenendomi pure,
fosse 'l farlo secondo i pensier miei.
Ché se libere in ciò fosser mie cure,
tal odierei, ch'adoro; e tal, ch'io sdegno,
con voglie seguirei salde e mature. (8.1–18)

(I wish it were the case, as you say it is,
that I lead my life free from Love, and frank,
not caught in his snare or pierced by his arrows;
and if in this affair I lack by far
the strength to resist the weapons of that god
who wearies heaven and earth and even hell,
my desire would still be that he nestled in my heart,
so that I could make him become
less resistant to what I most desire.
Not that I want to rule over him,
for I would be made even to imagine it,
nor would I presume to rule such a great god;
but I would like him to grant me as a gift
that even if I must fall in love,
I may do so according to my own design.
For if my feelings were free in this affair,
I would despise the man I adore;
and with steady, mature desire, I'd pursue the one I scorn.)[17]

Although Franco is disagreeing with the views put forth by the male author of poem 7, she strategically positions herself as agreeing with him, wishing he were right that she is immune to the power of Love. Mirroring his pun on her given name, she offers a pun of her own, on her surname, "franca" (frank; 8.2). She weaves a significant sound pattern, beginning with two labiodental fricatives (voiced /v/ and voiceless /f/) that are softened with sibilant /s/: "Ben **v**orrei **f**o**ss**e, come dite **v**oi, / ch'io **v**i**v**e**ss**i di Amor, libera e **f**ranca." These lines are all about desire in life, so it is not surprising that the words having to do

17 For Jones and Rosenthal's translation of "vivessi" as "led my life" in line 2, I have substituted "lead my life."

with desire and living are bound together with alliteration on *v* (vorrei, vivessi, volessi, vorrei, voglie). The hypothetically desired situations are hammered out in a series of imperfect subjunctives, a full seven of them in these first eighteen lines: fosse, vivessi, s'annidasse, facessi, volessi, credessi, fosser.

Franco then launches a series of arguments that rely on the phrase "I too" (anch'io). In lines 19–39 this phrase appears four times. "I, too, must complain of Love" (Amor anch'io biasmar convegno; 8.19), she writes to the author of poem 7. If Love brings suffering to his heart, her pain and sighs are "certainly no less" (certo non meno; 8.26). If he is overcome by his love for her, she too suffers from a cruel snake's bite to her heart ("anch'io d'un crudel angue / soffro al cor gli aspri morsi"; 8.29–30). Just as he presumably does not take pleasure in her pain, she too does not long for him to feel pain ("anch'io 'l vostro non bramo"; 8.35). This section concludes with a question: "if I lie abject and sick unto death, / how can I help you in your pain / when I shriek within and am outwardly silent?" (benché, s'oppressa inferma a morte giaccio, / com'è ch'a voi recar io possa aita / nel martír ch'entro grido e di fuor taccio?; 8.37–9.) The obvious Petrarchan echo in the antithesis between inward shriek and outward silence would appear to seal her likeness to a male poet lamenting a woman's cruelty toward him.[18]

Now we arrive at verses that will be crucial for understanding how Veronica Franco represents her own pain:

> Voi, s'a lagnarvi il vostro duol v'invita
> meco, nel mio languir soverchio impietra
> e rende un sasso di stupor mia vita:
> via più nel cor quella doglia penètra,
> che raggela le lagrime nel petto,
> e l'uom, qual Niobe, trasfigura in pietra. (8.40–5)

> (You, if your grief encourages you to complain
> to me, in my overwhelming travail, my life
> turns to stone and hardens into unfeeling rock:

18 Cf. canzone 105 in Petrarch's *Rvf*, in which he says, "et vo contando gli anni, et taccio et grido" (and I go counting the years and I am silent and cry out; 105.79), and sonnet 134, in which he says, "non ò lingua et grido" (I have no tongue and yet cry out; 134.9). For the Italian text and English translation, see Petrarca, *Petrarch's Lyric Poems*, trans. and ed. Durling.

such grief penetrates the heart far more deeply,
so that it freezes the tears within the breast,
and changes man, like Niobe, into stone.)[19]

The verses seem to begin with an address to the male poet, "Voi, s'a lagnarvi il vostro duol v'invita / meco," which I have translated here as "You, if your grief encourages you to complain / to me" in order to preserve the enjambment. One would think that the grammatical subject is the "you" (voi) of line 40, but then no verb can be found to go with this subject. The "you" is as if suspended. This is even clearer in the 1575 edition, where a semi-colon finalizes the utterance as a fragment:

Voi, s'a lagnarvi il vostro duol v'invita
Meco; ne'l mio languir soverchio impietra,
E rende un sasso di stupor mia vita:
Via piu nel cor quella doglia penetra,
Che raggela le lagrime nel petto,
E l'huom qual niobe trasfigura in pietra.[20]

In editing the 1575 edition to present it in 1913, Abdelkader Salza must have found the semi-colon ungrammatical, so he changed it to a comma, which links the fragment to what follows.[21] Every modern edition since then has followed his punctuation.

The 1575 edition has two other things that the modern editions, following Salza, change. The "ne'l mio languir souerchio" of line 41 reads "nel mio languir soverchio" (in my overwhelming travail) in all modern editions. But Franco was accustomed to use the articulated preposition "nel" in all other cases in the *Terze rime*, so it is unclear why the preposition and article are separated here. And in line 45, the 1575 edition does not capitalize "niobe," whereas all the modern editions do. It is unusual for the name of a mythological figure not to be capitalised in the *Terze rime*; to the best of my knowledge, this is the lone instance of non-capitalization.

Looking beyond the orthography and the graphic representation, one sees further instances of opaqueness. Consider lines 41–2, "nel mio languir soverchio impietra / e rende un sasso di stupor mia vita," which

19 I have modified Jones and Rosenthal's translation so that "You" appears at the beginning of 9.40, and the enjambment in 9.40–1 is preserved.

20 Franco, *Terze rime al Serenissimo Signor Duca di Mantova et di Monferrato*. To view the passage in the Google e-book, see https://play.google.com.

21 Stampa and Franco, *Rime*, ed. Salza, 258.

Jones and Rosenthal translate as "in my travail, greater yet, my life / turns to stone and hardens into unfeeling rock," with "mia vita" (my life) as the grammatical subject, which does seem to go with "impietra" (turns to stone) but fits uncomfortably with "rende un sasso di stupor," which I am not convinced means "hardens into unfeeling rock." One way to solve the puzzle of these lines would be to go back to the 1575 edition and correct "ne'l mio languir souerchio," not to "nel mio languir soverchio" (in my overwhelming travail) but to "il mio languir soverchio" (my overwhelming travail), which would then become the grammatical subject. I would translate lines 40–5 as follows:

> You, if your grief encourages you to complain
> to me, my overwhelming travail petrifies
> my life and turns it into a stupefied rock.
> That suffering penetrates ever more into the heart
> so that it freezes tears within the breast
> and transforms man, niobe-like, into stone.

Let us be clear. These are very bizarre verses. What can it possibly mean to petrify a life rather than a person? Why the insistence that the life both turns to stone ("impietra") and into a stupefied rock ("sasso di stupore")? Why link Niobe transformed into stone to a generic man ("uom") given that Niobe's fate is gender-specific? (Niobe was turned to stone after she hubristically boasted about her accomplishments, principally her reproductive accomplishments, and her husband and all fourteen of her children were slain by Apollo and Diana.) And why portray tears frozen in the breast, if this is not what happens to Niobe, whose body entirely turns to stone but who continues to weep?

Veronica Franco evokes stony petrification but makes it swerve away from her own body, partly by emphasizing that her life is turned to stone, partly by rethinking the body transformed into stone as a male body, and partly by denying the nature of Niobe's transformation.

A comparison to Ovid's account of Niobe's transformation in book 6 of the *Metamorphoses* will allow us to see how Veronica Franco is thinking differently about the representation of her own pain.

> [...] orba resedit
> exanimes inter natos natasque virumque
> deriguitque malis; nullos movet aura capillos,
> in vultu color est sine sanguine, lumina maestis
> stant inmota genis, nihil est in imagine vivum.
> ipsa quoque interius cum duro lingua palato

congelat, et venae desistunt posse moveri;
nec flecti cervix nec bracchia reddere motus
nec pes ire potest; intra quoque viscera saxum est.
flet tamen et validi circumdata turbine venti
in patriam rapta est; ibi fixa cacumine montis
liquitur, et lacrimas etiam nunc marmora manant.
(*Metamorphoses* 6.301–12)[22]

(Now does the childless mother sit down amid the lifeless bodies of her sons, her daughters, and her husband. Her hair stirs not in the breeze; her face is pale and bloodless, and her eyes are fixed and staring in her sad face. There is nothing alive in the picture. Her very tongue is silent, frozen to her mouth's roof, and her veins can move no longer; her neck cannot bend nor her arms move nor her feet go. Within also her vitals are stone. But still she weeps; and, caught up in a strong, whirling wind, she is rapt away to her native land. There, set on a mountain's peak, she weeps; and even to this day tears trickle from the marble.)[23]

Notably, when Ovid's Niobe rigidifies, it is her tongue that freezes in her mouth, rendering her speechless.[24] Both before providing this information and afterwards, Ovid catalogues the individual parts of Niobe, external and internal, and how they remain motionless. In Franco's poem, however, it is the tears that freeze within the breast ("raggela le lagrime nel petto"; 8.44), and, in stark contrast to Ovid, there is no other indication that parts of her body are rendered immobile. Even though she will go on to suggest that she is unable to express her pain because it remains locked within her heart, she continues to reaffirm her ability to speak and to write:

Il vostro duol si può chiamar diletto,
poiché parlando meco il disfogate,
del mio, ch'al centro il cor chiude, in rispetto.

22 The Latin text and English translation are from Ovid, *Metamorphoses*, trans. Miller. Subsequent citations appear in the text.

23 I have modified Miller's translation of this passage by removing his reference to Niobe sitting down "in stony grief," since the Latin does not include mention of such grief.

24 In *Lacan's Return to Antiquity*, 170, Oliver Harris observes: "Metamorphosis, in Ovid's poem, is always into the realm of speechlessness. Its victims lose control over expression. Instead, at the inexpressible limit of their experiences, they are frozen as symbols subject to others' readings; their interiority, at the moment of its greatest intensity, can only be revealed outside (like a blush, but on a larger scale)."

Io vi rispondo ancor, se mi parlate;
ma le preghiere mie supplici, il vento
senza risposta ognor se l'ha portate,
se pur ebbi mai tanto d'ardimento,
che in voce, o con inchiostro, addimandassi
qualche mercede al grave mio tormento.
E così portar gli occhi umidi e bassi
convengo, e converrò per lungo spazio
se morte al mio dolor non chiude i passi. (8.46–57)

(Your suffering could be called delight
since you ease it by speaking of it to me,
unlike mine, which my heart shuts up in its core.
I still answer you if you speak to me;
but the wind has carried my imploring prayers
off with it every moment, without an answer,
if ever I had sufficient daring
to appeal, through my voice or in ink,
for mercy in return for my dire pain.
And so I must lower my tearful eyes
and keep them low for a long time to come,
unless death cuts short the path of my woe.)[25]

It is worth reflecting on the imagined virtual body that Veronica Franco creates in poem 8 as she describes her suffering. Even as she uses the comparison to Niobe to evoke her pain, she keeps Niobe at arm's length. If she is Niobe, she is also not Niobe. There is no mention of her body turning hard and fixed like Niobe's, but her tears, frozen within, are also not like Niobe's. Unlike Niobe, she continues to speak. Whereas a powerful wind sweeps Niobe back to her homeland and fixes her to a mountain top, the wind manages only to carry off Franco's imploring prayers, rendering them without response. If Niobe is daring in her woe – "illa malo est audax" (6.288), says Ovid – Franco makes her own daring more tentative by placing it in an if-clause: "*se pur* ebbi mai tanto d'ardimento / che in voce, o con inchiostro, addimandassi / qualche mercede al grave mio tormento" (*if ever* I had sufficient daring / to appeal, through my voice or in ink, / for mercy in return for my dire pain; 8.52–4, emphasis mine).

25 I have modified Jones and Rosenthal's translation to make it clear, in line 52, that Franco is using an if-clause.

Franco continues to portray herself as a non-Niobe as she then turns to speak about her lover, cause of her woes:

Del mio amante non dico: che 'l mio strazio
è il dolce cibo, ond'ei mentre si pasce
divien nel suo digiun manco ognor sazio.
E dal suo orgoglio pur sempre in me nasce
novo desio d'appagar le sue voglie,
ch'unqua non vien, che riposar mi lasce;
ma dal mio nodo Amor l'arretra, e scioglie. (8.58–64)

(Of my lover, I say nothing; for my agony
is sweet nourishment to him, so that as he feeds on it,
it is ever less satisfied by its own starvation.
And even from his pride a strange desire
is born in me to satisfy all his wishes,
and it never allows me to rest;
but Love loosens and frees him from my embrace.)

If Franco's assertion is "I am like Niobe but I am not like Niobe," it is not surprising that in identifying her lover as the cause of her suffering, she uses the rhetorical figure of apophasis, speaking of him but claiming that of him she says nothing. Relevant to her description of herself and her lover is the following passage in which Ovid describes Niobe's response to Latona after Latona has killed Niobe's sons:

a quibus ad caelum liventia bracchia tollens
"pascere, crudelis, nostro, Latona, dolore,
pascere" ait "satiaque meo tua pectora luctu!
[corque ferum satia!" dixit, "per funera septem]
Efferor: exsulta victrixque inimica triumpha!
cur autem victrix? miserae mihi plura supersunt,
quam tibi felici; post tot quoque funera vinco!" (6.279–85)

(From them she lifted her bruised arms to high heaven and cried: "Feed now upon my grief, cruel Latona, feed and glut your heart on my sorrow. [Yes, glut your bloodthirsty heart! By the deaths of my seven sons] I am destroyed. Exult, and triumph in your hateful victory. But why victory? In my misery I still have more than you in your felicity. After so many deaths, I triumph still!")

Note the verb "pascere" (to feed), which Ovid's Niobe uses twice (6.280–1) as she cries out for Latona to feed upon her grief; note also the verb "satio," which Niobe uses twice as she tells Latona to "be done with" (e.g., sufficiently satiated with) feeding on her grief (6.281–2). When Ludovico Dolce translated this passage in the mid-sixteenth century, he gave particular importance to those two verbs, transporting them into the Italian forms "pascere" and "satiare," and positioning them at the end of one octave and the beginning of the following one:

E poi verso del ciel gli occhi inalzava,
Crudel (dice) Latona, ecco sì come
puoi trionfar del mio languir cotanto,
pasci, e *satia* il tuo petto del mio pianto.

Satia il tuo fero cor, gioisci affatto,
che di sette figliuoi, di rabbia accesa
m'hai fatto divenir orba ad un tratto
con morte non più vista e non più intesa.
Ma che? Per questo già non m'hai disfatto,
se ben l'empia tua man m'ha tanto offesa,
che più copia di figlie m'è restata,
Che non hai tu che sei nel ciel beata. (emphases mine)[26]

(And then she lifted her eyes toward the heavens,

"Cruel Latona," she says, "seeing how you can triumph in my deep suffering, *feed* on my tears and *sate* your breast.

"*Sate* your cruel heart, rejoice fully, that inflamed by rage, you deprived me at once of seven sons, with a death never before seen or comprehended. But so? You haven't undone me in this, even if your impious hand has so offended me, for an ample number of daughters remains to me – more than you, happy in the heavens, have.")

Franco uses "pascere" once (8.60) when she speaks of her lover feeding on the sweet food of her agony, and she echoes the Latin verb "satio" (Italian "satiare" or "saziare") as she describes her lover as ever less "satisfied" (sazio; 8.61) in feeding on her agony.

But if Franco marshals two of Niobe's key words, she also makes it clear that she is far from Niobe-like in her attitude. Niobe takes a

26 Ludovico Dolce's translation first appeared in 1553; I cite here from Dolce, *Le Trasformationi di m. Ludovico Dolce,* canto 13, p. 135. Available as a Google e-book, https://play.google.com. The English translation is mine.

defiant stance toward Latona, but there is nothing defiant in Franco's verses. Nor does she show more generally the kind of pridefulness that characterizes Ovid's Niobe. Pride ("orgoglio"; 6.62) is, instead, a characteristic of Franco's lover. Unlike Niobe who dares to look up to the heavens and challenge a divinity, Franco has already clarified in previous lines that her bodily stance is different: "portar gli occhi umidi, e bassi / convengo e converrò per lungo spazio" (I must lower my tearful eyes / and keep them low for a long time to come; 8.55–6).

At this point, Veronica Franco, in her strategy of cognitive reframing, opens up a wider perspective: "forse con lui fa un'altra donna quello, / ch'egli fa meco [...] / Fors'ancor voi del vostro amor conquisa / altra donna sprezzate [...] / Fors'anco Amor del comun pianto ride, / e, per far lagrimar più sempre il mondo, / l'altrui desir e discompagna, e divide" (Perhaps another woman does to him / what he does to me [...] / Perhaps you, too, disdain another woman / conquered by love for you [...] / Perhaps Love even laughs at the shared tears / and, to make the world weep even more / divides and sunders yet another's desire; 8.65–6, 8.70–1, 8.76–7).[27] What is interesting about this is the way that Franco reflects on systemic issues: she suggests that the subject positions of lover and object of love are mobile and that the disdaining lover could be male as well as female. Moreover, if Love is, as Franco suggests, a divisive force that takes delight in our common woes, calling upon Love to undo the cruelty of one's beloved is probably pointless.

Also pointless is any hope for beatific enjoyment of the sort that the unknown male author imagined Veronica Franco providing for other men:

> chè, s'uom potesse a suo diletto amare,
> senza trovar contrarie voglie opposte,
> l'amoroso piacer non avría pare.
> E, se tai leggi fûr dal destin poste,
> perché ne la soverchia dilettanza,
> al ben del cielo il mondan non s'accoste,
> tant'è più 'l mio dolor, quant'ho in usanza
> d'innamorarmi e di provar amando
> quest'amata in Amor disagguaglianza. (8.82–90)

27 I have modified Jones and Rosenthal's translation, replacing "Perhaps Love even laughs at these shared tears" with "Perhaps Love laughs at the collective tears too."

(for if man could love to his heart's delight,
without confronting contrary desires,
the pleasure of love would have no equal.
And if destiny has laid down the law
that in supreme delight, earthly good
may not attain the bliss of heaven,
my woe is all the greater as my habit is
to fall in love, and to feel, though loving,
this beloved disparity in love.)[28]

Setting the earthly ("il mondan") in tension with celestial bliss ("il ben del cielo"), which humans cannot achieve, Franco utilizes the rhetorical devices of alliteration and figura etymologica to place limits on the pleasure that humans can experience, but also to emphasize her own commitment to love. Alliteration on /d/ establishes that "delight" (diletto, dilettanza) is tied to "destiny" (destin), which then modulates to "woe" (dolor) and "disparity" (disagguaglianza). Figura etymologica – organized around the multiple words related to loving – pushes against the sense that we are condemned to dolefulness. This is especially notable in lines 88–90, "quant'ho in usanza / d'*innamorarmi* e di provar *amando* / quest'*amata* in *Amor* disagguaglianza" (my woe is all the greater as my habit is to fall in *love*, and to feel, through *loving*, / this *beloved* disparity in *love*).

Franco needs to reaffirm this commitment to love in order to make her next move, to preserve the possibility that she could bestow her affections on the man to whom she writes. (She is a courtesan, after all; she needs to hedge her bets.) To communicate the hypothetical situations, she returns to using the hypothetical constructions that characterized the first part of poem 8. She tells him that if she were able to take reason as her guide, "sarebbe nel mio cor la fiamma estinta / de l'altrui foco e di quel fôra in vece / del vostro l'alma ad infiammarsi accinta" (the flame for the other man would burn out / in my heart, and my soul would be prompt / to flare up with fire for you instead; 8.97–9). Once again she expertly uses alliteration (fiamma, foco, fora, infiammarsi) and figura etymologica (fiamma, infiammarsi), here presumably to keep his flame burning. In hedging her bets, she alternates between reaffirming the limitations on her and signalling her potential availability. Although she maintains that

28 I have modified Jones and Rosenthal's translation of "diletto" (8.80) and "disagguaglianza" (8.90) in order to preserve the alliteration.

she is not at liberty to undo or change the system, she offers that if the other man liberated her, she would give herself to him "as is more fit" (come conviene; 8.105). She describes the condition under which her joy would be complete (8.109–11), how she would gladly take her heart away from the cruel hands of her lover and give it to him (8.112–17). She reaffirms his valour – but notes that Love keeps her from being able to reward it (8.118–23). She tells him that she is considering how to accomplish this (8.124), but since "desire falls short of power" (al desio manca il potere; 8.125), he ought to take a calmer stance (8.127). Then "at a more propitious time, perhaps" (forse ch'a tempo di miglior ventura; 8.128), she will show him a good outcome. She ends with an exhortation that her unflagging interest ("cura"; 8.130) be of comfort to him and that he not judge her as harsh until one day she is once again free (8.130–3).

In this final section of conditional promises, two of the tercets present interpretive challenges. They are quoted here, with my translation:

> ma, ch'altro in ciò fuor del desir io spenda,
> e questo ancor con non picciola noia,
> non è, che più da voi, signor, s'attenda.
> Ben sarebbe compita la mia gioia,
> s'io potessi cangiar nel vostro amore
> quel ch'in altrui con diletto m'annoia. (8.106–11)

> (but, that I proffer something beyond desire
> – and this with not insignificant trouble –
> it is not that more is expected of you, sir.
> Certainly, my joy would be complete
> if I could exchange your love
> for that which in the other man, with delight, afflicts me.)

How do these tercets function in Franco's operation of cognitive reframing? The entire project in this poem depends on her ability to modify the man's perception of things: his perception of what she is willing to do, what the constraints on her are, and what his appropriate response should be. As we can see in these tercets, she first tells him that there is no need for him to do more right now. This is an important message to send to a man who in poem 7 was grasping for ways to get her to change her mind about him. Then she says she would be most glad to swap his love for what the other man offers her (which is not a promise that she will switch her love from another man to him, even though it might seem to move in that direction).

In the final verses of the poem, Franco seeks to secure the male poet's good will while simultaneously extricating herself from binding obligation to him. Here we witness her persistently seductive ways. She underscores his "high distinction" (alto valore; 8.114), his "valor [...] clearly evident" (Chiaro il vostro valore; 8.121), and his virtue (virtute; 8.118). She states that she would give him her heart but for the fact that "Love keeps me from availing myself of so much good" (Amor non vuol che tanto ben adopre; 8.123). No sooner does she communicate impossibility than she dangles the possibility of something happening in the future: "Com'io 'l potessi far, da me si pensa" (As for how I might do this, I am going to think about this; 8.124).[29] After telling him that "certainly your duty is to make peace with me" (che v'acquietate meco è ben dovere; 8.127), she tells him that "perhaps" (forse; 8.128) in the future she will be able to show him a positive result. Of course, her success also depends on reframing his perception in the present, and so the poem ends with an exhortation that, up until the time that she is free again, his being certain of her solicitude ("l'esser certo di mia cura"; 8.130) can be a comforting force that will alleviate his grief and allow him not to perceive her as callous ("mi faccia stimar da voi non dura"; 8.132).

In poem 8, Veronica Franco reveals for the first time in the *Terze rime* an impressive ability to shift the terms of discourse and to offer a different perspective. Responding to a male author's rambling and disjointed account of suffering, she calls attention to systemic imbalances, she highlights how she too suffers (though not so much that her ability to express herself is affected), she subtly crafts a story of herself as not proud and not cruel, and she ably navigates her rejection of him by repeated reminders that she is currently constrained in her options but might be able to reconsider in the future.

29 I have substituted my own translation of this line for Jones and Rosenthal's version, "I consider how I might be able to do so."

5 Seductive Insinuation and Obliquely Frank Refusal: *Terze rime* 9 and 10

In poem 9, a lover complains that Veronica Franco, with her absence, has brought him cruel death; he pleads with her to return to see the pain he endures for her, promising that "every pain will be a great joy" (fia d'alta gioia ogni dolore; 9.79) provided that she returns soon. In poem 10, Veronica Franco responds with the same rhyme scheme to explain that she departed to curb his desire and to ensure that she was not tormenting him and herself. In this chapter, I shine light on the male author's dual attempt to control Franco, first, by his quite unsettling insinuation of himself into Franco's interior space and, second, by his demand that she function as witness to his being. I document also the way in which Franco constructs her refusal of him around an oblique frankness that will allow her to present any disapproval as benevolent.

Poem 9 begins with a direct address that puts a spotlight on the woman and the speaker:

> Donna, la vostra lontananza è stata
> a me, vostro fedel servo ed amante,
> morte tanto crudel quanto insperata. (9.1–3)

> (Lady, your being so far away has been
> to me, your faithful servant and lover,
> a death as cruel as it was unhoped for.) (translation mine)[1]

The opening verse, an iambic hendecasyllable *a minore* (with major accent on the fourth syllable) may seem properly solemn, as it reproduces the metrical rhythm of the opening line of Petrarch's *Rerum*

1 Here I have substituted my own translation for Jones and Rosenthal's in order to preserve the enjambment and to translate "insperata" (9.3) as "unhoped for."

vulgarium fragmenta, "Voi ch'ascoltate in rime sparse il suono" (You who hear in scattered rhymes the sound).[2] But this line also leaves us uneasily in suspension, as we wait for the enjambment to resolve: how indeed will the male poet define Franco's being so far away? With the second line the poet further defers the answer until the beginning of the third line. The enjambment of lines 1 and 2 ("è stata / a me"), combined with accented first syllables ("Donna," "morte") in lines 1 and 3 will bond together "Lady," "me," and "death."

Line 2 of the poem is metrically unsettling. It is a non-canonical hendecasyllable, with accents on syllables 2, 3, 7, and 10 as follows: "a **me**, **vo**stro fedel **ser**vo ed a**man**te." Why the rhythmical deviation? The lack of expected accentuation on either the fourth or the sixth syllable forces us to dwell on the phrase "vostro fedel servo ed amante" (your faithful servant and lover). The actual accentuation further underscores the labels the male poet wishes to apply to himself – "me," "your," "servant," "lover" – and takes the accents off the word "fedel" (faithful). We could conceivably wrench the verse into a canonical form by shifting the accent from the seventh syllable to the sixth, reading "fedel" as a noun ("your faithful one") rather than as an adjective modifying the word that follows, and heightening the caesura: "a **me**, vostro fe**del** **ser**vo ed a**man**te." But to my mind, that creates quite an ugly-sounding verse, even if it is a canonical hendecasyllable *a maiore* (with major accent on the sixth syllable). To maintain mellifluousness we find ourselves having to accept a man who is willing to break a code, established implicitly by Petrarch and reinforced by Pietro Bembo, about the construction of hendecasyllables.

A man willing to break with expectations about versification is a man who might well break other boundaries. And that is what we begin to see in the verses that follow. I cite the passage along with my own translation:

> Nel gentil vostro angelico sembiante
> abitar l'alma e 'l mio cor vago suole,
> e ne le luci sì leggiadre e sante:
> Queste fûr risplendente unico sole
> sovra i miei dì, senza lor tristi e negri,
> e di quel pieni, ond'uom via più si duole,
> Come sono a me adesso orbati ed egri,
> in questa sepoltura de la vita,
> che non fia, senza voi, che si reintègri. (9.4–12)

2 Petrarch, *Rvf* 1.1, in Petrarca, *Petrarch's Lyric Poems*, trans. and ed. Durling.

(In your genteel, angelic features
and in your beautiful and saintly eyes,
my soul and my desiring heart are wont to live.
These eyes were the lone resplendent sun
on my days, which, without them, were sad and blackened,
and full of that which man most bemoans;
as now my days are bereaved and infirm
in this sepulcher of life
which, without you, will not recover.) (translation mine)

What happens when I imagine these lines addressed to me? I feel contaminated by a foreign presence. I understand that the speaker wishes to proclaim my divinity and sanctity, but now I have a male heart and soul so inhabiting me that I feel I cannot easily rid myself of them.[3]

The contamination I feel as I read these verses becomes more marked as the verses go on and the man describes his days without the "lone resplendent sun" of my eyes. The words and phrases used to describe those days are: "tristi" (sad), "negri" (blackened), "di quel pieni, ond'uom via più si duole" (full of that which man most bemoans), "orbati" (bereaved), "egri" (infirm). His life is a sepulchre. Granted, he is describing his days and his life in this way; technically, the representation is not of his heart and soul. But remembering that his heart and soul – crucial to his life day after day – inhabit my features and eyes, I feel a deathly darkness overcoming me as well.

The infiltration of a woman's body continues:

Con voi l'anima mia s'è dipartita,
anzi 'l mio spirto e l'anima voi sete,
e tutta la virtù vitale unita:
e s'uom morto parlar vien che si viete,
non io, ma di me parla in cambio quella
che ne le vostre man mia vita avete.
Questa non pur vi scrive e vi favella,
per miracol d'amor, in cotal guisa,
che, ne l'esser io morto, in voi vive ella;

3 I feel this less when I read the translation of lines 4–6 that Jones and Rosenthal have provided: "My soul and my enamored heart *once lived* in your angelic face / and in your eyes, so beautiful and blessed" (emphasis mine). They offer a verb in the past tense, "lived," for the present indicative "suole" (are wont to) in line 2, and they turn the man's "desiring heart" (vago cor) into an "enamored heart." This attenuates the peculiarity of these verses.

ma stando dal cor vostro non divisa,
vi susurra a l'orecchie di segreto,
e 'l mio misero stato vi divisa.
Né perciò del mio male altro ben mieto,
se non ch'agli occhi vostri ei si figura
con spettacolo a voi gioioso e lieto;
e mentre meco ognor v'innaspra e indura,
superate ne l'essermi crudele
le fiere mostrüose a la natura. (9.13–30)

(With you my soul took leave of me,
or, rather, you are my spirit and soul
and all my vital strength conjoined in one;
and if a dead man is barred from speaking,
not I but my life, which you hold in your hands,
speaks here in exchange for me.
My life not only writes and speaks to you,
by a miracle of love, in such a way
that in my death, it lives in you;
not being divided from your heart,
it whispers secretly in your ears,
and describes my wretched state to you.
Nor do I win any ease for my pain,
except that it appears before your eyes
in a spectacle joyful and pleasant to you;
and as it sharpens and hardens you toward me,
in your cruelty to me you surpass
the monstrous wild beasts of nature.)[4]

Although this section begins with the idea that the male poet's soul has, on account of the woman, left him, he quickly moves to define her not only as holding his life in her hands but also as being his spirit, his soul, and all of his vital strength. If he is dead (and thereby, presumably, mute), he offers up a stunning solution: his life lives in her, one with her heart, able to communicate in an intimate fashion. Since he represents his life as being her, being in her hands, being one with her heart, and since his life writes, speaks, and whispers in her ears, he covers all

4 I have modified Jones and Rosenthal's translation of "orecchie" in line 23, changing "ear" to "ears," and I have clarified that the grammatical subject of line 28 is not "you" but rather "it" (referring possibly to the spectacle described in line 27 or the pain of line 25).

the bases. It appears that there is no way for her to rid herself of him. An equivocal rhyme underscores his infiltration of her bodily space. Because his life is "not divided" (non divisa; 9.22) from her heart, it is able to whisper in her ears and describe his pain to her ("'l mio misero stato divisa"; 9.24).

Toward the end of the passage, however, the male poet gets himself into difficulty. He has insinuated himself into the woman, taking her over and occupying her fully, but in order to represent her as cruel toward him and to represent his pain as a spectacle in which she takes pleasure, and in order to express the desire that she be witness to his pain, he has to render himself external to her. Only once he is outside her can he launch the accusation that in her cruelty she surpasses the wildest beasts of nature.

Perhaps it is the mention of the wildest beasts of nature in line 30 that activates the comparisons to natural phenomena that allow the male poet to express his frustration at not being able to persuade Franco with his tears and his laments:

Lasso, ch'io spargo ai venti le querele,
anzi è un percuoter d'onde a duro scoglio,
quanto mai di voi pianga e mi querele.
Mosso s'insuperbisce il vostro orgoglio,
sì come 'l mar a l'impeto de' venti,
mentre a ragion con voi di voi mi doglio;
ed or, per far più gravi i miei tormenti,
per levarmi 'l ristoro ch'io sentia
nel formarvi propinquo i miei lamenti,
n'andaste a volo per diversa via,
quando men sospettava, a dimostrarvi
in tutti i modi a me contraria e ria. (9.31–42)

(Alas, that I cast my laments to the winds –
rather, it's the beating of waves on a stone,
no matter how much I weep and complain.
Shaken, your pride grows haughtier still,
much like the blast of winds on the sea,
while I rightly complain of you to yourself.
And now, to make my torments more grievous still,
to deny me the comfort I used to feel,
close to you declaring my woe,
you flew away on a different path
when least expected, in order to appear
in all ways contrary and cruel to me.)

Certain rhetorical features in this passage underscore the sense of iterative pounding that is communicated in the image of waves pounding against a hard rock. The poet says, "I cast my laments [*querele*] to the winds" and suggests this is useless, no matter how much "I weep and lament [*mi querele*]." Winds ("venti") appear in line 31 and then again in line 53. "Con *voi* di *voi* mi doglio" (To *you* I complain about *you*; emphasis mine), he tells her.

Now come some very puzzling verses, in which the relationship between the male poet and Franco, which he had taken care to define earlier in the poem, becomes truly garbled. I offer my translation of these lines, with two different possibilities for line 48:

Qual neve sotto 'l sol, piangendo sparvi
con quest'orma di vita, e con quest'ombra
vana e insufficiente a seguitarvi;
anzi, da' miei sospir cacciata e sgombra,
col vento, ch'a voi venne, si risolse,
che spirando al bel sen fors'or v'ingombra. (9.43–8)

(Like snow under the sun, I vanished, weeping,
with this mere trace of life, and with this vain shade
that is powerless to follow after you,
or rather, driven out by my sighs and disencumbered,
this trace of life dissolved in the wind that came to you
and as it blows softly on your fair breast, perhaps encumbers you now.

Like snow under the sun, I vanished, weeping,
with this mere trace of life, and with this vain shade
that is powerless to follow after you,
or rather, driven out by my sighs and disencumbered,
this trace of life dissolved in the wind that came to you,
and as it expires before your fair breast, perhaps encumbers you now.)

In the immediately preceding verses, the male poet has spoken of Franco having left suddenly. Thus, one might well think that when he uses the verb "sparire" (to vanish) in line 43, he would continue to speak about her departure.[5] But "sparvi," a first-person verb in the past tense, can only mean "I vanished" or "I faded away," which is quite startling. As the male poet shifts from using the wind and sea imagery in 9.31–6 to the

5 Line 43 is so strange that it predictably creates confusion in readers. Jones and Rosenthal, for example, take "sparvi" to mean "you vanished," and thus to refer to Veronica Franco's departure.

image of snow in the sun in 9.43, we might initially see him as emphasizing his copious tears, as that is how Petrarch and Boccaccio had used the image of snow melting in the sun.[6] It soon becomes clear that he is describing the total annihilation of his being.[7] Through sonic texturing on the nouns "orma" (trace) and "ombra" (shade), he appears to be trying to hold on to what remains of him. Lines 46–8 present significant challenges to interpretation because the adjective "cacciata" (9.46) can mean both "driven out" (as I translate it) and "pursued" (as Jones and Rosenthal translate it), and the adjective "sgombra" (9.46) can mean both "disencumbered" (as I see it) and "weighed down" (the choice of Jones and Rosenthal). According to my reading, the male poet claims in 9.43–5

---

6 See Petrarch, *Rvf* 30.19-24, in Petrarca, *Petrarch's Lyric Poems*, trans. and ed. Durling:

Non fur giammai veduti sì begli occhi
o nella nostra etade o ne' prim' anni,
che mi struggon così come 'l sol neve,
onde procede lagrimosa riva
ch' Amor conduce al pie' del duro lauro
ch' à i rami di diamante et d'or le chiome.

(There never have been seen such lovely eyes,
either in our age or in the first years;
they melt me as the sun does the snow:
whence there comes forth a river of tears
that Love leads to the foot of the harsh laurel
that has branches of diamond and golden locks.)

See also Boccaccio, *Corbaccio*, ed. Padoan, 413–614, at comma 67, with English translation from Boccaccio, *The Corbaccio or the Labyrinth of Love*, trans. and ed. Cassell, 12: "Dalla qual conoscenza una contrizione sì grande e pentimento mi venne delle non ben fatte cose che non solamente mi parve che gli occhi di vere lagrime e assai si bagnassero ma che il cuore, <non> altrimenti che faccia la neve al sole, in acqua si risolvesse" (From this knowledge, such great contrition and repentance for my evil deeds came to me that not only did it seem that my eyes were wet with many real tears, but also that my heart melted into water, just as snow in sunshine).

7 Similarly, Dante Alighieri uses the image of snow in the sun in this fashion in "Amor, da che convien pur ch'io mi doglia." See Alighieri, *Dante's Lyric Poetry*, ed. and trans. Foster and Boyde, vol. 1, pp. 206–7:

Ben conosco che va la neve al sole,
ma più non posso: fo come colui
che, nel podere altrui,
va co' suoi piedi al loco ov'egli è morto.

(Well I know that it is snow going to the sun, but I can do nothing else: I'm as a man in another's power who goes on his own two feet to the place where he is killed.)

to cease to exist except for a trace of life and an empty shade, but then he offers an alternative in which the trace of life or the vain shade is recuperated because it is "driven out by his sighs and disencumbered"; what is left of him then dissolves in the wind, which has travelled toward Franco, and specifically to her fair breast. It is as if, atomized and transported by the wind, he can recolonize her by settling on her body.

The verse in which the male poet's diminished presence reaches Franco is, as my translations of line 48 show, ambiguously perched between an erotic advance and a ghastly threat. On the one hand, his trace of life might be "blowing softly" (spirando) upon her fair breast, the way that the wind blows softly; on the other, his trace of life might be breathing its last ("spirando" in the sense of "expiring" or "dying") as it reaches her. Whether the male poet comes as a sexual or as a deathly presence, the image remains quite unsettling.

In the final portion of the poem, as the male poet laments Franco's absence, he repeatedly calls attention to the fact that, being far from him, she cannot witness his pain. Cruel fate, he says, took her away "far from the sight of my ruin and pain / which, endless, has settled in my heart through you" (dal mirar mio strazio e quella pena, / che infinita al mio core per voi s'accolse; 9.50–1). He recalls how a kind heaven "shone down upon me the light of your eyes" (la luce de' vostr'occhi a me rifulse; 9.60). In the final lines of the poem he opens and closes with his request for her return and underscores the importance of her as witness to the pain that she inflicts on him:

 Deh tornate a veder il mio gran pianto,
venite a rinovar l'aspre mie piaghe
senza lasciarmi respirar alquanto
 di ciò contente fían mie voglie e paghe,
che 'l mio duol, da voi fatto ancor maggiore,
mirin da presso l'alme luci vaghe.
 A me fia d'alta gioia ogni dolore;
e in gran pietà riceverà lo strazio,
e in dolce aita ogni aspra offesa il core,
 pur ch'a noi ritorniate in breve spazio. (9.73–82)

 (Pray, return to see my flood of tears,
come to reopen my bitter wounds,
not letting me take a single breath;
 by this all my wishes would be met and fulfilled:
that your kind, noble eyes, close by, should see
the pain that you constantly increase in me.

To me every pain will be a great joy,
and my heart will interpret torment as compassion
and every harsh injury as sweet relief,
provided that you come back to us soon.)

The final tercet appears to seal the situation as Petrarchan by setting up a series of antitheses: pain will be joy, torment will be compassion, and harsh injury will be sweet relief. But how Petrarchan is it, really? Let us compare what happens in the concluding lines of poem 9 to a sonnet by Petrarch, *Rvf* 351, which mobilizes a series of oxymorons:

Dolci durezze et placide repulse
piene di casto amore et di pietate;
leggiadri sdegni che le mie infiammate
voglie tempraro (or me n'accorgo), e 'nsulse,

gentil parlar in cui chiaro refulse
con somma cortesia somma onestate,
fior di vertù, fontana di beltate,
ch' ogni basso penser del cor m'avulse,

divino sguardo da far l'uom felice,
or fiero in affrenar la mente ardita
a quel che giustamente si disdice,

or presto a confortar mia frale vita:
questo bel variar fu la radice
di mia salute, ch' altramente era ita.[8]

(Sweet rigors and placid repulses full of chaste love and pity, charming angers which (I now see) tempered my inflamed and foolish desires,

noble speech in which highest chastity brightly shone with highest courtesy, flower of virtue, fountain of beauty which uprooted from my heart every low thought,

a glance so divine as to make a man blessed, now fierce in reining in my daring mind from what is justly forbidden,

8 The Italian text and English translation are taken from Petrarca, *Petrarch's Lyric Poems*, trans. and ed. Durling.

now swift to comfort my frail life: this lovely variety was the root of my salvation, which otherwise was gone.)[9]

In the first quatrain Petrarch describes Laura's response to him with three oxymorons; he sets her chaste love in antithetical opposition to his untoward desires. In the second quatrain he focuses on her noble, chaste, and courteous speech; her virtue and beauty are placed in opposition to his lowly thoughts. The first tercet turns to her "divine glance" that, capable of bringing happiness to a man, is fierce in curbing what justly should be rejected. But lest that fierceness be our final memory of Laura, the second tercet quickly notes that the opposition is not simply between the look that is "divine" and one that is "fierce." The divine look alternates between being "fierce" and being "quick to comfort." The closing lines of the second tercet offer a pithy summary: his salvation lay in this beautiful variation.

There are significant differences between the situation that Petrarch describes in *Rvf* 351 and the situation we see in the conclusion to poem 9. In the final accounting, the effect of Laura's harsh behaviour toward the speaker of *Rvf* 351 is not further suffering; rather, Laura's harshness serves to temper his desire. The purpose of her gaze is not to affirm her as witness to the speaker's pain; in its fierceness her gaze serves to rein in overweening ardour, but it also serves as a comforting force. The speaker of *Rvf* 351 takes time to praise the woman not only for her divine gaze but also for her noble speech and, more generally, her physical and moral qualities (beauty and virtue). The male poet of *Terze rime* 9, however, remains exclusively focused on securing Veronica Franco's gaze. Nowhere in his poem does he refer to her speech, and nowhere in this poem does he speak about her virtue. The main focus, I would say, is on himself and the continuation of his suffering. Unlike Petrarch, he does not view a woman's turn away from him as leading him to a higher level. The antitheses he creates (pain will be joy, torment will be compassion, and harsh injury will be sweet relief) are not in the service of a nobler purpose; rather, they stabilize the male poet in a dynamic where, if he evidently cannot successfully persuade Franco to be less cruel, he may be able to persuade her to torment him not at a distance but proximately.

---

9 The Italian text and English translation are from Petrarca, *Petrarch's Lyric Poems*, trans. and ed. Durling, though I have modified the translation of line 9, "divino sguardo da far l'uom felice," because Durling's translation of "sguardo" as "glance" makes Laura's gaze too brief, and his translation of "felice" as "blessed" projects a spirituality onto the happiness in a way I believe is not warranted.

In her response in poem 10, Veronica Franco makes some atypical moves. First of all, as is clear from the very first line, "In disparte da te sommene andata" (I went away, departing from you; 10.1), she addresses the man with the informal second-person singular pronoun "tu"; in previous poems addressed to men, she has always used the respectful second-person plural "voi."[10] And she responds to him using the same rhyme scheme, the only time in the *Terze rime* that she does this.[11] The use of informal address combined with the decision to second the man's rhyme scheme suggest a certain residue of affection, particularly given the instances of men responding to Franco using her rhyme scheme: the author of poem 4 begs her to return to Venice, and the author of poem 6 communicates his appreciation for her speech and guardedly expresses his hope that he will be worthy of her affection.

The opening fifteen lines of the poem, in their combination of obliqueness and frankness, and in their combination of benevolence and censure, are classic Veronica Franco:

> In disparte da te sommene andata,
> per frastornarti da l'amarmi, avante
> ch'unqua mostrarmi a tanto amore ingrata:
> né mia colpa fia mai ch'alcun si vante
> giovato avermi in opre od in parole,
> senza mercede assai più che bastante;
> ma s'uom, seguendo ciò che 'l suo cor vuole,
> di quel m'attristi, ond'ei via più s'allegri,
> meco non merta, e mi sprezza, e non cole.
> Quei sì, che son d'amor meriti intègri,
> quando, per far a me cosa gradita,
> per me ti sono, i tuoi dì tristi, allegri!

10 Subsequently Franco will use informal address with the man to whom she writes in poem 13, "Non più parole: ai fatti, in campo, a l'armi" (No more words! To deeds, to the battlefield, to arms!); he will respond in poem 14 with the respectful "voi," pleading for peace. She will also use informal address in poem 17, "Questa la tua Veronica ti scrive" (This letter your Veronica writes to you), an angry reproach to a man who has been unfaithful; and also in poem 22, "Poi ch'altrove il destino andar mi sforza" (Since destiny forces me to go elsewhere), a poem addressed principally to the city of Venice that also includes Veronica Franco's address to an ungrateful and cruel lover whom she addresses with the informal "tu."

11 Likely because of the restrictions that the rhyme scheme imposes, poem 10 flows less easily than do other poems by Franco in the collection; in large part, this is due to the greater than usual number of enjambments. I count eighteen enjambments in the 82 lines; compare this with poem 2, for example, where I count ten enjambments in 190 lines.

E nondimeno tu con infinita
doglia sentisti che mai cose liete
non m'incontrâr dal tuo amor disunita. (10.1–15)

(I went away, departing from you,
in order to force you out of loving me,
not at all to seem thankless for so much love;
nor is it my fault if anyone boasts
of giving me favors in word or deed
without having received more than ample reward.
But if a man, following his heart's desire,
makes me regret it, which delights him even more,
he deserves nothing, and scorns and dishonors me.
But those are certainly love's just rewards
when, to please me, your sad days
turn to happy ones, on my account.
And yet you've heard with infinite sorrow
that any joy has ever come to me
since I was parted from your love.)

In stating why she departed in order to keep the man from loving her, and in raising the issue of her feelings about that love, she is careful both to make herself seem grateful for the man's love and to communicate that, had she not left, she would have turned ungrateful. Jones and Rosenthal's translation ("to force you out of loving me / not at all to seem thankless for so much love") successfully captures Franco's recognition of the man's love, but they leave out the adverb "before" (avante), which so tantalizingly suspends a reader at the end of line 2. I would suggest that we translate 10.2–3 as follows: "to dissuade you from loving me, before / ever showing myself to be ungrateful for such love." She reasserts her blamelessness decisively. Her declaration that "né mia colpa fia mai" (10.4) can be translated, as Jones and Rosenthal have it, as "nor is it my fault"; but if we attend to the adverb "mai," on which the major accent falls in this line, we will likely hear "nor will it *ever* be my fault" (emphasis mine). While she maintains her innocence, she begins to move toward censure of her addressee. She advances her criticism obliquely by speaking about a generic man: the man who boasts of giving her favours (10.4–5) and the man who delights in making her regret things (10.7–8). Only then does she let loose the arrow with a stinging "meco non merta, e mi sprezza, e cole," which I would render as "[he] does not deserve me, and he scorns and dishonours me." Having pronounced this authoritative judgment about a generic man, she returns to addressing the male poet specifically. Before criticizing him for his less than noble response to reports that she might experience joy after she was parted from him (10.13–15), she cushions her reproach by outlining the condition under which his days would be happy ones and he would have love's just rewards – that is, when he seeks to please her (10.10–12).

Franco then elaborates further on why she cannot reciprocate his love:

Che mi prendesti a l'amorosa rete,
presa da un altro pria, vietò mia stella,
non so se per mio affanno, o per quïete:
basta che, fatta d'altro amante ancella,
l'anima, ad altro oggetto intenta e fisa,
rendersi ai tuoi desir convien rubella.
Con tutto questo, e ch'al mio ben precisa
la strada fosse, e fattomi divieto,
dal tuo seguirmi poco men che uccisa,
con giudicio amorevole e discreto
tanto stimai 'l tuo amor senza misura,
quanto più al mio voler fosti indiscreto:
e di te preso alcuna dolce cura,
bench'a me tu temprasti amaro fele
col tuo servirmi, in ciò non ti fui dura;
e per te non avendo in bocca il mèle
di quell'affetto ch'entro 'l sen raccoglio,
che in altrui pro convien che si rivele,
liberamente, come teco soglio,
ti raccontai ch'altrove erano intenti
i miei spirti, e mostraiti il mio cordoglio. (10.16–36)

(My star forbade you to trap me in love's net,
for I was caught already by another man,
for woe or peace I do not know;
it's enough that my soul, beholden to another lover,
intent and fixed on this other man,
rightly rebels against sharing your desire.
In spite of all this, and that my path to joy
was straight and direct, yet I was pushed off it
and all but slain by your persistence,
with a loving and tempered judgment,
I believed your love was as boundless
as, in fact, you failed to respect my will;

having taken loving care of you,
though you mixed bitter bile with your duty to me,
I was not harsh to you as a result;
and since toward you my mouth lacks the honey
of the affection I feel in my breast,
which I must reveal only to another,
freely, as is my custom with you,
I told you that my thoughts were turned
elsewhere, and I showed you my regret.)[12]

Franco defends herself from the persistent lover. He had wanted her gaze; she prioritizes verbal communication instead. In telling him that her thoughts were turned elsewhere (10.35–6), she states, "[T]i raccontai ch'altrove erano intenti / i miei spiriti," where "raccontai" means "I told you" with the sense of "I gave you an account" rather than "I said," thus communicating that her repulse was likely not peremptory. In this context, when she adds that "I showed you my regret" (mostraiti il mio cordoglio; 10.36), we are likely to understand that "to show" (mostrare) can be achieved through verbal exposition as well.[13] As she continues to reject her addressee, she does so obliquely in order to hold herself blameless. The active agents are "her star" (mia stella) that forbade him to entrap her, and the "other man […] another lover" (un altro […] altro amante) who entrapped her first and to whom she is beholden. It is her soul that "rightly rebels" (rendersi […] convien rubella). Prior to accusing him of vile actions toward her – murderous persistence, indiscreet failure to respect her will, and the passive aggressiveness evidenced by his having mixed "bitter bile" (amaro fele) with service to her – she highlights her "loving and tempered judgment" (giudicio amorevole e discreto) and "loving care" (dolce cura). Even in the lines where she describes not having in her mouth the honey of the affection she holds in her breast, she manages to make it seem that honeyed affection might be for her addressee as well, even though she can rightfully express it verbally only to another man, and even though

12 Jones and Rosenthal translate "d'altro amante ancella" as "enslaved to another"; I have modified the translation so that it reads "beholden to another lover."

13 The *Grande dizionario della lingua italiana*, vol. 10, p. 1010, reaffirms this meaning of "mostrare": "10. Dire, dichiarare, affermare, esporre; far conoscere, comunicare, riferire, rendere noto a voce o per scritto (una notizia, un'informazione, un progetto, un fatto, ecc.). – In partic.: rivelare un segreto; confessare i peccati, le colpe." (10. To say, declare, affirm, lay out; to make known, communicate, report, render known orally or in writing [news, information, project, fact, etc.]. Especially: to reveal a secret, to confess sins and faults.)

she locates in him negative emotions (indiscretion and the bitterness of bile) that contrast with her own positive ones (discretion and sweetness of honey).

In the central portion of the poem (10.37–60), Franco outlines her reasons for having left: not to do so would have been torture both to him and to herself (10.37) because she needed to curb his desire to keep him from a precipitous fall (10.50–1), and because her refusals would have certainly brought him to death (10.57–8). For the first time in the poem she addresses the effects of her gaze (10.58–60). One might well think that Franco, who emphasizes how truthful ("veridica"; 10.41) she has been, would seize the opportunity to be fully frank. But if we look closely at lines 46–60, we will see that she supplies a heavy dose of obliqueness in order to blur her agency:

Benché, se vaneggiando erra ed adombra
il tuo pensier, che da ragion si tolse,
seguendo Amor per via di lei disgombra,
non però quel ch'ad util tuo si vòlse
da me, da cui 'l desir tuo si raffrena,
che d'ir al precipizio i piè ti sciolse,
a meritar alcun biasmo mi mena;
anzi di quel ch'aiuto in ciò ti diede,
la mia chiara pietà si rasserena:
che s'io mossi da te fuggendo 'l piede,
fu perché le presenti mie repulse
m'eran de la tua morte espressa fede.
E quante volte fu che ti repulse
da se 'l mio sguardo, o ti mirò con sdegno,
so che 'l gran duol del petto il cor t'evulse. (10.46–60)

(Although your thought, straying from reason,
wanders aimless and disturbed,
following Love unimpeded by judgment,
even so, I am not to be held to blame
for anything that I did to help you,
on my side, as I curb your desire,
and I kept you from a precipitous fall.
On the contrary, the help I gave you
clearly shows my exceptional good will;
so if I fled from you, the reason was
that the refusals I am making now
were a firm guarantee to me then of your death.

And whenever my glance drove you away
or I looked at you with scorn, I know
that great pain tore your heart from your breast.)

In their translation Jones and Rosenthal organize Franco's statements around the first-person singular pronoun "I," which appears nine times in these lines and underscores Franco's agency. This is logical, given that to do otherwise would create significant issues for readability. It is important to note, however, that in Italian, Franco depends much more on grammatical subjects in the third-person singular. The gaze holds on to its position as grammatical subject, so that "ti repulse / da se 'l mio sguardo, o ti mirò con sdegno" (10.58–9) means "my glance drove you away or looked at you with scorn." To speak about a glance that "looks" sounds truly peculiar. So Jones and Rosenthal offer "my glance drove you away / or I looked at you with scorn." Lines 46–54 present even more of a challenge for the English translation, which begins, reasonably enough, with "your thought" (il tuo pensier; 10.47) as the grammatical subject of a subordinate clause in lines 46–8 that asserts that the man's thought has moved away from reason in order to follow Love. But then what is the grammatical subject of the main clause and the other subordinate clauses in lines 49–52? The grammatical subject is not "I," though understandably the English translation has "I am not to be held to blame / for what I did to help you / [...] I curb your desire / [...] I kept you from a precipitous fall." Rather, the grammatical subject of the main clause in lines 49–52 is the demonstrative pronoun "quel" (that; 10.49) with "desire" (desir) as the grammatical subject of the subordinate clause of line 50, and "kindness" (pietà) as the grammatical subject of the subordinate clause of line 54. Tracking the grammatical subjects of the Italian text, I translate: "Even so, that [*quel*] which for your own good turned to me [*si volse da me*], by whom your desire curbs itself [*si raffrena*], [and] which released [*sciolse*] your feet from going to the precipice, does not bring me to deserve any blame; quite to the contrary, my clear kindness [*pietà*] is illuminated [*si rasserena*] on account of the help that it gave [*diede*] to you." Quite murky! No wonder Jones and Rosenthal seek to clarify.

Having pushed to make emotions rather than individuals the prime actors in this drama, Franco speaks to her inability to resist Cupid's power, in a concluding passage that allows her to move sinuously between object position and subject position:

Ch'io ti vedessi d'alta doglia pregno
morirmi un dì davante, eccesso tale
era a me sconvenevole ed indegno.

Da l'altra parte, assai potev'io male
risponder al tuo amor: non men che fosse
il tentar di volar non avendo ale.
E che far potev'io contra le posse
di quell'arcier che, del tuo bene schivo,
d'oro in te, in me di piombo il suo stral mosse?
Ma d'òr prima anco al mio cor fece arrivo
la sua saetta, stand'io ferma intanto,
mirando incauta l'altrui volto divo.
Quinci un lume, ch'al sol toglieva il vanto,
m'abbagliò sì, che non fia che s'appaghe
d'alcun ben altro mai l'anima tanto.
E perch'errando 'l mio stil più non vaghe,
io partí' per disciôrti dal mio amore,
con le mie piante a fuggir pronte e vaghe.
So che la lontananza il suo furore
mitiga; e quando tu, del viver sazio,
pur vogli amando uscir di vita fuore,
te, con quest'occhi, e me insieme non strazio. (10.61–82)

(That I should see you, overwhelmed
with grief, die before me one day –
such an extreme seemed wrong and unfit.
On the other hand, I could hardly return
your love, especially because
it was an attempt to fly without wings.
And how could I resist the power of that archer,
who, shunning your well-being, shot you
with a golden arrow, me with one of lead?
But earlier still, his gold shaft reached my heart,
as I stood firm, incautiously gazing
at the other man's celestial face.
There a light that robbed the sun of its pride
so dazzled me that never will my soul
be as contented by any other love.
And so my wavering style would no longer stray,
I left, to free you from love for me,
with feet eager and longing for flight.
I know that absence lessens love's fury;
and when you, having lived to the full,

still loving, decide to leave life behind,
with these eyes I'll not torture both you and myself.)[14]

The reference to Cupid's arrows of gold and lead bring to mind the moment in book 1 of the *Metamorphoses* when Cupid shoots Apollo with a golden arrow and then shoots Daphne with a leaden one (*Metamorphoses* 1.468–71). No sooner, however, does Franco put the man of poem 9 into the position of Apollo, and herself into the position of a fleeing Daphne, than she rejects that analogy. She describes having been struck earlier by a golden arrow – almost as if she herself were Apollo – with the object of her love a godlike figure upon whom she happened to be gazing and whom she represents as Apollo-like in his radiance.

By the time that she returns to describing herself in flight, in lines 76–8, she has placed all three actors (the man she addresses, herself, and the object of her love) in the position of Apollo. And describing herself in flight, she again declines to put herself into the position of Daphne. I am struck by Franco's reasoning in line 77, "io partí' per disciôrti dal mio amore," which Jones and Rosenthal translate as "I left, to free you from love for me." But doesn't "dal mio amore" mean "from my love" rather than "love for me"? Compare what a jealous Bradamante says in *Orlando furioso* 45.32.5–8:

ch'impossibil mi par, ch'ove concesso
ne sia il veder, ch'ogni donna e donzella
non ne sia accesa, e che non usi ogni arte
di sciorti dal mio amore e al suo legarte.[15]

(I cannot conceive that any woman, married or single, can be offered a glimpse of you and not catch fire, and not use every device to free you of my love and bind you each to her own.)

Just as Bradamante's "Di sciorti dal mio amore" could not possibly mean "to free you from love for me," Franco's "disciorti dal mio amore" should not be thus translated. Franco alerts us to this by using the possessive pronoun "my" both in the preceding verse ("my style"

14 In line 68, I have substituted Jones and Rosenthal's translation of "del tuo bene schivo" (opposed to your desire) with my own ("shunning your well-being").

15 The Italian text is taken from Ariosto, *Orlando furioso*, ed. Segre, and the English translation is from Ariosto, *Orlando Furioso*, trans. Waldman.

['l mio stil]) and in the subsequent verse ("le mie piante" [my feet]), thus firmly anchoring this love as hers ("[il] mio amore").

What is Franco doing? With the reference to Cupid and his arrows of gold and lead, she represents her addressee as Apollo-like and herself as Daphne-like. She then points out that she herself was already in the role of Apollo, struck by Cupid's golden arrow as she gazed on a man – himself Apollo-like – who became the object of her love. When she calls attention to authorship by referencing her style, and she tells her addressee that she left to free him from her love, she is, in effect, an Apollo figure who *makes the choice not to pursue a love object.* (Granted, she justifies her turning away from her addressee by maintaining that she has absolutely no choice but to love another man. But such are the paradoxes of argument.)

In the final lines of the poem Franco returns to the question of her eyes, which the male poet had claimed to inhabit and which he begged to be witnesses to his ever-increasing pain. In essence, she tells him that she does not intend to return to look upon him even at some moment in the future when he is dead. Here too, however, she seals her frank refusal in oblique language. Any talk of his death is rendered in words that have to do with life. The future moment will be when he will "have lived to the full" (del viver sazio) and he will "leave life behind" (uscir di vita fuore); she further lessens the blow of this moment by representing it as a wish and an active decision on his part: "quando [...] / pur *vogli* amando uscir di vita fuore" (when you [...] / still loving, *decide* to leave life behind; emphasis mine).

In poem 10, Veronica Franco lays out another way to sidestep male advances. As in poem 8, she reaffirms that she belongs to another. But for the first time in the poetic collection she shows a repertoire of disapproving statements that she weaves into a fabric of reassuring half promises. She is both conciliatory and non-conciliatory, oblique and frank. Just as previously she was like Orpheus and not like Orpheus, and like Niobe but not like Niobe, she is now like Apollo and not like Apollo, whether that is because she flees like Daphne or because she renounces desires as Apollo could not. She reaffirms thus her ability to occupy multiple subject positions and to mobilize them as needed in order to manage her relations with a male interlocutor.

6 Verona, Venezia, Veronica: *Terze rime* 11 and 12

In poem 11, "Invero una tu sei, Verona bella" ("Truly, fair Verona, you are one of a kind"), an unknown male author praises the city of Verona because Veronica Franco is staying there; he pays tribute to Franco's celestial beauty, laments the fact that another man enjoys her favours, comments on his own sadness and jealousy, and requests that Franco return to Venice as soon as possible. In poem 12, "Oh quanto per voi meglio si faria" ("Oh, how much better you would do"), Franco summarily rejects the male poet's praise of Verona and of her beauty, offering that if he wanted her to return, he should have chosen to praise Venice instead. In closing, she proclaims her disdain for his love and announces that she will not return to Venice any time soon.

Commentaries on the poems have called attention to the male poet's hyperbolic and misplaced praise[1] and have emphasized Franco's "appeal to civic pride and verisimilitude"[2] and her "rhetoric of truth."[3] The reading of these poems that I offer in this chapter will allow us not merely to affirm that Franco gets the upper hand by aligning herself with Venice over Verona and with truth over hyperbolic falsity, but also to evaluate the specific strategies that the male poet uses to praise Franco and gain favour with her and the specific strategies that Franco adopts in her response; moreover, I ask us to consider how Franco manages the only occasion in the *Terze rime* in which she bluntly rejects a man.

Poem 11 is striking for the energy it puts into mobilizing the conceits of earlier Italian poetry written in praise of the beloved woman.

1 See Graf, *Attraverso il Cinquecento*, 303–4, and Rosenthal, *The Honest Courtesan*, 186–8.
2 Jones, *The Currency of Eros*, 190.
3 Finotti, "Il teatro cortigiano di Veronica Franco," 526.

In comparison with other poems in the *Terze rime* written by an unknown male author, it is considerably more gracious. As he lavishes abundant praise on Franco, the male poet takes care not to represent her as cruel, opting instead to represent celestial bodies (a cruel planet in 11.25, and a cruel star in 11.69) as the source of cruelty.

The first twenty-four lines of the poem provide a fine sense of the strategies that the male poet will use:

Invero una tu sei, Verona bella,
poi che la mia Veronica gentile
con l'unica bellezza sua t'abbella.
Quella, a cui non fu mai pari simíle
d'Adria ninfa leggiadra, or col bel viso
t'apporta a mezzo 'l verno un lieto aprile;
anzi ti fa nel mondo un paradiso
il sol del volto, e degli occhi le stelle,
e 'l tranquillo seren del vago riso;
ma l'intelletto, che sì chiaro dielle
il celeste Motor a sua sembianza,
unito in lei con l'altre cose belle,
quegli altri pregi in modo sopravanza,
che l'uman veder nostro non perviene
a mirar tal virtute in tal distanza.
A pena l'occhio corporal sostiene
lo splendor de la fronte, in cui mirando
abbagliato e confuso ne diviene:
questa la donna mia dolce girando,
l'aria fa tutta sfavillar d'intorno,
e pon le nubi e le tempeste in bando.
Di rose e di vïole il mondo adorno
rende 'l lume del ciglio, con cui lieta
primavera perpetua fa soggiorno. (11.1–24)

(Truly, fair Verona, you are one of a kind,
now that my gentle Veronica
beautifies you with her unique beauty.
She, who's never had an equal or peer,
Adria's nymph, now with her fair face
brings you in midwinter an April full of joy;
the sun of her face and the stars of her eyes
and the calm serenity of her sweet laugh
turn you, indeed, to a heaven on earth;

but the brilliant intellect that the heavenly Mover
gave her, in his image, united
with her other beautiful qualities,
so far surpasses all those other gifts
that our human vision cannot reach far enough
to perceive such great virtue at such a distance.
The bodily eye can scarcely bear
the splendor of her brow; beholding it,
human sight becomes dazzled and dazed:
this lady of mine, gently turning around,
sets the air all about her to sparkling
and banishes tempests and clouds far away.
The gleam of her eye bedecks the world
with roses and violets, and with her,
gay, everlasting spring comes to stay.)[4]

The unknown male poet is reaching back into the poetic tradition to praise Veronica Franco, pulling on the praise of the beloved's beauty that we find in the poetry of Dante, Petrarch, and Guido Cavalcanti. There is the play on her name (Veronica) and that of the city of Verona, to emphasize her true uniqueness with the play on "una" (one of a kind) and "unica" (unique). Repeatedly, he describes the resplendent qualities of her body and her mind: the sun of her expression, the stars of her eyes, the light of her brow, the clarity of her intellect. Her power is such that she is able to alter distant meteorological phenomena and convert a wintry chill into a pleasing springtime. Like the woman described in Cavalcanti's "Chi è questa che vèn, ch'ogn'om la mira" (Who is this woman that comes, watched by all) who "makes the air tremble brightly" (fa tremar di chiaritate l'âre), she illuminates the air around her and makes it sparkle.[5] And as in Cavalcanti's poem, which emphasizes man's inability to know the beloved fully, those who look upon Franco experience the limitations of human comprehension.[6]

---

4 For Jones and Rosenthal's translation of "Verona bella" (fair Verona; 14.1), I have substituted "beautiful Verona," and for their translation of "bel viso" (fair face; 14.5), I have substituted "beautiful face."

5 See Cavalcanti, *Rime*, ed. Rea and Inglese, 56–7; the English translation is mine.

6 In the final tercet of "Chi è questa che vèn, ch'ogn'om la mira," Cavalcanti writes, "Non fu sì alta già la mente nostra / e non si pose 'n noi tanta salute, / che propiamente n'aviàn canoscenza" (Our intelligence was not so profound, and we were not given such virtue, that we can arrive at full knowledge of her). See Cavalcanti, *Rime*, ed. Rea and Inglese, 59; the English translation is mine.

The attention to Franco's beauty is exceptionally heavy handed, particularly in the first six lines where words indicating beauty (i.e., "bella," "bel," "bellezze," "abbella," "belle," "bel," "vago") abound. Probably in order to make the poem seem less clunky, Jones and Rosenthal seek to attenuate this by translating "Verona bella" as "fair Verona" rather than as "beautiful Verona," and "bel viso" as "fair face" rather than as "beautiful face." In modifying their translation of these lines, I have sought to reproduce the effect of the abundance of words indicating beauty.

To see a masterful praise of beauty, even with repetitions of the adjective "beautiful" (bello), we need go no farther than Petrarch's "Chiare, fresche e dolci acque," the most famous canzone of the *Rerum vulgarium fragmenta*. This poem came into prominence in the sixteenth century after Pietro Bembo extolled it for its gracefulness, sweetness, and pleasantness.[7] Here is the first stanza of the poem:

Chiare, fresche et dolci acque,
ove le belle membra
pose colei che sola a me par donna,
gentil ramo ove piacque
(con sospir mi rimembra)
a lei di fare al bel fianco colonna,
erba et fior che la gonna
leggiadra ricoverse
co l'angelico seno,
aere sacro sereno,
ove Amor co' begli occhi il cor m'aperse:
date udienzia insieme
a le dolenti mie parole estreme. (*Rvf* 126.1–13)[8]

(Clear, fresh, sweet waters
into which she, who alone seems
woman to me, slipped her beautiful limbs:
noble branch where it pleased her
(I think of it again, sighing)
to make a columnar support for her beautiful body:
grass and flowers which her graceful
dress did cover

7 "Gracefulness," "sweetness," and "pleasantness" are my translations of Pietro Bembo's "vaghezza," "dolcezza," and "piacevolezza." See Bembo, *Prose della volgar lingua*, II, xiii, in Bembo, *Prose e rime*, ed. Dionisotti, 156.

8 The Italian text is from Petrarca, *Petrarch's Lyric Poems*, trans. and ed. Durling.

as likewise it did the angelic breast:
serene and sacred air,
where Love pierced my heart with beauteous eyes:
listen together
to my last sad words.)[9]

When Petrarch uses the adjective "bello" (beautiful) to describe Laura's limbs, the side of her body, and the eyes that Love uses to wound his heart, he distributes the adjective throughout the stanza at verses 2, 6, and 11, and he varies the way in which he applies the adjective so that in the third usage we have to make a concerted effort to understand that the eyes of which he speaks are Laura's rather than Love's. Moreover, while the first two usages of the adjective "bello" focus the look on Laura's beautiful body, the third instance reminds us that Love and Laura work in concert to make Petrarch fall in love with Laura. Unlike the male author of poem 11, who flatly repeats the claims of Verona's and Veronica's beauty, Petrarch strives for variation.

Moreover, Petrarch offers a scene that is deeply pleasing and beautiful because it engages the reader's imagination, creating wonder and a sense of sacred mystery. A review of readings of this stanza from the sixteenth century to modern times reveals how Petrarch created a scene that allows the imagination to flow among various possibilities.[10]

When Laura arrives at these clear, fresh, and sweet waters, how much of her body is visible?[11] As Nancy Howe points out, the passage might

---

9 My translation. Robert Durling translates as follows: "Clear, fresh, sweet waters where she who alone seems lady to me rested her lovely body, / gentle branch where it pleased her (with sighing I remember) to make a column for her lovely side / grass and flowers that her rich garment covered along with her angelic breast, sacred bright air; / where Love opened my heart with her lovely eyes: listen all together to my sorrowful dying words."

10 As Nancy Howe notes, this is "created by a studied vagueness of descriptive detail." She adds, "This vagueness […] artfully allows the reader to fill in the outlines of the scene with his own dreams" ("Laura in the Grass, Alas?," 193).

11 Petrarch says that the waters are where Laura "le belle membra / pose colei che sola a me par donna" (she, the only one who seems woman to me, slipped her beautiful limbs). The Italian verb that Petrarch uses, "porre," meaning "to place" or "to set down," creates challenges for any translation. Robert Durling chose to translate the first lines as follows: "Clear, fresh, sweet waters where she who alone seems lady to me rested her lovely body." In my translation, "Clear, fresh, sweet waters / into which she, the only one who seems woman to me, / slipped her beautiful limbs," I have chosen to render the Italian "pose" as "slipped." This is consistent with Italian paraphrases of *Rvf* 126 that understand "pose" to mean "immersed" (immerse) or "placed" (mise).

suggest "anything from [Laura's] getting her feet wet to swimming."[12] As Mark Musa notes, "early commentators argued over whether [Laura] first appears naked in the waters. Castelvetro (1582) thought modesty would forbid this; Carducci (1899) disagreed."[13] If instead we see the waters as the place where Laura rests her body, are we to imagine Laura in the waters (perhaps floating on them?) or resting beside them?

How Laura manages to lean on a branch is also somewhat puzzling.[14] Musa resolves the problem by specifying that the branch is the laurel, whose "branches are low enough for her to lean against."[15] But as Alessandro Tassoni points out, if Petrarch had wanted, he could have specified that Laura was leaning against a tree;[16] and to this I would add that there would be no metrical obstacle to writing about a "gentil lauro" (noble laurel) rather than a "gentil ramo" (noble branch). Laura's body, in relation to the tree as in relation to the waters, is left mysterious.

The relation between the grass and the flowers ("l'erba et fior") on the one hand and Laura's dress ("gonna") on the other hand is also quite unstable. Does Laura's garment cover the grass and flowers (as in my translation), or should the grass and flowers be understood as a singular collective so that they can bind to the singular verb "ricoverse" and be understood to cover Laura's garment? Is the "gonna" just the bottom part of Laura's dress, or should it be understood as the entire dress? What about the reference to the "angelico seno"? In the vast majority of readings and translations it is the "angelic breast" covered by Laura's dress. But the esteemed poet Giosuè Carducci suggested that we hear the reverberation of the Latin "sinus" (i.e., the folds and hem of a garment) in "angelico seno."[17] In reviewing scholarly understandings of lines 7–9, Howe argues that we should understand them as follows: "grass and flowers, which her charming dress covered as it did her angelic breast."[18] In her reading, "Laura's vitality and dignity are preserved, the formal structure of the stanza becomes harmonious

12 Howe, "Laura in the Grass, Alas?," 193.

13 Petrarca, *Petrarch: The Canzoniere*, trans. Musa, 596.

14 Maria Bufalini documents the various understandings of the "gentil ramo" (noble branch) in "Sulla canzone del Petrarca," 395.

15 Petrarca, *Petrarch: The Canzoniere*, trans. Musa, 596.

16 Petrarca, *Le rime di Francesco Petrarca, s'aggiungono le Considerazioni rivedute e ampliate d'Alessandro Tassoni, le Annotazoni di Girolamo Muzio, e le Osservazioni di Lodovico Antonio Muratori*, 268. https://books.google.com/books?id=4lxcAAAAcAAJ&printsec=frontcover#v=onepage&q&f=false.

17 See Petrarca, *Le rime di Francesco Petrarca di su gli originali.*

18 Howe, "Laura in the Grass, Alas?," 197.

in its parallelism of thought, suspect Latinisms remain unsuspected."[19] To make this argument for a more simple and straightforward reading of these lines, however, she had to argue against editors of the *Rvf* such as Carducci, who had asserted Laura's nakedness.

What does this kaleidoscope of interpretations tell us? Although most of these readings of the opening stanza of *Rvf* 126 are driven by an impulse to resolve ambiguities in the text, I believe that we should realize that the poetic language derives its power precisely from these ambiguities, which render Laura a figure of transcendent humanity in this natural landscape. We are encouraged to see her both in the water and beside it, to see her clothed (or partially clothed) and unclothed, to imagine that she is so light and supple that leaning on a branch is no problem at all. For us, as for Petrarch, Laura is always just a bit beyond our grasp – and not because Petrarch tells us explicitly that this is the case but because the poetic language acts this out.

I have paused over Petrarch's accomplishments because if we see what Petrarch achieves when he invokes the landscape with which Laura interacts, we can more easily understand why it is that the unknown male author of poem 11 falls short of creating wonder despite his repeated assertions of Veronica Franco's marvellous beauty and its impact on the city of Verona. Poem 11 begins with the play on the name of the city, Verona, said to be "verily unique" ([i]nvero una) because Veronica graces the city with her presence. The effect is to meld Veronica with the cityscape. When Petrarch had the opportunity to do something similar, with a play on Laura's name, he avoided any descent into paronomasia. As I noted earlier, he could have portrayed Laura leaning against a noble *laurel* (gentil *lauro*). To describe the "serene and sacred air," he could have spoken of "*l'aura* sacra, serena" rather than the "aere sacro, sereno" (though, granted, this would have required a change to the preceding verse to produce a rhyme for "serena"). Later in the poem, in speaking about Laura's hair that looked like "oro forbito" (burnished gold; *Rvf* 126.48), Petrarch could have had recourse to speak not about "oro" but about "auro," using the Latinate alternative that we also find in the *Rvf*. The paronomasia pattern of "Laura," "l'aura," "lauro," and "l'auro" is a signature Petrarchan move, and it can be used to create wonder, as in the marvellous madrigal "Non più al suo amante Diana piacque" (Not more did Diana please her lover; *Rvf* 52) and in sonnet 90, "Erano i capei d'oro a l'aura sparsi" (The golden hair was scattered in the breeze). But it is not used at all in *Rvf* 126.

19 Howe, 197.

After the first twenty-four lines, in which the poet speaks to the city of Verona, described as paradisiacal thanks to the divine presence of Veronica, and in which Verona is described as a source of light, warmth, and springtime renewal, the tone changes in line 25. Previously the male poet had addressed the city of Verona, had praised it for its celestial qualities of light and warmth, and had attributed to Veronica Franco the ability to make heaven on earth, but he now punctuates with an exclamation of pain and loss:

> Oimé! qual empio influsso di pianeta,
> unica di quest'occhi e vera luce,
> subito mi t'asconde e mi ti vieta? (11.25–7)

As these are complicated lines and ripe for misunderstanding, I provide here both Jones and Rosenthal's translation and my own:

> Alas! what cruel planet's influence,
> unique and truthful light of her eyes,
> suddenly hides you and keeps me away? (Jones and Rosenthal's translation)

> Alas! what cruel planet's influence,
> unique (to my eyes) and true light,
> suddenly hides me from you and bans me from you? (my translation)

This is an important turning point in the poem. In the previous twenty-four lines the male poet addressed the city of Verona and spoke about Franco in the third person. Now he addresses the "light" (luce; 11.26), which he qualifies as "unique" (unica; 11.26) and "true" (vera; 11.26). To whom, however, do the eyes belong? Jones and Rosenthal understand the "eyes" (occhi) referred to in 11.26 as Franco's; according to them, her eyes project a "unique and truthful light." But in the original Italian there is no possessive pronoun to link the eyes to Franco; presumably Jones and Rosenthal are responding to the play on what is "true" (vera) and "unique" (unica) in this line that thus link the light to her, just as Verona is linked to her by the play on "invero" and "unica" in the first tercet of the poem. I, on the other hand, would suggest that we understand "questi occhi" of line 26, literally "these eyes," as "my eyes." This would be a usage of the demonstrative pronoun "questo" that is consistent with Petrarchan practice in the *Rvf*, where "questi occhi" is translated as "these eyes" when it is clear that the demonstrative pronoun refers to the speaker; it can also be translated as "my eyes."[20] The sense of these lines would be something like what Petrarch claims in *Rvf* 23 when he speaks of Laura as a figure who "sola a me par donna" (the only one who seems woman to me).

The unique and true light continues to shine even as the unknown male author is hidden from it and banned from it. Is that "true light"

---

20 Consider the following examples from Petrarch's *Rvf*. In *Rvf* 30.16–18, Petrarch writes: "seguirò l'ombra di quel dolce lauro / per lo più ardente sole et per la neve, / finché l'ultimo dì chiuda quest'occhi" (in the scorching sun and in the snow I will follow the shadow of that sweet laurel until the last day closes these eyes); here, "quest'occhi" (these eyes) clearly are the speaker's (i.e., Petrarch's). In *Rvf* 243, Petrarch writes: "il mio cor [...] / va or contando ove da quel bel piede / segnata è l'erba et da quest'occhi molle" (my heart [...] now goes counting when the grass is marked by that lovely foot and made wet by these eyes; 243.5, 243.7–8); again "quest'occhi" are clearly Petrarch's. In *Rvf* 252.5–8, Petrarch writes: "Or fia giammai che quel bel viso santo / renda a quest'occhi le lor luci prime, / (lasso, non so che di me stesso estime) / o li condanni a sempiterno pianto" (Now will it ever be that that beautiful, holy face / will give back to these eyes their first light / (alas, I know not what to think of myself) / or will it condemn them to eternal weeping); again, "quest'occhi" (these eyes) refers to Petrarch's eyes. The Italian text is taken from *Petrarch's Lyric Poems*; the English translations from *Rvf* 30 and 243 are mine; the English translation from *Rvf* 252 is from *Petrarch's Lyric Poems*.

The difficulty in translating the demonstrative pronoun "questo" in 11.26 raises questions about the translation of this pronoun in line 11.19, "Questa la mia donna dolce girando." Jones and Rosenthal translate it as "this lady of mine, gently turning around," but I believe that "questa" in this line refers back to "fronte" (brow or forehead, and, by extension, face) in 11.17, so that 11.19 should be translated as "my lady gently turning her face [toward me]." For a comparable usage of "girare la fronte" with the sense of "to see (by turning one's brow)," see the opening stanza of Giambattista Marino's "L'amore incostante":

Chi vuol veder, Marcello,
Proteo d'amor novello,
novel camaleonte,
a me giri la fronte,
ch'ognor pensier volgendo,
forme diverse e color vari apprendo.

(Let all, Marcello, see
new Proteus in me,
a love's chameleon
in all my longings shown,
for, though my thoughts I turn,
different colors, various forms I learn.)

The Italian text and its English translation, by Joseph Tusiani, can be found in the *Journal of Italian Translation* 5.1 (2010): 152.

(typically associated with the divine godhead) to be understood as the city of Verona itself? As Veronica Franco? That is not clear.

From here, where the poem introduces the loss experienced by the male speaker, the poem establishes, in 11.28–45, fundamental oppositions: between joy and springtime in Verona (where Franco is), and sadness, winter, and roaring seas in Venice (where the male poet is). Once these oppositions have been established, there appears to be no place to go but somewhere even more hyperbolic. So when the male poet stops addressing Venice and returns to addressing Verona, he offers over-the-top praise of Veronica Franco in 11.46–108, tediously repetitive of the first twenty-four lines. Grasping the absurdity of the hyperbole, Arturo Graf ridiculed it.[21] Throughout the over-the-top praise, the unknown male author intersperses laments about how miserable he is at being separated from Franco and knowing that she is with another man.

As the unknown male author moves to a conclusion, he presents his plea in a single tercet that binds his praise for the divine heavenly light and his lament at having been abandoned by it:

> Deh torna, luce mia, del raggio impressa
> de la divinità, qui dove mai
> pianger la tua partita non si cessa. (11.106–8)

> (Pray, my dear light, do come back,
> marked by the ray of divinity, to the place
> which never ceases to mourn for your going.)

While it would appear that this tercet is addressed directly to Veronica Franco, we discover in the concluding thirteen lines of the poem that the unknown male author's address to the light in line 106, as previously his address to the light in line 26, is quite apart from his direct address to Franco. Addressing her as "madonna" (my lady), he turns away from the familiar pronoun "tu" that he had used in addressing Verona, Venice, and the light and opts instead for the courteous pronoun "voi":

> Tempo è di ritornar, madonna, omai
> a consolar de la vostr'alma vista
> di questa patria i desïosi rai,

21 Graf, *Attraverso il Cinquecento*, 303–4.

a dar a la mia mente inferma e trista,
col dolce oggetto del bel vostro lume,
rimedio contra 'l duol che sì l'attrista:
e se troppo 'l mio cor di voi presume,
datemi in pena che del vago volto
da vicin lo splendor m'arda e consume;
né de' begli occhi altrove sia rivolto
il doppio sol, fin che 'n polve minuta
non mi vediate dal mio incendio vòlto;
e per farlo, affrettate la venuta. (11.109–21)

(It is time, my lady, at last to return,
to bring comfort, with your blessed sight,
to the longing eyes of this, your native land,
and to grant my ailing and sorrowful mind
by the sweet visibility of your fair light
a remedy for the woe that so aggrieves it:
and if my heart demands too much of you,
let my penance be that your fair face's splendor
may consume and burn me at close hand;
and let the double sun of those lovely eyes
be turned nowhere else, until you see me
reduced to fine dust by this fire of mine.
And in order to do this, speed your return.)

Why would the unknown male author create a situation in which he allows a reader to believe that he could be addressing Franco in a familiar manner, only to reverse strategy in the final thirteen lines to address her in the respectful manner that a woman of high status would merit? I believe this is the result of a tension that he creates between what can be possessed and what cannot be possessed.

Throughout poem 11, he repeatedly uses the possessive pronoun "mio" (my) to mark Veronica Franco, heavenly presence and source of light, as *his*. He calls her "la mia Veronica gentile" (my gentle Veronica; 11.2), "la donna mia dolce" (this lady of mine; 11.19), "[i]l vago mio splendor celeste" (my beautiful heavenly radiance; 11.32), "[i]l mio bel sol" (my beautiful sun; 11.49), "la mia dolce terrena dea" (my sweet goddess on earth; 11.65), "del mio bel sol la luce" (the light of my fair sun; 11.71), "luce mia" (my light; 11.106).[22] This is most striking.

22 For 11.32 and 11.106, I have substituted my own translations for those of Jones and Rosenthal.

In none of the other poems attributed to an unknown male author (poems 1, 4, 6, 7, 9, 14) do we see such insistent assertions that Veronica Franco belongs to the male speaker. When the male poet complains in 11.70–2 that another man enjoys the light that Franco brings, the jealousy is made all the more palpable by the sense that he has lost what he truly believes belongs to him, and that he proclaims to be "unica di quest'occhi e vera luce" (unique [to my eyes] and true light; 11.26).

At the same time that the unknown male author emphasizes that Franco is his, he highlights Franco's divine-like nature, featuring her as a figure that conceivably belongs to all. She is, he says, a "true light" (vera luce; 11.26), daring to use for her an epithet applied to Christ both in the Bible and in the Italian literary and religious traditions.[23] A contradiction is born, for to the extent that Franco is such a "true light," her enlightenment must be available to all who do not choose to remain in the darkness. She would not be able to be an object of singular possession because all would be able to participate in loving her charitably. Union with her would not be sexual but mystical. There would be no place for the kind of envy that the unknown male author feels because someone else experiences her light.

Here it is instructive to consider the pronouns that Dante uses with Beatrice in his *Commedia*. For the entire time that Beatrice is serving as his guide in purgatory and paradise, he uses the honorific "voi" with her. But in *Paradiso* 31.79–90, after Beatrice has entrusted Dante to Bernard of Clairvaux and has returned to her seat in heaven, Dante suddenly uses the informal "tu" with her. Commenting on the eleven second-person-singular pronouns and verb endings that Dante uses in these twelve verses, Robert Hollander argues that Dante addresses Beatrice with "tu" in heaven when "they are on an equal footing as lovers of one another in God."[24] While it appears that Hollander would agree with Manfredi Porena, who views the affectionate "tu" as the pronoun one would use with a saint, God, or Mary, Hollander appears not to want to see the distancing effect that Porena sees in the informal

23 In John 1:9, Christ is said to be "the true light that enlightens every man that comes into the world" (lux vera quae inluminat omnem hominem venientem in mundum). The English translation is mine; for the Latin original, see *Biblia sacra iuxta vulgatam versionem*, ed. Weber. In chapter 49 of the *Fioretti di san Francesco*, Christ is said to be the "vera luce delle anime" (true light of souls); see *I fioretti di san Francesco*, ed. Davico Bonino; the English translation is mine. In the *Vita nova* 15 [XXIV] 4, Dante creates an analogy in which Beatrice is like Christ, referred to as "la verace luce" (the true light); see Alighieri, *Vita nova*, ed. Gorni; the English translation is mine.

24 See Hollander's note to *Paradiso* 31.79–90 in Alighieri, *Paradiso*, trans. Hollander and Hollander, 780.

pronoun; instead Hollander reads "tu" as indicating "a more personal sense of affection."[25]

This tells us that the informal and affectionate "tu" can instantiate an intimate and familiar relationship between a human and a divine being and it can, at the same time, remind us of the divide between what is human and what is divine. When Franco is represented as divine and as a celestial light in poem 11, the unknown male author uses "tu" because he is addressing her as that light. When at the end of the poem he pleads with her to return, and he focuses firstly on her ability to aid him in his distress, he shifts to the honorific "voi."

The poem ends with the unknown male author asserting that Franco is a divine presence, the sight of which, at a closer distance, is not permitted of mere mortals, at least if they wish to continue to live. Let us look again at the closing lines of the poem:

> e se troppo 'l mio cor di voi presume,
> datemi in pena che del vago volto
> da vicin lo splendor m'arda e consume;
> né de' begli occhi altrove sia rivolto
> il doppio sol, fin che 'n polve minuta
> non mi vediate dal mio incendio vòlto;
> e per farlo, affrettate la venuta. (11.115–21)

> (and if my heart demands too much of you,
> let my penance be that your fair face's splendor
> may consume and burn me at close hand;
> and let the double sun of those lovely eyes
> be turned nowhere else, until you see me
> reduced to fine dust by this fire of mine.
> And in order to do this, speed your return.)

The unknown male author figures Veronica Franco as Phoebus-like, able to incinerate a mortal being with her splendour; the comparison to Phoebus-Sol is underscored by and amplified by the mention of the "double sun" (doppio sol; 11.19) of her eyes. In effect he states that he wants her to return and to keep her gaze on him whether this bring him life or death. In her response in poem 12, Franco will reject the unknown male author's comparison of her to Phoebus-Sol. In my discussion of poem 12, I will comment on the passage in which she does

25 Alighieri, *Paradiso*, trans. Hollander and Hollander, 780.

this (12.67–78). Here, however, I would like to put a different passage next to the unknown male author's comparison of Franco to Phoebus-Sol. The following passage is taken from poem 19, one of the monologic poems of the *Terze rime*; in it Franco reflects on the love that she felt for a man of the church.

Or sicura ho 'l pericolo a la mente,
quando da' be' vostr'occhi e dal bel volto
contra me spinse Amor la face ardente:
ed a piagarmi in mille guise vòlto,
dal fiume ancor de la vostra eloquenza
il foco del mio incendio avea raccolto.
L'abito vago e la gentil presenza,
la grazia e le maniere al mondo sole,
e de le virtù chiare l'eccellenza,
fûr ne la vista mia lucido sole,
che m'abbagliâr e m'arser di lontano,
sì ch'a tal segno andar Febo non suole. (19.16–27)

(Safely now I recollect
the danger when Love reached forth to me
the flaming torch of your fair eyes and face,
and, set on wounding me in a thousand ways,
he had intensified the fire of my passion
even further with the flow of your eloquence.
Your becoming attire and noble presence,
your grace and manners, unique in the world,
the excellence of your luminous virtues
were a brilliant sun to my sight,
which dazzled and burned me from far away,
to a degree that Phoebus himself does not reach.)

What distinguishes a passage like this from the way in which the unknown male author speaks about Franco at the end of poem 11? For one thing, in describing the brilliant light that emanates from the man she speaks about, Franco positions it not only in his eyes and face but also in his attire (which is to say in items that can be put on and removed), in his social behaviour and presence (i.e., his grace and manners), and in his virtues. While the male author of poem 11 does at one point early in his poem comment on the "brilliant intellect that the heavenly Mover gave her, in his image" (l'intelletto, che sì chiaro dièlle / il celeste Motor a sua sembianza; 11.10–11), he focuses primarily on the effect of Franco's corporeal beauty, especially that of her eyes and her face. When he describes what emerges from her mouth, it is not clear that he considers Franco's verbal expression. He lauds instead the "mild air and precious scent / exhaled from the rosy lips / of this daughter of Pallas and Love" (L'aura soave e 'l prezïoso odore, / che da le rose de la bocca spira / questa figlia di Pallade e d'Amore; 11.55–7) and "the harmoniousness of her angelic voice" (de la voce angelica il concento; 11.61). The former appears simply to be the perfumed breath, and the latter could well be music without words. And while the unknown male author grants Franco Orphic powers when he states that the harmoniousness of her angelic voice "stops rivers in their course and convinces the hills to pause and listen, / and heaven stops, intent on hearing" (i fiumi affrena, e i monti ad udir move, / e 'l ciel si ferma ad ascoltarla intento; 11.62–3), Franco highlights the power of the man's eloquent speech to intensify the passion ignited by the beauty of his eyes and face. In the final accounting, Franco's showcasing of the man's eloquent speech in poem 19 places into relief the fact that the unknown male author in poem 11 does not showcase Franco's expertise with words.

In her response in poem 12, Veronica Franco seeks to take the upper hand. As I noted at the beginning of this chapter, previous scholars have demonstrated how she does this by aligning herself with the city of Venice (as opposed to Verona) and by aligning herself with a rhetoric of truthfulness (in opposition to what she characterizes as hyperbolic mendaciousness). I intend here to focus on how she adopts a far more direct and insistent style of critical questioning and how, atypically, she concludes with a brutally unpleasant retort that can be read as heartless. I shall also show how, in poem 12, she returns to a strategy that she adopted in her much shorter poem 5, invoking spirituality to advance a criticism of focusing on earthly things.

Here I document the poem's individual moves, paraphrasing what Franco says as she addresses the unknown male author:

12.1–15: The first criticism

It would be better for you to use the lofty intellect heaven gave you more appropriately, by disdaining the frail world. If you have to praise a mortal thing, you should have praised Venice (which, though earthly, has the true form of heaven on earth). This – not hollow versifying – was the subject matter for your intellect.

12.16–21: The second criticism

Instead of engaging in hyperbolic lies, you could have praised Venice.

12.22–30: The third criticism

You should have praised Venice; but you recited the marvels of another city, and you said of me what blind love dictated to you.

12.31–48: The fourth criticism

Verona is special but not for the reasons you give. Furthermore, Venice is more beautiful than Verona. Venice is built upon waters in a way that is completely otherworldly. Heaven gave Venice joy that exists nowhere else on earth.

12.49–54: The fifth criticism

You were aware of this but then Love blinded you.

12:55–60: The sixth criticism

I don't believe your lies about me, though I appreciate the style. The over-the-top praise of me both pleases and annoys me.

12:61–6: The seventh criticism

So if you want to praise me, why don't you praise Venice, where I was born? If you have to praise a place, why are you directing your thought elsewhere?

12:67–75: An interpolated address to Venice

The east is privileged; Phoebus unleashes his divine ray in the east; thus, without comparing myself to the sun, I think of you, Venice, as my east.

12.76–8: The eighth criticism

If you sought to please me, you should have praised this city and in this way call me back to my usual place of sojourn.

12.79–84: How I, Veronica Franco, feel about this

While I am away from Venice, I enjoy a lone hope: that you will be freed from me or bonded to another. Continuing in this hope, I shall delay returning as long as possible – that is how strong my disdain for your love is!

12.85–8: Why I do not intend to return to Venice

This is what the man I love commands. Out of revenge, he may perhaps scorn my love no less than I do yours. In any case, however, I won't hasten to return.

In considering this sequence of moves, I am struck by how insistently and repeatedly Franco states that the unknown male author should have praised Venice, failed to praise Venice, should think about praising Venice. She enumerates each cause for the unknown male author's failure: his failure to use his lofty intellect appropriately, his hyperbolic lies, his displaced attention, his being blinded by love. Her insistence is underscored by recurrent repetitions throughout the poem. She tells him that if he were to praise a mortal thing, he should "*praise* what is valued by good judgment, / *praise* the happy, noble retreat of Adria" (*lodar* quel ch'al giudicio ancor poi vale, / *lodar* d'Adria il felice almo ricetto; 12.9–10, emphasis mine). In lines 16–17, she hammers on how he could have written "*Without* running on in poetical fashion, / *without* using hyperbolic figures of speech" (*Senza* discorrer poeticamente, / *senza* usar l'iperbolica figura; 12.16–17, emphasis mine). Exalting Venice, she sits on the demonstrative pronoun "this" (questa), giving it a privileged position at the beginning of two tercets:

> *Questa* dominatrice alta del mare,
> regal vergine pura, invïolata,
> nel mondo senza essempio e senza pare,
> *questa* da voi deveva esser lodata,
> vostra patria gentile, in cui nasceste,
> e dov'anch'io, la Dio mercé, son nata. (12.22–7; emphases mine)

> (*This* high ruler of the sea,
> lofty virgin, inviolate and pure,
> without equivalent or peer in the world,
> *this* is what you should have praised,
> your noble fatherland, in which you were born,
> and where I, too, thank God, was born.)[26]

In praising the city of Venice, Franco uses anaphora to great effect:

> Una invero e, qual dite voi, Verona,
> per le qualità proprie di se stessa,
> e non per quel che da voi si cagiona;[27]
> ma tanto più *Vinegia* è bella d'essa,
> quanto e più bel del mondo il paradiso,
> la cui beltà fu a *Vinegia* concessa.
> In modo dal mondan tutto diviso,
> fabricata è *Vinegia* sopra l'acque,
> per sopranatural celeste aviso. (12.31–9; emphases mine)

> (Verona is indeed unique, as you say,
> but for her own qualities,
> not for those you attribute to her;

26 For "vostra patria gentile" in line 26, I have substituted my translation, "your noble fatherland," for Jones and Rosenthal's "this gentle land."

27 I have changed "ragiona" to "cagiona," since "cagiona" is what the 1575 edition has.

but the beauty of *Venice* exceeds hers
as far as the earth is surpassed by paradise,
with whose beauty *Venice* was endowed.
In a way set apart from what is seen on earth,
Venice was built upon the waters
according to supernatural, heavenly intent.)

Franco creates a high sense of solemnity not simply through her use of anaphora but also through her decision to use the form of the city's name that Dante used in the *Commedia* and Boccaccio used in the *Decameron*. Moreover, in the verses where the city's name appears, Franco begins with a hendecasyllable *a maiore* (12.34), then modulates to a hendecasyllable *a minore* (12.36), then returns to a hendecasyllable *a maiore* (12.38). This creates a very pleasing and stabilized rhythm.

The final insistent repetition is on "why?" (perché?), thus putting Franco decidedly into the position of a judge who persists in questioning:

Ma se pur tal di me concetto fate,
*Perch'*al nido, ov'io nacqui, non si pensa
da voi, e 'n ciò *perch'*ognor nol lodate?
*Perch'*ad altr'opra il pensier si dispensa,
se per voi deve un loco esser lodato,
che dia al mio spirto posa e ricompensa? (12.61–6; emphasis mine)

(But if you make such a conceit even of me,
why do you not consider the place I was born,
and *why* do you not constantly sing its praise?
Why do you devote your thought to other tasks,
if you must praise some place or another
that can give repose and reward to my spirit?)

These are the only interrogatives in poem 12. With her repeated questioning of why the unknown male author did not choose to praise Venice, Franco responds obliquely but pointedly to the interrogatives the man made in poem 11, none of which were addressed directly to Veronica Franco. In poem 11 the unknown male author used interrogatives to ask the city of Venice who was responsible for taking their paradise elsewhere (11.28–30), to ask why, if Franco hears his grief, she does not come to relieve him of his jealousy (11.73–5).

With her insistent repetitions throughout the first three quarters of poem 12, Franco portrays herself as adamant, persistent, unfaltering. She bolsters her position further by aligning herself and her views with higher, spiritual forces. Unusually, she references the supreme celestial power three times in poem 12, when she affirms that Venice is dear to God (12.12), when she thanks God that she was born in Venice (12.27), and when she describes the privileged place that Venice has for the King of heaven (12.40).[28] By criticizing the focus of the unknown male author on unworthy objects in this frail world (i.e., Verona, Franco herself) and by branding him as someone unable to see clearly because he is blinded by love, she lays claim to being committed to higher values. In effect, poem 12 is a more sustained version of poem 5 in which Franco asserted her commitment to a higher love, and it portrays Franco as unwavering also in her love of virtuous thinking (and, unlike poem 5, makes no mention of any moment in her life in which she might not have been so staunch in her commitment to virtue).

What has happened to the Franco who previously, in poems 8 and 10, blunted her criticisms so as not to offend her male interlocutor? For the vast majority of poem 12, she is courteous without appearing particularly concerned to assuage the ego of the unknown male author. She grants that his intellect is lofty (12.2) and that his style is not entirely displeasing to her (12.55–7), but overall she sticks with her forthright and repeated criticisms of the choices he made in poem 11. She can sustain her criticism of him without conceding that she might not really mean it because she has aligned herself with a higher purpose and a higher vision.

Franco's conclusion to her poem is quite startling, however. She has, up to now, delivered her criticisms with a golden mean in mind: neither too biting nor too faint. In the final lines she shows a side of herself that I do not see anywhere else in the *Terze rime*, namely, the ability to be harsh and merciless:

> Lunge da lei, di nullo altro ben godo,
> se non ch'io spero che la lontananza
> dal mio vi scioglia o leghi a l'altrui nodo.

28 In previous poems, if Franco referenced a god, it was typically Cupid in order to speak about the power of earthly love. In 3.49 she writes about "il piccolo dio, bendato arciero" (the little god, blindfolded archer) that had made her fall in love; in 5.21 she writes about the "little archer god" (il dio picciolo arciero) that had bound her with chains from which she stated she was now free; and in 8.5–6 she refers to "quel dio / che 'l cielo e 'l mondo e fin gli abissi stanca" (that god / who wearies heaven and earth and even hell; 8.5–6). Furthermore, Franco will not mention God again until the final poem of the collection, in praise of Fumane and the villa of Marcantonio della Torre (see 25.187 and 25.460). It seems fair to say that Franco refers to God in poem 25 in order to proclaim the exceptional beauty of Fumane and its art, just as in poem 12 she refers to God in order to reaffirm Venice's supreme beauty on earth.

Continuando in cotal mia speranza,
prolungherò più ch'io potrò 'l ritorno:
tal che m'amiate ha lo sdegno possanza!
Così vuol chi nel cor mi fa soggiorno:
amor di tal, che per vostra vendetta
forse non meno il mio riceve a scorno;
ma, come sia, non ritornerò in fretta. (12.79–88)

(Away from her, I enjoy nothing else,
except to hope that our separation may free you
from your bond to me or tie you to another.
Persisting in this hope of mine,
I will delay my return as long as I can:
so much do I disdain your love for me!
This is what the man who dwells in my heart wants:
whose love, perhaps to right your wrong,
responds to mine with no less scorn; but
be that as it may, I will not come back soon.)

For all that she has been accused in certain of the poems by men to be the classic cruel woman, oblivious to their suffering,[29] she has never previously taken on a nasty tone. Perhaps because the unknown male author of poem 11 never portrays her as a cruel lady, choosing instead to blame the cruelty of planetary and astral influences for his misery (see 11.25 and 11.69), Franco can adopt here the stance of the haughty and uncaring woman.

What makes these concluding lines seem gratuitously caustic is that there are two moments in them in which Franco could have broken off and managed to avoid a cruel jab at her interlocutor. She could have ended her poem with a succinct comment about Venice: "Lunge da lei, di nullo altro ben godo" (Away from her, I enjoy nothing else; 12.79). In that way she could have avoided commenting on the delight that she feels at the thought that the separation might bring the unknown male author to cease loving her or begin loving someone else, and she could have avoided an open declaration (punctuated with an exclamation mark at 12.84) of her intense disdain for his love. Furthermore, if she wanted to skirt responsibility for her actions, as she has done in some previous poems, she could have ended the poem with the line "Così vuol chi nel cor mi fa soggiorno" (This is what the man who dwells

29 See *Terze rime* 1.2, 1.15, 4.1–6, 7.1–3, 7.130–2, 7.142, 7.175–7, 9.34–42.

in my heart wants; 12.85). Instead, she doubles down on her pitiless response. Even if this other man scorns her love for him, she will not return.

Why the acerbic cruelty? In other poems, not rejecting a man too summarily meant that Franco could keep her options open: if not one lover, then perhaps another. At the end of poem 12, we see her carving out a space that she might occupy alone, as a woman who feels desire but is unwilling to respond to the offers of any and all men, not even when they engage in elaborate praise of her.

7 Attacks and Concessions under Erasure: *Terze rime* 13 and 14

In the first chapter of this book, where I analysed the opening poetic exchange between a man and Veronica Franco, I showed how, in poem 2, Franco manages the male aggression that appears in poem 1, how she responds to it, how she uses it when necessary, and how she redirects it. Whereas the male poet sought to bend Franco to his will, Franco's strategy of persuasion, I argued, depends not on control and on threats of violence but on identification among speakers and on free choice of a higher good. She seeks to create connections, mutuality, and reciprocality, and she imagines a future situation, dependent on conditional factors, in which she would indeed love the male author of poem 1.

Having arrived at the final exchange between Franco and a man (poems 13 and 14), I propose to explore what happens when Franco imagines herself attacking her male opponent. What benefits and disadvantages are there when a woman takes up an aggressive stance? How are writing, violence, and desire connected for Franco? What differences are there, if any, between the rhetorical strategies that Franco uses in poem 13 to threaten a man with violence and the rhetorical strategies that male poets use when they turn aggressive? Are responses to threatened aggression gendered, and if so, how?

In poem 13, "Non più parole, ai fatti, in campo a l'armi" ("No more words! To deeds, to the battlefield, to arms!"), the central poem of the collection, Franco turns away from words to action, invites her male opponent to choose either the arms or the battle-place, then both; she invites him even to choose her bed, minister of her undoing; she announces all of the ways in which she might mutilate her opponent; she then imagines his entrance into a bedroom battle-field, the piercing weapon she will take from him, the sight of his exposed breast, and – one can already see where this is going – her staunch performance until death at the end.

Given that this poem has been lauded for its strong, confident voice, its affirmation of Franco's feminine and erotic identity, and its embrace of a "sane hedonism,"[1] it has often been viewed as representative of Franco's poetics and is among those most frequently selected for inclusion in anthologies, be they for scholarly or simply personal use.[2] Highlighting the poem's refusal of victimization, Sara Maria Adler sees Franco refusing the Petrarchan notion that unfulfilled desire and the acceptance of love's torments are a prerequisite for writing.[3] Patricia Phillippy maintains that Franco, by refusing the role of the silent and chaste woman and utilizing martial discourse as a metaphor for erotic discourse, undermines Petrarchan and heroic epic traditions.[4]

Unlike other readers, who see an unqualifiedly victorious Franco in this poem, I am not fully convinced that a woman who displays her strength through hostility, physical aggression, and violence can always be certain she will live to tell the tale. Rather than viewing poem 13 as affirming a strong woman on top, I maintain that it is characterized by deep ambivalences. True, the poem offers a surface message about Franco's triumph over a man in battle and in bed. But if we look closer at the poem's rhetorical texturing and its intertextual recalls, we will see that in this verbal duel there is at some level an awareness that, for a woman, to threaten hostility in writing is an imperfect strategy and can backfire.

---

1 See Adler, "Veronica Franco's Petrarchan *Terze Rime*," 218–19.

2 In *Lirici del Cinquecento*, ed. Baldacci, Luigi Baldacci includes a portion of poem 2, two sections of poem 25, and poems 3, 13, and 19 in their entirety. In *Poesia italiana: Il Cinquecento*, ed. Ferroni, 238–43, Ferroni offers poems 3 and 13. Poem 13 is the lone selection from Veronica Franco in *Zehn italienische Lyrikerinnen der Renaissance*, ed. Scarpa, 58–65. Martha Feldman and Bonnie Gordon feature the first twelve lines of poem 13 on track 6 of the compact disc that accompanies *The Courtesan's Arts*, ed. Feldman and Gordon; see also their "Appendix: CD Notes and Texts," in *The Courtesan's Arts*, 357–8. Irma Jaffe gives special attention to portions of poems 1, 2, 13, 14, 15, 16, 19, 22, and 25 in Jaffe, *Shining Eyes, Cruel Fortune*, 338–85. In *Il nuovo La scrittura e l'interpretazione*, ed. Luperini, Cataldi, Marchiani, and Marchese, poem 13 is the lone selection from Veronica Franco. The full text of poem 13 and a portion of poem 19 appear in Cox, *Lyric Poetry by Women of the Italian Renaissance*. Tatiana Crivelli chooses to include *Terze rime* 2, 13, 16, and 24 in her presentation of Veronica Franco in *Liriche del Cinquecento*, ed. Farnetti and Fortini, 277–325. Terry Clitheroe features poem 13 (described as "a playful challenge to a lover") on his website, *The Poets Garret*, among the poems selected for 2015: http://www.thepoetsgarret.com, accessed 11 January 2020.

3 Adler, "Veronica Franco's Petrarchan *Terze Rime*," 218.

4 Phillippy, "*Altera Dido*," 2, 13–14.

The poem begins – contradictorily – by renouncing words: "Non più parole" (No more words; 13.1). This serves as the prelude to a series of double-edged statements. I would like to pause over the one that strikes me as most significant:

> Non so se 'l mio «cartel» si debba dire,
> in quanto do risposta provocata:
> ma perché in rissa de' nomi venire? (13.4–6)

> (I don't know if one should call this thing I'm writing a challenge to a duel,
> inasmuch as I am responding to a provocation;
> but why get into a brawl over words?) (translation mine)[5]

Given that Franco speaks of responding to a provocation, readers understand the "cartel" of line 4 as a "cartel di sfida" (a challenge to a duel). But "cartel," a semantically rich term, can also mean "a piece of slanderous or libellous writing." Could Franco, aware that she may be considered an aggressive offender of another as well as a righteous defender of herself, also be saying, "I don't know if my writing should be called defamatory"?

And there is more. Punctuation tamps down ambivalence that lurks in line 4. If one strips out the punctuation, the line reads, "Non so se 'l mio cartel si debba dire." We could translate this as "I don't know if one should call this thing I'm writing a *cartel*" (where "cartel" hovers between meaning a "challenge to a duel" and a "defamatory writing"). But we could also translate as follows: "I don't know if this *cartel* should be uttered" (where again "cartel" hovers between meaning a "challenge to a duel" and a "defamatory writing").

The original 1575 edition controls the punctuation tightly by inserting two commas that create a stumbling, stuttering rhythm and force us to read the verse as a hendecasyllable *a minore*, with a major accent on the fourth syllable: "Non so, se 'l *mio*, cartel si debba dire" (emphasis mine).[6] Such punctuation creates a shield against ambivalence. Modern editions, such as the one I quoted earlier, rely instead on the punctuation provided by Abdelkader Salza in his 1913 edition: "Non so se

5 Jones and Rosenthal translate these lines as follows: "Should I call this a challenge? I do not know, / since I am responding to a provocation; / but why should we duel over words?" I have substituted my translation because the lines have only one question, not two, and because I believe "rissa" (13.6) is translated better as a "brawl" than as a "duel."

6 Franco, *Terze rime al Serenissimo Signor Duca di Mantova et di Monferrato*.

'l mio «cartel» si debba dire."[7] By eliminating the commas and placing the word "cartel" within guillemets, Salza smooths out the rhythm of the line (which I suspect he found problematic) and permits a reading of the line as either a hendecasyllable *a minore* (major accent on the fourth syllable) or a hendecasyllable *a maiore* (major accent on the sixth syllable). How we understand the sense of the line depends on how we parse it metrically. A hendecasyllable *a minore*, "Non so se 'l *mio* cartel si debba dire" (emphasis mine), keeps nomenclature front and centre: Is "cartel" the proper name for this piece of writing? A hendecasyllable *a maiore*, "Non so se 'l mio car*tel* si debba dire" (emphasis mine), poses a question about the legitimacy, or not, of speaking out.

Dismissing any ambivalence about writing and fighting, Franco asks, "[M]a perché in rissa de' nomi venire?" ([B]ut why get into a brawl about words?; 13.6). By refusing to engage in a brawl, which is a noisy and disorderly fight that typically involves multiple people, Franco stabilizes the terms of her attack as one that will be limited to two people and conducted in an orderly fashion. Furthermore, she underscores the privileging of deeds over words, as proclaimed in the opening line of this poem and on which she has relied in previous poems to affirm that she is committed to rightful and virtuous action.

The ambivalence will not go away, however. It bubbles up later in the poem too, when Franco threatens three forms of mutilation:

E, se non cede l'ira al troppo amore,
con queste proprie mani, arditamente
ti trarrò fuor del petto il vivo core.
La falsa lingua, ch'in mio danno mente,
sterperò da radice, pria ben morsa
dentro 'l palato dal suo proprio dente;
e, se mia vita in ciò non fia soccorsa,
pur disperata prenderò in diletto
d'esser al sangue in vendetta ricorsa;
poi col coltel medesmo il proprio petto,
de la tua occisïon sazia e contenta,
forse aprirò, pentita de l'effetto. (13.16–27)

(And unless my rage yields to overwhelming love,
with these very hands I will, in all boldness,
tear your living heart from your very breast.

7 Stampa and Franco, *Rime*, ed. Salza, 274.

The deceiving tongue that lies to my detriment
I shall tear out by its root, though only after it's been soundly bitten
within the palate by its own tooth;
and if this brings no relief to my life,
abandoning all hope, I will rejoice
at having turned to bloodshed for my revenge.
Then with the same knife, my own breast,
satisfied and appeased by slaying you,
I may cut open, regretting my deed.)[8]

In threatening to rip out her opponent's heart and then possibly turn the knife on herself, Franco makes the references to her opponent and herself absolutely clear: "*ti* trarrò fuor del petto il vivo core [...] poi col coltel medesmo il *proprio* petto [...] forse aprirò" (I will [...] tear *your* living heart from your very breast [...] Then, with the same knife, *my own* breast [...] I may cut open; 13.18, 13.25–7, emphases mine). When she threatens violence against the false tongue, however, she does not specify to whom that false tongue belongs: "La falsa lingua, ch'in mio danno mente, / sterperò da radice; pria ben morsa / dentro 'l palato dal suo proprio dente" (The deceiving tongue that lies to my detriment / I shall tear out by its root, though only after it's been soundly bitten / within the palate by its own tooth; 13.19–21). The adjectival force of "proprio" (its own) wavers here, especially since, four lines later, Franco uses "proprio" to refer to her own breast ("il proprio petto"; 13.25). Franco could have banished the ambiguity had she written, "La *tüa* lingua, ch'in mio danno mente, / sterperò da radice; pria ben morsa / dentro 'l palato dal *tuo proprio* dente" (*Your* tongue that lies to my detriment / I shall tear out by its root, though only after it's been soundly bitten / within the palate by *your own* tooth).[9] Why speak about the lying tongue and the tooth without using pronouns or adjectives to clarify to whom they belong? Can we be we certain beyond the shadow of a doubt that the false tongue to be ripped out is the

8 In 13.19–21, I have substituted my own translation for Jones and Rosenthal's.

9 To those who would question the dieresis on "tüa," I acknowledge that this would be an unlikely choice for a poet respecting metrical rules established by Petrarch, but would be an option within the metrical rhythms that Dante used. As Mario Casella has shown, Dante pronounced "io" (I), "tuo" (your), and "suo" (his/her/its) as two syllables when he sought to communicate special emotional charge ("Studi sul testo della *Divina Commedia*," 35–40.). For an overview of dieresis, and a list of examples in Dante, see Beccaria, "Dieresi."

opponent's? Might the language suggest that the false tongue lying to her detriment is her own?

What sort of identity will Franco fashion? Will she perpetrate acts of violence that make her look like men taking revenge on women they love?[10] That would be a Franco who removes the heart of her opponent the way Guiglielmo Rossiglione removes the heart of Guiglielmo Guardastagno in *Decameron* 4.9. In threatening to remove the man's tongue in order to keep him from speaking, might she not be like Tereus who cuts out Philomela's tongue in order to keep her from ruining his name and reputation?[11] It appears that Franco is unable to follow through fully. As she threatens violence, she mutes the force of the threats by noting that she will rip out his heart if anger does not give way to excessive love (13.16) and by offering that perhaps she will repent and turn the knife on herself (13.25–7).

Having floated the possibility of violent acts that are gendered male, Franco re-establishes a female identity as she recalls the bed where she received her opponent as a lover:

> Or mi si para il mio letto davante,
> ov'in grembo t'accolsi, e ch'ancor l'orme
> serba dei corpi in sen l'un l'altro stante.
> Per me in lui non si gode e non si dorme,
> ma 'l lagrimar de la notte e del giorno
> vien che in fiume di pianto mi trasforme.
> Ma pur questo medesimo soggiorno,
> che fu de le mie gioie amato nido,
> dov'or sola in tormento e 'n duol soggiorno,
> per campo eleggi, accioch'altrove il grido
> non giunga, ma qui teco resti spento,
> del tuo inganno ver' me, crudele infido. (13.34–45)

10 While I read these threatened acts of violence as gendered male, Mary Rogers argues that poem 13 "could be seen as [Franco's] adoption of another aspect of Minerva, that of a fierce warrior in a just cause." Although Franco never reveals what the lover's wrongdoing has been, Rogers believes that Franco seeks "revenge for a lover's betrayal of her with another woman"; perhaps because Rogers reads the man's wrongdoing as sexual, rather than slanderous (the way that Margaret Rosenthal sees it), she describes Franco's challenge as "allowing her to assume ferociously 'masculine' characteristics." See Rogers, "Fashioning Identities for Venetian Courtesans," 98.

11 Ovid recounts the story of Tereus, Procne, and Philomela in *Metamorphoses* 6.401–674. See Ovid, *Metamorphoses,* vol. 1, bks. 1–8, trans. Miller.

(Here before me now stands the bed
where I took you in my arms, and which still
preserves the imprint of our bodies, breast to breast.
In it I find now neither joy nor sleep,
but only weeping, by night and by day,
which transforms me into a river of tears.
But this very place, which once was
the cherished shelter of my joys,
where I now live alone, in torment and grief,
choose this as a battleground, so that the news
of your betrayal will reach no other place
but die here with you, cruel, faithless man.)

This is the first time in the *Terze rime* that Franco refers to sexual activity in a bed. She uses the bed both to call attention to intimate activity and to present herself as a spurned woman. Recalls of two Ovidian heroines spurned by men they love raise questions about what kind of wronged woman Franco is and how she uses writing and speech in order to seek redress.

In referring to the bed that "still / preserves the imprint of bodies" (ancor l'orme / serba dei corpi; 13.35–6), Franco suggests that she might be like Ariadne, abandoned by the man she loves. In *Heroides* 10.51–8, Ariadne speaks of the bed that had received her and Theseus:

saepe torum repeto, qui nos acceperat ambos,
sed non acceptos exhibiturus erat,
et tua, quae possum pro te, vestigia tango
strataque quae membris intepuere tuis.
incumbo, lacrimisque toro manante profusis
"pressimus," exclamo, "te duo – redde duos!
venimus huc ambo; cur non discedimus ambo?
perfide, pars nostri, lectule, maior ubi est?"[12]

(Oft do I come again to the couch that once received us both, but was fated never to show us together again, and touch the imprint left by you – 'tis all I can in place of you! – and the stuffs that once grew warm beneath your limbs. I lay me down upon my face, bedew the bed with pouring tears, and cry aloud: "We were two who pressed thee – give back two! We

12 The Latin text and English translation are drawn from Ovid, *Heroides and Amores*, trans. Showerman.

> came to thee both together; why do we not depart the same? Ah, faithless bed – the greater part of my being, oh, where is he?")

Moreover, in noting that her constant weeping transforms her into a river of tears (13.38–9), Franco suggests she might be like Ovid's Byblis, turned into a fountain (*Metamorphoses* 9.649–65).

Significantly, Franco chooses Ovidian heroines whose communication is both effective and ineffective. Like Orpheus, Ariadne is able to move rocks and surrounding nature to respond in chorus with her (*Heroides* 10.21–4). But it is not clear how Theseus will be able to see the visual signs she creates (e.g., sending signals with her hands, and fixing her veil to a long tree branch (*Heroides* 10.39–41); nor is it clear how her letter can be delivered to Theseus, given that she is entirely alone on an island that has no other sign of human life or civilization (*Heroides* 10.59–62). Writing allows Byblis to communicate her passion to her brother, Caunus; still, she decides in retrospect that writing was far riskier than direct speech: "et tamen ipsa loqui, nec me committere cerae / debueram, praesensque meos aperire furores. / vidisset lacrimas, vultum vidisset amantis; / plura loqui poteram, quam quae cepere tabellae" (And yet I should have told him with my own lips, I should in person have confessed my passion, and not have trusted my inmost heart to waxen tablets! He should have seen my tears, he should have seen his lover's face; I could have spoken more than any tablets could hold; *Metamorphoses* 9.601–4).[13] Both Ovidian subtexts reinforce our sense of Franco's ambivalence about the effectiveness of her written challenge. If she is like Ariadne and like Byblis, her communication – like theirs – may prove futile. Simultaneously, in a move that is typical of her, she introduces doubts about whether she is truly like Ariadne and Byblis. Franco, unlike Ariadne, will address not the bed but her male interlocutor, and she certainly would not refer to her male interlocutor as "the greater part of my being" (pars [...] maior; *Heroides* 10.58). And unlike Byblis, spurned by her brother when she revealed her desire for him, Franco has been intimate with the man to whom she writes.

Franco deflects her anger throughout. She introduces threats of violence with if-clauses, which make her action conditional on the dominant emotion, anger or "overwhelming love" (troppo amore; 13.16),

13 The Latin text and English translation are taken from Ovid, *Metamorphoses*, vol. 1, bks 1–8, trans. Miller.

and on whether she finds relief once she acts (13.22).[14] She promises to rip out the false tongue but only after a self-inflicted mutilation of that tongue (13.19–21). The qualifying adverb "perhaps" (forse; 13.27) also communicates that Franco is not fully committed to violent action.

By purposefully confusing imperatives and indicatives in the central portion of the poem, Franco allows her opponent a space in which to choose the narrative into which he will read himself, even as she ineluctably orders him to assume his battle position. When Franco writes, "Or, mentre sono al vendicarmi intenta, / *entra* in steccato, amante empio e rubella / […] pur questo […] soggiorno […] / per campo *eleggi* […] / qui *vieni*" (13.28–9, 13.40, 13.43, 13.46), these lines could be translated as "Now, while I'm intent on pursuing revenge, / enter the arena, cruel, rebellious lover / […] but this very place […] / choose this as a battleground […] / come here," as Jones and Rosenthal do, but the verbs in these lines do not always feel securely tied to an imperative mood. They strain toward another translation: "Now, while I'm intent on pursuing revenge, / there enters into the arena, cruel and rebellious lover […] / but this very place […] / you do choose as a battleground […] you do come here." The double message works both in the man's favour and against him. The verbs in the imperative mood indicate that he can

14 See 13.16–24, where the if-clauses appear in line 16 and 22:

E se non cede l'ira al troppo amore,
con queste proprie mani, arditamente
ti trarrò fuor del petto il vivo core.
La falsa lingua, ch'in mio danno mente,
sterperò da radice, pria ben morsa
dentro 'l palato dal suo proprio dente;
e se mia vita in ciò non fia soccorsa,
pur disperata prenderò in diletto
d'esser al sangue in vendetta ricorsa.

(And if my rage does not yield to overwhelming love,
with these very hands I will, in all boldness,
tear your living heart from your very breast.
The deceiving tongue that lies to do me harm
I will tear out by its root, after it's been bitten
against the palate with repentant teeth;
and if this brings no relief to my life,
abandoning all hope, I will rejoice
at having turned to bloodshed for my revenge.)

I have modified Jones and Rosenthal's translation at line 16 in order to retain the if-clause that is present in the Italian original.

choose how the battle will proceed (although Franco is the one commanding him to choose); alternately, if the verbs are read in the present indicative mood, they present him as the one who, in dramatic fashion, enters into her bedroom, chooses it as a battleground, and therefore can be blamed for having initiated conflict in an intimate space.

Franco uses both of these strategies to her advantage, casting both herself and the man as the primary agents who will determine the focus and the action. While she repeatedly acknowledges her opponent's ability to determine the course of action, a series of verbs in the first-person singular, clustered in the first nine lines, establish her as the primary agent: "voglio" (I want), "do risposta" (I am responding), "da te mi chiamo disfidata" (I will say you challenged me), "ti disfido" (I challenge you), "prendo" (I'll take) (13.2, 13.5, 13.7, 13.8, 13.9). The impersonal exhortatives that follow – "a te stia" (yours be the choice; 13.10) and "ambo nel tuo arbitrio sia" (let both be your decision"; 13.12) – offer her opponent the ability to choose, while at the same time depriving him of an active role as a grammatical subject. When Franco describes her opponent's advance, she does so in fairly neutral terms, stating, "Quando tu meco pur venissi a questo" (Were you finally to come to this point with me; 13.76).[15] The more violent actions, tinged with eroticism, are ones that she herself regulates: "Debbo continuar teco anco in guerra?" (Must I continue to battle with you?), "e quivi, teco guerreggiando stesa" (and here, lying in battle with you), "teco morrei d'egual colpo ferita" (I would die with you, wounded by the same blow) (13.73, 13.80, 13.85; translations mine). Franco's relation to her male opponent wavers in phrases like "non ti cederei" (13.81), which could mean both "I would not give in to you" and "I would not give you up." And in the end her opponent has the opportunity to read Franco's threat as his own desire, for what initially appears to be a transitive use of the gerund, given the poet's place as grammatical subject – "ti verrei sopra, ed nel contrasto ardita, / scaldandoti" (I would get on top of you, and bold in fight, / as I fire you up; 13.83–5, translation mine) – suddenly shifts into a reflexive use, suggesting that the opponent gets fired up on his own –"ti verrei sopra, e nel contrasto ardita, / scaldandoti ancor tu ne la difesa / teco morrei" (I would get on top of you, and bold in fight – with you getting fired up too in the defense – I would die with you; 13.83–5, translation mine). This ambivalence culminates in the poem's concluding statement, "tronca il tuo scempio" (end your

15 Here, in order to preserve the hypothetical, I have modified Jones and Rosenthal's translation of 13.76, which reads, "When you finally came to this point with me."

massacre; 13.91, translation mine). Once Franco's aggression has been directed toward the other who causes torment, will she then turn her weapon on herself?

The verses march toward resolution, but the resolution is destined to be imperfect, as indicated already by the defective rhyme "ferite/lite/diffinita":

> Dal petto ignudo ogni arnese sia tolto,
> al fin ch'ei, disarmato a le *ferite*
> possa 'l valor mostrar dentro a sé accolto.
> Altri non s'impedisca in questa *lite*,
> ma da noi soli due, ad uscio chiuso,
> rimosso ogni padrin, sia *diffinita*. (13.52–7; emphases mine)

> (Let all armor be stripped from your naked breast,
> so that, unshielded and exposed to blows,
> it may reveal the valor it harbors within.
> Let no one else intervene in this conflict,
> let it be resolved by the two of us alone,
> behind closed doors, with all seconds sent away.)[16]

Thus, the poet Veronica Franco comes down firmly on the fence. Her poem expresses moral superiority on the one hand and complicity on the other; it celebrates violent and erotic aggression at the same time that it deflects and defers aggression; it makes claims to identify and punish the (male) culprit, while blurring agency. It would be possible to affirm an integral resolution only if we turn a blind eye to the message communicated by the poem's use of semantic ambiguities and stylistic liberties. For Veronica Franco, ambivalence – and the denial of ambivalence – is one with her style of communicative exchange.

In poem 14, "Non più guerra, ma pace: e gli odi, l'ire" ("No more war, but peace! and may the hate and rage"), we find the last of the poems in the *Terze rime* under the signature of the unknown male poet. Curiously, the poem has received very little attention, even though one would think that as the final poetic offering from a male, it might receive at least as much attention as the first poem of the collection, also by a man.[17]

16 For Jones and Rosenthal's translation of "lite" (13.55) as "match," I have substituted "conflict," and for their translation of "diffinita" (13.57) as "limited," I have substituted "resolved."

17 Adler is quite dismissive of poem 14; given that her analysis depends on showing how Franco distances herself from Petrarch and "revises the portrait of the typical

In responding to a threat of violence that appears to turn into an offer of passionate sex, the unknown male author does not take Franco up on either count. Rather, as I shall demonstrate, his principal objective appears to be to de-escalate. The first nine lines of the poem establish strategies that will be crucial:

> Non più guerra, ma pace: e gli odi, l'ire,
> e quanto fu di disparer tra noi,
> si venga in amor doppio a convertire.

---

lover-poet-victim," she is predisposed to view the male respondent as trapped within a Petrarchan scheme designed to "insure and perpetuate his torment" (see Adler, "Veronica Franco's Petrarchan *Terze Rime*," 218, 219). The contrast for Adler is clear, as Franco "dispels the passivity and depression characteristic of love's torment," and as the unknown male author "sustains his suffering as a lone, powerless victim of love denied" (Adler, "Veronica Franco's Petrarchan *Terze Rime*," 219). In *The Honest Courtesan*, 186–90, Rosenthal comments briefly on poem 14 as the last poem by the unknown male author, who, in her view, remains unaware that Franco has all along been operating on the assumption that her male interlocutor is Maffio Venier, the author of an obscene poem denigrating her, "Veronica, ver unica puttana" ("Veronica, veritably unique whore"). Rosenthal cites as evidence for this letter 47 of Veronica Franco's *Lettere familiari a diversi* (Familiar letters to various people) published in 1580, five years after the *Terze rime* appeared. In this letter, Franco apologizes to an unknown man for having believed he was the author of a satiric piece denigrating her; she writes:

> [M]'è occorso per mio passatempo di scriver il capitolo del quale, sì come sono rimasa sodisfatta ch'Ella degnasse tenerlo presso di sé, così mi rallegro che sia stato mandato a lei per errore. E con certezza che ciò così sia, e che un gentiluomo par suo onoratissimo non dicesse una cosa per un'altra, cesso con lei dall'occasione del duello e del cartello. (Franco, *Lettere*, ed. Bianchi, 114)

> [I]t occurred to me for my own amusement to write the *capitolo*, which has so pleased me, given that you have been willing to keep it, that I was even glad it was sent to you by mistake. And in the certainty that it happened this way and that a gentleman as honorable as you are wouldn't say one thing and mean another, I no longer have a reason for a duel or a challenge. (Franco, *Poems and Selected Letters*, ed. Jones and Rosenthal, 45)

I am not fully persuaded that we should use a statement from Franco's 1580 letters to read the 1575 poetry. While we know that Maffio Venier's poem was written prior to the publication of the *Terze rime*, we do not know when Franco discovered that she had sent her poem to another man in error. Might she have discovered the error even prior to the publication of the *Terze rime*? Might she have sent her poem to more than one man, just to cover all possibilities? I therefore believe that it behoves us to keep in mind a reading of poems 13 and 14 that does not take account of information that Franco provided a full five years after the *Terze rime* were published.

La mia causa io rimetto in tutto a voi,
con patto che, per fin de le contese,
amici più che mai restiamo poi:
non mi basta che l'armi sian sospese,
ma, per stabilimento de la pace,
d'ogni parte si lievino l'offese. (14.1–9)

(No more war, but peace! and may the hate and rage,
and whatever disagreement has arisen between us
be transformed into twice as much love.
I entrust my case completely to you,
on the condition that, to end the quarrel,
we remain better friends than we ever were.
To me it's not enough that the weapons get hung up,
but in order to establish peace, let attacks
be lifted on all sides.)[18]

The male poet echoes and transforms Franco's call to arms. He opens by exclaiming, "No more war, but peace" (Non più guerra, ma pace; 14.1), in contrast to Franco's "No more words" (Non più parole; 13.1). Then he ups the ante in 14.7–9 by reinforcing the peaceful message of the first line, by proposing not just to hang up weapons but to end all attacks. He adopts an impersonal voice, taking attention away from who might be responsible for the conflict. He speaks about "the hate, the rage / and whatever disagreement has arisen between us" (gli odi, l'ire / e quanto fu di disparer tra noi; 14.2) as if these emotions had a life of their own apart from human agents, and he makes these emotional reactions the subject of the exhortative "si venga in amor doppio a convertire" (may [all these things] be transformed into twice as much love; 14.3),

18 I have substituted my own translation for that of Jones and Rosenthal in order to maintain the more impersonal voice that I believe is crucial to the male poet's strategy. Jones and Rosenthal's translation reads thus:

No more war, but peace! and may the hate and rage,
and whatever disagreement has arisen between us
be transformed into twice as much love.
I entrust my case completely to you,
on the condition that, to end our quarrel,
we remain better friends than we ever were.
To me it's not enough that we hang up our weapons,
but to ensure peace, let attacks
be put an end to on both sides. (14.1–9)

thus skirting the question of who will have to do what in order for this to happen. That strategy continues in 14.7, where he adopts the passive voice in speaking about "weapons get[ting] hung up" (non mi basta che l'armi sian sospese), and in 14.9, where he expresses his interest in attacks being lifted on all sides ("d'ogni parte si lievino l'offese").

The adversative conjunction "but" (in Italian, "ma") appears with unusual frequency in this poem (fifteen times in 151 lines), nearly replicating the frequency with which it appears in Franco's poem 13 (eight times in 91 lines).[19] Of particular interest are the six cases in which the male poet combines the adversative "but" with a negative. Initially, he uses a "not x but y" construction in order to de-escalate. He seeks not war but peace (14.1), not just hanging up weapons but ending all attacks (14.7–9). He says he too burns at times, "and not from anger but from great pain" (e non per ira, ma per dolor molto; 14.47). However, beginning in line 64, he utilizes this particular adversative structure for different effect: to emphasize his lack of certainty. He says he is not sure, but perhaps there is someone who was offended by their living together (14.64–6); he is not sure if he has offended her, but he tells her to persist in her cruelty (14.67–72) even as his love will not diminish; he is not sure how she will react when she sees him weeping, but he will enter the field, already defeated, and offer her his bare right hand (14.79–87).

With different content injected into the adversative structure, the male poet succeeds in introducing information that shores up his own image and chips away at Franco's. When he advances a tentative hypothesis about the conflict originating perhaps with someone who was disturbed that he and Franco had lived together (14.64–6), he reveals himself as a man who has previously enjoyed Franco's sexual favours, presumably on a longer-term basis. (This is the only such reference to cohabitation in the *Terze rime*, so it places this male poet in a relatively privileged position.) When he says that he is not sure if he has offended her (14.67–8), he implies that she too might want to be somewhat unsure about whether he offended her; thus, when he invites her to persist in cruelty, it is as if he is saying, "Go ahead, persist in your cruelty while I persist in my love, even if it's not clear I did anything to offend you." When he says he is not sure that she will react to seeing him weep, but he will enter the field already defeated and offer her his bare right hand (14.79–87), he not only seeks to defuse the violence but

19 The only other poem in which "but" appears with comparable frequency is poem 18 (four times in a thirty-one-line poem).

also takes control of the situation by deflecting the erotic physicality of her poem.

From the opening nine lines of the poem, we might assume that the male poet will consistently redefine the terms of the relationship so that it will be about peace, love, and friendship rather than war, hatred, anger, and quarrelsomeness. But he shifts his tactics in order to be able to occupy, simultaneously, the semantic space of warfare as well as the semantic space of peace. There remains a battle to be had, and he focuses on the kind of weapons that will grant him victory:

e se pur ragion vuol ch'io mi risenta
e vendicata sia l'ingiuria mia,
de la qual foste ognor ministra intenta,
voglio con l'armi de la cortesia
invincibil durar tanto a la pugna,
che conosciuto alfin vincitor sia.
Né questo da l'amor grande repugna,
anzi con queste e non mai con altre armi
ogni spirto magnanimo s'oppugna. (14.13–21)

(and even though reason requires of me
that I resent and avenge the injury
that you were always intent on dispensing to me,
I intend, through the use of the weapons of courtesy,
to stand up so well to this battle, unvanquished,
that in the end I am acclaimed the victor.
True love has no objection to this;
with these and never with any other weapons
every great-hearted spirit undertakes battle.)

With curious argumentation the male poet asserts that reason requires that he take revenge, thus putting his subsequent choice, approved of by true love and by the magnanimous, on the side of the irrational. Why do this? For one thing, it allows him to state what he avoided saying earlier when he used impersonal forms, that Franco treated him badly, and this is not something he himself thinks but something acknowledged by reason itself. Moreover, by declining to avenge the injury, he portrays himself as taking the high road even as he engages in battle with the expectation that he will be recognized (presumably by all) as the victor. Can he be the victor without Franco being a loser? I suppose the answer to this question depends on how we imagine the weapons of courtesy to work. He skilfully positions the adjective "invincibil" (unvanquished, invincible) at the beginning of line 17 so that it may or may not be the *rejet* of an enjambment. Does the descriptor "unvanquished" stick firmly to his own person, or is there a possible enjambment in lines 16–17 so that we might initially read them as "I intend, through the use of the weapons of invincible courtesy, to stand up so well to this battle"?

Consistent with the offer of peace, the male poet adopts a courteous tone. Franco had addressed him with the informal second-person singular "tu" (you), a pronoun that allows for aggression and contempt as well as familiar intimacy. He chooses to address Franco with the formal respectful pronoun "voi" (you), with the first instance of this in 14.4. He signals that the emotions will not be simply positive; they will be extremely so: love will be doubled (14.3), and the friendship will be better than it was previously (14.6).

How might we respond to the male poet's expressions of courtesy if we were inclined to view them more positively that readers have thus far? We might well assert that resorting to courtesy and civility is most welcome. We might embrace courtesy as a form of caring attention to other people. We might recall that politeness and good manners were much lauded in the sixteenth century, when, as Michael Curtin notes, courtesy writers such as Baldassare Castiglione "create[d] the courtier out of the warrior."[20] We might quote a passage such as the following from Giovanni della Casa's *Galateo*:

> E, come i piacevoli modi e gentili hanno forza di eccitare la benivolenza di coloro co' quali noi viviamo, così per lo contrario i zotichi e rozzi incitano altrui ad odio et a disprezzo di noi."[21]
>
> (And, just as pleasant and polite manners have the power to stimulate the benevolence of those with whom we live, rough and uncouth manners lead others to hate and disdain us.)

Furthermore, we might also look to more contemporary efforts to promote civility, such as those of the psychologist Giovanna Axia, whose *Elogio della cortesia* (In praise of courtesy) promotes civility as a form of intelligence,[22] or the Civility Initiative, co-founded in 1997 by Pier

20 Curtin, "A Question of Manners," 398.

21 For the Italian text see Giovanni della Casa, *Galateo*, ed. Prandi, 6–7, and for the English translation see Giovanni della Casa, *Galateo*, trans. Eisenbichler and Bartlett, 4.

22 Axia, *Elogio della cortesia*.

Massimo Forni, author of *Choosing Civility: The 25 Rules of Considerate Conduct*.[23]

Now one must recognize, of course, that although the poem begins with a declaration of "No more war!" and although the male poet states that he will arm himself with courtesy, he continues to conjure up scenes of conflict between himself and Franco. How he manages this conflict is worth further examination. Here is a first critical passage:

> O se voleste incontra armata starmi,
> se voleste tentar, con forza tale,
> se possibil vi sia di superarmi,
> fôra 'l mio stato a quel di Giove eguale;
> forse troppo è la speranza ardita,
> che studia di volar non avendo ale. (14.22–7)

> (Oh, were you to want to face me, armed yourself,
> were you to want to test, with such strength,
> whether you are able to overcome me,
> my state would be equal to that of Jove;
> perhaps my hope is too daring,
> for it seeks to fly without wings.) (translation mine)

The male poet's bold claim that in an armed conflict with Franco he would be like the supreme god, Jove, looks to be an apotropaic move where the message is, "Think you're going to come out on top? Think again, because I'll crush you." The punctuation in this threatening line is somewhat unusual in the poem, however. Generally speaking, the end of any clause, independent or dependent, coincides with the end of a tercet. That is not the case here, where the semi-colon that closes the claim that "my state would be equal to that of Jove" (fôra 'l mio stato a quel di Giove eguale) is found at the end of the tercet's first line. This alerts the reader that there is more to come in the next two lines of the tercet. But rather than redoubling on his threat, the male poet quickly backtracks: "forse troppo è la speranza ardita, / che studia di volar non avendo ale" (perhaps my hope is too daring, / for it seeks to fly without wings; 14.26–7).

Following a meandering section of the poem in which the male poet comments on how happy he would be if Franco were to reconsider and

---

23 Forni, *Choosing Civility.*

stop being angry, and in which he reaffirms his undying love and his desire to please her, he once again imagines a scene where he faces an armed Franco:

> Ecco che nel düello mi preparo,
> con l'armi del mio mal, de le mie pene,
> de l'innocenzia mia sotto 'l riparo.
> Non so se 'l vostro orgoglio ne diviene
> maggior, o se s'appiana, mentre mira
> ch'io verso 'l pianto da le luci piene:
> ben talor l'umiltà estingue l'ira,
> ma poi talor l'accende, onde quest'alma
> tra speranza e timor dubbia si gira.
> Ma d'armi tali pur sotto aspra salma,
> mi rendo in campo a voi, madonna, vinto,
> e nuda porgo a voi la destra palma.
> Se non s'è l'odio nel cor vostro estinto,
> mi sia da voi col preparato ferro
> un mortal colpo in mezzo 'l petto spinto:
> pur troppo armata, e so ben ch'io non erro,
> contra me sète; ed io del seno ignudo
> l'adito ai vostri colpi ancor non serro. (14.76–93)

> (Here I am, getting ready in the duel,
> with the arms of my suffering, my sorrows,
> my innocence underneath protective cover.
> I do not know whether your pride
> will swell or decline as it watches
> how I weep with eyes full of tears;
> often humility extinguishes anger,
> but sometimes it fuels it; so my doubtful soul
> hesitates between hope and fear.
> But even so, under the oppressive burden of such armaments,
> I present myself on the field, defeated, to you, lady,
> and offer you my bare right hand.
> If the hatred has not died down in your heart,
> may a mortal blow from your ready sword
> be struck into the center of my breast;
> unfortunately, you are armed – and I know I'm not wrong –
> against me; and I this naked breast
> still do not close off from your blows.) (translation mine)

The scene begins with a dramatic "Ecco che nel düello mi preparo" (Here I am, getting ready in the duel; 14.76), which calls attention to how the male poet prepares his body during a struggle with another human body. Although previously he announced that he would stand victorious, like Jove, wielding the weapons of courtesy, now he changes strategy; his arms are the arms of unjustified distress, and they are weighty; he will stand defeated, essentially calling off the duel. Though he has claimed to be armed, his armour appears to do nothing to protect him from the mortal blow to his breast, and in fact, by lines 91–3, we find that in this imagined encounter Franco is armed, and his uncovered breast is open to attack.

With this passage the male poet also rewrites the sexual encounter at which Franco had hinted in poem 13, beginning in the following lines, which come after her invitation to have the conflict take place in a bedroom:

qui vieni, e pien di pessimo talento,
accomodato al tristo officio porta
ferro acuto e da man ch'abbia ardimento.
Quell'arme, che da te mi sarà porta,
prenderò volontier, ma più, se molto
tagli, e da offender sia ben salda e corta.
Dal petto ignudo ogni arnese sia tolto,
al fin ch'ei, disarmato a le ferite,
possa 'l valor mostrar dentro a sé accolto.
Altri non s'impedisca in questa lite,
ma da noi soli due, ad uscio chiuso,
rimosso ogni padrin, sia diffinita. (13.46–57)

(Come here, and, full of most wicked desire,
braced stiff for your sinister task,
bring with daring hand a piercing blade.
Whatever weapon you hand over to me,
I will gladly take, especially if it is sharp
and sturdy and also quick to wound.
Let all armor be stripped from your naked breast,
so that, unshielded and exposed to blows,
it may reveal the valor it harbors within.
Let no one else intervene in this match,
let it be limited to the two of us alone,
behind closed doors, with all seconds sent away.)

Franco embraces sexual innuendo; she divests her opponent of his armour, at least from the waist up; she guards the intimacy of the scene so that we are virtually certain to read it as sexual. The male poet does not specify where the duel will take place, and it certainly does not appear to take place in a bedroom. He does not speak about the presence or absence of witnesses. Most important, he rethinks nudity. Highly clever is the line "e nuda porgo a voi la destra palma" (and offer you my bare right hand; 14.87). As this verse begins, the reader might wonder whether the feminine adjective "nuda" (bare, naked, uncovered) could suddenly be applied to Franco herself; however, the male poet addressed her as "madonna" (my lady) in the previous verse, making this virtually impossible, and the verse resolves with him offering her his bare right hand. Furthermore, he secures the nudity as non-sexual in 14.91–3. In 14.91, he affirms that she is "unfortunately [...] armed" (purtroppo armata), thus presumably not nude, and then he engages in a bit of suspense as he continues, "ed io del seno ignudo" (and I this naked breast), leading one to ask, And might the naked breast now be hers? That possibility extinguished, the male poet gives Franco the power to wound him but divests her of her sexual power.

Should that message not be clear, the male poet restages the scene and, defenceless, offers himself up to a cruel attack. The restaging begins with his declaration, "Ecco che disarmato a voi ritorno" (Here I am, returning to you unarmed; 14.124), which recalls the earlier dramatic announcement, "Ecco che nel düello mi preparo" (Here I am, getting ready in the duel; 14.76). Ignoring Franco's invitation to him that would allow him to bring a sharp, sturdy, and piercing weapon that she would take in hand, the male poet defines the weapon that he has her taking in hand as the "cutting sword" (tagliente spada; 14.127) of her own disdain.

The poem closes with lines that simultaneously affirm and delimit Franco's power:

> Potete, se vi piace, essermi ria;
> e quando usar l'asprezza non vi piaccia
> potete, se vi piace, essermi pia.
> Quanto a me, pur ch'a voi si sodisfaccia,
> vi dono sopra me podestà franca,
> legato piedi e mani e gambe e braccia;
> e vi mando per fede carta bianca,
> ch'abbiate del mio cor dominio vero,
> sì che veruna parte non vi manca.

Del resto assai desío più, che non spero,
né so se in via di strazïar m'abbiate
fatto l'invito, o se pur da dovero.
Aspetterò che voi me n'accertiate. (14.139–51)

(You can, if you wish, be cruel to me;
and when you don't wish to adopt harsh ways,
you can, if you wish, be compassionate to me.
As for myself, as long as it is your wish,
I grant you complete authority over me,
bound hand and foot and legs and arms;
and I send you, in faithful guarantee, carte blanche
to have total dominion over my heart,
so that no part of it does not belong to you.
Besides, I wish for far more than I hope,
nor do I know if you made your invitation
to torture me or because you truly meant it.
I shall wait for you to clarify this for me.) (translation mine)

The choice of how to respond remains with Franco, who is represented as having complete control. The male poet repeats "potete" (you can) twice and uses the verb "piacere" (to like, to wish) three times, thus highlighting Franco's powers and wishes. He leaves Franco with the option of deciding whether or not she will accept his submissive stance. He offers her carte blanche ("carta bianca"; 14.145). He secures her dominance and his submissiveness through oblique evocations of her given name, Veronica, and her family name, Franca. She will have authority over him that is "franca" (complete; 14.142) and a dominion that is "vero" (total and true; 14.146); she has his heart in which "veruna parte" (no part; 14.147) does not belong to her.

Along with the resounding affirmation of Franco's powerful authority, however, there remains a challenge to it. When the male poet substitutes his "carta bianca" for Franco's challenge to a duel on an open battle-field or in a bedroom ("cartel"; 13.4), he quashes the threatened violence and the sexual charge of her poem. When he states that matters remain to be decided by her, he undercuts the projected finality of her message.

Here the dialogic poems will come to a close, with Veronica Franco infusing ambivalence into her declarations of violent victory and with an unknown male author contemporaneously conceding and withholding power. Attacks and concessions remain under erasure, essentially leaving Franco and the unknown male author in a stalemate, where neither is clearly victorious and neither is vanquished. Whether they pursue conflict or they pursue peace, both Franco and her unknown male interlocutor allow that they could adopt alternate stances. The power dynamic they instantiate looks less tidy and less reassuring than readers might wish to see if they want to affirm that Franco emerges as unqualifiedly victorious against an opponent who is no match for her. That Franco chooses, in this central and climactic moment of the *Terze rime*, to portray both herself and her male interlocutor as more nuanced in their interactions and in their responses to conflict shows her to be, I believe, an astute judge of human behaviour.

Conclusion

I began this book by asking, "What do we see in Veronica Franco?" Highlighting the consequences of embracing her as a feminist icon, I asserted that if we let her poetry speak to us in its fullness, we could hear yet other stories. So what are the other stories that emerge from the sustained close readings that I have provided here?

In answering this question, it will help to return to a statement by Margaret Rosenthal that I quoted in my introduction because it captures so well what Franco has meant for readers:

> When I first read Veronica Franco's poems and letters many years ago, I was struck, as I still am, by her forthright polemical stance. She writes passionately in support of women unable to defend themselves. She writes with conviction about social and literary inequalities. Deploying an eroticized language in her epistolary verses, Franco calls attention to the performative, seductive nature of all poetic contests – courtesanry, like courtiership, relies on debate, contest, and competition. It is Franco's insight into the power conflicts between men and women, and her awareness of the threat she posed to her male contemporaries, who were also aspiring writers, that makes her literary works and her interaction with Venetian intellectuals so forceful and so extraordinarily modern. Franco is dramatic in her indignation – comic, coy, and vehement in her repudiation of social injustices. She adopts the epistolary form in all of its literary manifestations in the Renaissance – as poetic debate, familiar letter, verse epistle, elegy – to engage in a conversation with her male contemporaries.[1]

When I commented on this passage earlier, I highlighted how it frames Veronica Franco as a champion for women, justice, and truth

1 Rosenthal, *The Honest Courtesan*, 10.

and how it asserts her range as a writer and intellectual. Revisiting the passage now, I am moved to comment on the following key phrases: "forthright polemical stance," "support of women unable to defend themselves," "writ[ing] about social and literary inequalities," and "repudiation of social injustices."

I too tend to think of Veronica Franco as forthrightly polemical. However, I am now struck by how much she palliates her polemicism in the dialogic poems. Any criticisms she advances in poem 2 are cloaked in qualifying clauses. In poems 3 and 5 there is no ground for polemics. Poem 8 is better described as an exercise in cognitive reframing than as a polemical rejection. In poem 10 she resorts to oblique frankness, presenting as benevolent any disapproval she expresses of her male interlocutor. Only in poem 12 does she turn more direct and insistent, and only at the very end of poem 12 does she bluntly reject the advances of the unknown male author. Poem 13, in which she challenges the unknown male author to a duel, bespeaks the kind of polemicism and battle readiness that we tend to associate with Franco, which explains why this poem is so often included in anthologies. As I have shown, however, the polemicism is infused with ambivalence.

This indicates that in the dialogic poems Franco tempers her polemicism until she approaches the central poems of the collection. Even there, she is not unqualifiedly polemical. Her forthright polemicism emerges only twice in the later monologic poems, that is, in poem 16, "D'ardito cavalier non è prodezza" ("It is not a brave knight's gallant deed"), in which she defends herself against the attacks in Maffio Venier's satirical verses, and in poem 17, "Questa la tua Veronica ti scrive" ("This letter your Veronica writes to you"), in which she excoriates an unfaithful lover. Even in poem 24, "Sovente occorre ch'altri il suo parere" ("It often happens that a person declares"), in which Franco writes to a man who has threatened a woman – to make the case for women's worth and to request that he change his ways – she does not adopt a polemical tone. We have thus labelled Franco forthright and polemical because evidently the poems in which she threatens military-style action (i.e., poems 13 and 16) and in which she writes with seething anger (i.e., poems 13 and 17) have spoken to us more loudly than other poems in which she writes with studied tentativeness.

As for Franco's support of women unable to defend themselves, and her speaking out against inequalities and injustices, it is noteworthy that Franco becomes a standard-bearer for women and a denouncer of social injustices only after she has left behind the dialogic poems. This is curious since in all of the eleven monologic poems except two

Franco continues to address men.[2] It seems that she is able to engage in the debate about women and speak in their defence only after she is no longer responding to words of men that we have available to us on the page and only when she does not include any responses to her from men.

What then does Franco gain by including the seven poems attributed to an unknown male author (or by including a first poem attributed to Marco Venier and six poems attributed to an unknown male author)? Franco could have published her collection of poems in terza rima with eighteen poems, all of them written by her. Granted, this would deny us the possibility of seeing how the four poems in which she responds to men seeking her favours (poems 2, 8, 10, and 12) function as responses to the specific requests and complaints that male authors put forward in poems 1, 7, 9, and 11, but the remaining poems (numbered 3, 5, and 13) could easily stand by themselves, just as all the monologic poems do.

By beginning her *Terze rime* with the dialogic poems, Franco creates a foil against which she can craft her image of herself as neither condescending nor haughty but still the equal or better than most of her male interlocutors. Franco is politic toward men who are controlling and accusatory, even in the instances where they do not write especially good poetry. She reveals that she is not a courtesan who has to accommodate all men and that she is not given to accepting easy flattery. She holds to ideals of noble love and friendship. She is cognizant of a community beyond one-on-one exclusive relationships, and she is a supremely committed Venetian citizen and lover of her city. She too can threaten violence (but maybe not really mean it). Poems 4 and 6, in which men respond using a rhyme scheme that Franco has established, allow her to reaffirm that she is a member of an elite group in which conversations require significant poetic skill, and poem 10, in which Franco responds using a rhyme scheme that an unknown male author uses in poem 9, offers proof that she remains undaunted by such a technical challenge.

In crafting her image in the dialogic poems, Franco resorts time and again to a pattern of affirmation and denial. Mythological figures incarnate imperfectly what she is. She is like Orpheus and not like him, like Ariadne and not, like Byblis and not, like Niobe and not, like Apollo and not. She affirms her adherence to higher values but without turning away from the things of this world. Criticisms and rejections can be

2 The two exceptions are poem 21, which is an interior monologue, and poem 25, written in praise of Marcantonio Della Torre's villa of Fumane.

blunted and made to seem toothless. She threatens revenge that seems to ricochet as self-mutilation. Violence might not be violence but rather inflamed union.

While I am not alone in calling attention to how Franco tells her story with reference to mythological figures, the particular mythological figures that I have brought to light – especially Orpheus in poem 3, Niobe in poem 8, and Apollo in poem 10 – offer stories about Veronica Franco that are different from the stories that other scholars have identified.

Mary Rogers, for example, focuses on Venus, goddess of love, and on Minerva, goddess of wisdom and war. She notes that Franco, in poem 2, accepts that the male author of poem 1 has characterized her as Venus, but then "reinterprets Venus not simply as a passive object of desire, but as a beneficent being, fostering mutual love, and as an active and skilled practitioner of the arts of love."[3] Rogers also reminds us: "In life, [Franco] named one of her children Aeneas – the son of Venus – thus in a sense accepting an enduring comparison with the goddess of love."[4] In Franco's poem 12, Rogers sees Franco's encomium of Venice as a Minerva-like and statesman-like response to the male author's having called Franco the daughter of Minerva and Love in poem 11, an allusion that "was perhaps meant as conventional flattery for her wisdom and beauty."[5] According to Rogers, Minerva would also serve as a model for Franco's portrayal of herself as "a fierce warrior for a just cause" in poem 13.[6] Rogers offers that "Franco, whom we know to have been aware of the art of her day, would have looked with interest at the forceful female characters, particularly of a mythological kind, that it presented, and seen their possibilities for providing her with starting points for novel literary identities."[7] In Rogers' assessment, "[t]hese fictive identities allowed her to extend her tone and subject-matter, to transcend the limitations of current gender stereotypes, and to create verses whose energy and variety go beyond the lachrymose languishings of the conventional love cycle."[8]

It is incontrovertible that Franco looked to mythological figures as she carefully crafted her own identity as a woman, courtesan, Venetian citizen, and writer and that these fictive identities allowed her to transcend the limitations of current gender stereotypes. However, I would

3 Rogers, "Fashioning Identities for Venetian Courtesans," 97.
4 Rogers, 97.
5 Rogers, 98.
6 Rogers, 98.
7 Rogers, 99.
8 Rogers, 99.

urge us not to assume that, in crafting her identity, Franco looked only to female characters. The fact that she could evoke mythological figures such as Orpheus and Apollo to explore her poetic and sexual identity tells us otherwise. I would also urge us to keep in mind that Franco does not completely renounce the possibility of representing herself as a languishing, lachrymose woman, nor does she renounce the possibility of evoking a mythological bereaved figure such as Niobe. As she does elsewhere, she tweaks the fictive identity in order to reaffirm the vitality of her body and her spirit and her communicativeness.

Looking forward, where might our investigations of Veronica Franco's writing go? At the present time I foresee three main areas for future research: exploring how digital technologies can illuminate aspects of her writing; engaging in sustained linguistic and stylistic analyses; and promoting further close readings both of the dialogic poems that I have analysed here and of the eleven monologic poems with which Franco concludes the *Terze rime*.

Digital technology could be highly useful to those of us seeking to understand writers like Veronica Franco. The Oregon Petrarch Open Book project, an ongoing web-based system devoted to the study and teaching of Petrarch's *Rerum vulgarium fragmenta*, could serve as a source of inspiration. Writing about this project, its creator, Massimo Lollini, reports that through digital close reading and encoding, the participants in the project identified five major themes in selected poems of the *Rvf*: metaphysics, the poet, Laura, nature, and urban life.[9] They then added metamorphosis to the themes and conducted a distant reading of all the poems of the *Rvf*. Significantly, the digital close reading and the distant reading were able to show that nestled within the *Rvf* were different stories:

> On the one hand, the outcome of our digital close reading had Metaphysics as a prominent theme and the Poet and Laura as second and third, followed by Nature and Urban life; on the other hand, the result of the distant reading had the Poet as the principal theme immediately followed by Laura, and then, at a farther remove, metaphysics, metamorphosis, nature, and finally urban life. Thus, the thematic picture suggested by the distant reading is coincident with traditional readings of the *Rvf* as a love story that has two main protagonists and a prevalent metaphysical orientation. In this reading, nature does not deserve the role of protagonist and metamorphosis is just one theme among others.

9 Lollini, "Reading, Rewriting, and Encoding," 115–16.

> On the other hand, the digital close reading based on an attentive semantic encoding of Petrarch's poems tells a different story. In this case, poet and metaphysics have a prominent role but the distance between them and Laura and nature is not so large as to rule out the interpretation that they play a role of co-protagonists in the *Rvf*. In other words, the close reading via encoding triggered an interpretation of the *Rvf* conceived not as a static and finished reality around the subjectivities of the poet and Laura but rather as a relational structure in which all the parts are mirroring each other in multiple perspectives.[10]

In the case of Veronica Franco, digital tools could help us tease out the differences and the similarities between the poems under Franco's signature and the poems attributed to male authors. They could help us understand better how the language and themes of the poems by Franco in the dialogic section of the *Terze rime* (i.e., poems 2, 3, 5, 8, 10, 12, and 13) compare to the language and themes of her monologic poems (i.e., poems 15 through 25). They could be used to analyse metrical patterns in the verses, which would help us understand better the musicality of the poetic language.

Whether or not we apply digital tools, the language in the *Terze rime* begs for more attentive linguistic and stylistic analysis. To what extent is the language "Petrarchan"? Does it conform to Pietro Bembo's ideals of gracefulness, sweetness, and pleasantness? When the language is not Petrarchan and does not conform to Bembo's ideals, how would we characterize it? How does Franco's language change when she adopts different stances (enamoured, mournful, supplicant, resistant, determined, angered, polemical, exuberant)? How different is her poetic language in the *Terze rime* from the poetic language in her sonnets? And how different is it from the language that she uses when she writes her letters in prose?

Finally, I would invite us to continue the endeavour of reading Veronica Franco's poetry closely. In *Veronica Franco in Dialogue* I have provided my own close readings of poems 1 through 14 of the *Terze rime*. I hope that these close readings will inspire others to contribute their own close readings. What I see and hear in these poems is undoubtedly conditioned by my own experiences with love, sexuality, friendship, separation, loss, aggression, and violence, and it is undoubtedly conditioned as well by all the linguistic experiences I have had, both in Italian and in English. Others who come to these poems with different experiences may well bring different stories to light.

10 Lollini, 116–17.

The eleven monologic poems call for sustained close readings. Seven of these poems deal with love, and in them Franco almost always portrays herself as a woman made unhappy by love. Although poem 15 is presented as Franco's apology for not having visited the man to whom she writes (presumably Domenico Venier), most of the poem is dedicated to complaining about her love woes with another man. In poem 17, Franco launches an angry reproach of her lover. Poem 18, an expression of gratitude to a man who counselled her not to send her verses to a certain friend, turns out to be a request that her addressee help her revise verses that she could use to change her lover's scorn for her into pity. In poem 19 she writes to a man who appears to be a member of the clergy (though strangely this detail does not emerge until lines 91–105 of the poem) to tell him how she had once unhappily burned with love for him but now has transformed her unfulfilled passionate longings into friendship. In poem 20 she takes up the question of mismatches in love, since she loves the man to whom she addresses this poem, but he loves another woman. Poem 21 is written to a lover from whom she is separated, and poem 22 is written both to Venice and to a distant lover. In the monologic poem that has drawn the greatest attention, poem 16, "D'ardito cavalier non è prodezza" ("It is not a brave knight's gallant deed"), Franco responds to the attacks that Maffio Venier launched against her in his satirical poems. In two of the poems she asks for advice: poem 23 is a plea to a man for help in deciding whether she should take aggressive action against a man who seeks to defame her; poem 24, addressed to a man who had threatened a woman verbally and was on the verge of physical violence, shows the rhetorical strategies that Franco adopts in counselling an abuser. Poem 25, by far the lengthiest composition in the *Terze rime* with its 565 lines, is the lone poem in the collection for which the 1575 edition has a rubric that proclaims its subject matter: "In lode di Fumane, luogo dell'illustrissimo signor conte Marcantonio della Torre, preposto di Verona" (In praise of Fumane, the villa of the illustrious count Marcantonio della Torre, canon of Verona; translation mine).[11]

We should want to hear more fully what stories the monologic poems transmit, and this can be done only if we perform the kinds of close textual readings that I have proposed for each of the dialogic poems. In poems 15 through 25, what rhetorical strategies does Franco retain from the dialogic poems, and what new strategies does she adopt? In poem 3, Franco describes her unhappiness at being separated from her

11 See Franco, *Terze rime al Serenissimo Signor Duca di Mantova et di Monferrato*.

lover in Venice and concludes with an image of her being "vanquished by him in loving war" (da lui vinta in amorosa guerra; 3.64), bringing pleasure to him, and ending her own torment (3.72–3). What purpose does it serve, in the monologic poems, for her to present her amorous desires as consistently unfulfilled? The male authors of poems 1, 4, 7, 9, and 14 accuse Franco of cruelty toward them; when Franco writes of male cruelty toward her in the monologic poems and when she begs a man to bestow his affections on her, what do her strategies share (or not) with the kinds of strategies that male authors have used to try to win her over? What roles do violence, deflection of violence, and wielding of violence play? How does Franco craft her identity with reference to mythological figures? Will we see the same pattern of affirmation and denial that we have seen in the dialogic poems?

As we read the monologic poems with such questions in mind, we should consider the order in which Franco arranged these poems and the way in which she uses them to provide an extended reflection on power and powerlessness. Sara Maria Adler has aptly identified in the *Terze rime* a "general dialectic pattern … of victimization and rallying from victimization."[12] No doubt there are distinct moments in Franco's poetry of rallying from victimization, and it is to those moments that many readers have been drawn. The supreme rally cry appears in poem 16, where, as Hannah Chapelle Wojciehowski has expertly demonstrated, Veronica Franco counters Maffio Venier's representation of her body as abject, monstrous, syphilitic, and plague ridden by "envision[ing] an alternative body for herself and her audience," a body that is "healthy, beautiful, and exceedingly strong."[13] While I fully agree with this assessment of poem 16, I caution us from assuming that Franco's assertions of triumph and harmonious integration are untroubled by doubts, uncertainties, ambiguities, and ambivalences. This is the point I have made here in my analysis of poem 13, "Non più parole, ai fatti, in campo, a l'armi" ("No more words! To deeds, to the battlefield, to arms!"), and it is the point that Irene Eibenstein-Alvisi has made in her analysis of Franco's praise of Marcantonio Della Torre's villa at Fumane in the concluding poem of the *Terze rime*,[14] a poem that, according to others, shows that "victimization is transcended,"[15] that "all traces of alienation, disorientation, and entrapment have been

12 Adler, "Veronica Franco's Petrarchan *Terze Rime*," 222.

13 Wojciehowski, "Veronica Franco vs. Maffio Venier," 377. For another key reading of this poem see Rosenthal, *The Honest Courtesan*, 190–7.

14 Eibenstein-Alvisi, "Dialoguing with the Past," 137–63.

15 Adler, "Veronica Franco's Petrarchan *Terze Rime*," 223.

given up,"[16] and that Franco "recuperates a world where nature and reason coexist and where individuals come together freely in mutual friendship and in love."[17] But, as Eibenstein-Alvisi has maintained, "embedded in the necessarily congratulatory tone of the eulogy, [there are] many signs of anxiety and puzzlement that contradict ... optimistic view[s] of the poem," and Fumane proves to be a place "in which art is used in ways that mask violence to the point of rendering it part of the artistic success the estate embodies."[18]

The predilection for Franco that many readers have shown has depended on their approval of her open embrace of sexuality, her polemicism, her deft self-fashioning, and what they see as her integral self. It also depends on a narrative that has been constructed to keep troublesome elements at bay. Will these readers still find Franco as appealing when they see how she deals in ambiguities, ambivalence, and studied tentativeness? I hope they will. Moreover, I hope my analyses in this book will bring readers to weigh the merits of all the dialogic poems and to appreciate the considerable rhetorical and poetic skills that Franco displays. Above all, I ask that when we are confronted with the dialectic of victimization and the rally from victimization that we find in Franco's poetry, we not rush to resolve this in triumphant overarching narratives but instead remain faithful to nuance and complexity.

16 Adler, 223.

17 Rosenthal, *The Honest Courtesan*, 255.

18 Eibenstein-Alvisi, "The Dialogic Construction of Woman in the Italian Renaissance," 141, 142. Irene Eibenstein-Alvisi and I are currently co-authoring an analysis of *Terze rime* 25, which expands on the reading of this poem that she included in her doctoral dissertation.

Bibliography

Adler, Sara Maria. "Veronica Franco's Petrarchan *Terze Rime:* Subverting the Master's Plan." *Italica* 65, no. 3 (1988): 213–33.

Ariosto, Ludovico. *Opere minori*. Edited by Cesare Segre. Milan: Ricciardi, 1954.

– *Orlando furioso*. Edited by Cesare Segre. 3rd ed. Milan: Mondadori, 1982.

– *Orlando Furioso*. Translated by Guido Waldman. Oxford: Oxford University Press, 1983.

Axia, Giovanna. *Elogio della cortesia: L'attenzione per gli altri come forma di intelligenza*. Rev. ed. Bologna: Il Mulino, 2012.

Baldelli, Ignazio. "Rima." In *Enciclopedia dantesca*, vol. 4, edited by Umberto Bosco, 930–49. Rome: Istituto dell'Enciclopedia Italiana, 1970–8.

Barolini, Teodolinda. "*Inferno* 24: Metamorphosis (Ovid)." In *Commento Baroliniano*, Digital Dante. New York: Columbia University Libraries, 2018. https://digitaldante.columbia.edu/dante/divine-comedy/inferno/inferno-24/.

– "Petrarch as the Metaphysical Poet Who Is Not Dante: Metaphysical Markers at the Beginning of the *Rerum vulgarium fragmenta* (*Rvf* 1–21)." In *Petrarch and Dante: Anti-Dantism, Metaphysics, Tradition*, edited by Zygmunt G. Baranski and Theodore J. Cachey, 195–225. Notre Dame, IN: University of Notre Dame Press, 2009.

Bassanese, Fiora A. "Defining Spaces: Venice in the Poetry of Gaspara Stampa and Veronica Franco." In *Medusa's Gaze: Essays on Gender, Literature, and Aesthetics in the Italian Renaissance, in Honor of Robert J. Rodini*, edited by Paul A. Ferrara, Eugenio Giusti, and Jane Tylus, 91–105. West Lafayette, IN: Bordighera, 2004.

– "Private Lives and Public Lies: Texts by Courtesans of the Italian Renaissance." *Texas Studies in Literature and Language* 30, no. 3 (1988): 295–319.

– "Veronica Franco." In *Encyclopedia of Italian Literary Studies: A-J*, edited by Gaetana Marrone, 777–80. New York: Routledge, 2007.

– "Veronica Franco's Poetics of Redemption." In *From Rome to Eternity: Catholicism and the Arts in Italy, ca. 1550–1650*, edited by Pamela M. Jones and Thomas Worcester, 43–61. Leiden: Brill, 2002.

Beccaria, Gian Luigi. "Dieresi." In *Enciclopedia dantesca*, edited by Umberto Bosco. Rome: Istituto dell'Enciclopedia Italiana Treccani, 1970–8. http://www.treccani.it.

Bembo, Pietro. *Prose e rime*. Edited by Carlo Dionisotti. Turin: Unione tipografico-editrice torinese, 1960.

Bernardo, Aldo S. *Petrarch, Laura, and the "Triumphs."* Albany: State University of New York Press, 1974.

Bianchi, Stefano. *La scrittura poetica femminile nel Cinquecento Veneto: Gaspara Stampa e Veronica Franco*. Manziana (Rome): Vecchiarelli, 2013.

Biblia sacra iuxta vulgatam versionem. Edited by Robert Weber. 2 vols. Stuttgart: Württembergische Bibelanstalt, 1969.

Boccaccio, Giovanni. *Corbaccio*. Edited by Giorgio Padoan. In *Tutte le opere di Giovanni Boccaccio*, vol. 5, tome 2, edited by Vittore Branca, 413–614. Milan: Mondadori, 1994.

– *The Corbaccio or the Labyrinth of Love*. Translated and edited by Anthony K. Cassell. 2nd ed. rev. Binghamton, NY: Medieval and Renaissance Texts and Studies, 1993.

– *Ninfale fiesolano*. Edited by Armando Balduino. In *Tutte le opere di Giovanni Boccaccio*, vol. 3, edited by Vittore Branca, 273–421. Milan: Mondadori, 1974.

Botting, Fred, and Scott Wilson. *Bataille*. Basingstoke, UK: Palgrave, 2001.

Brundin, Abigail. "Vittoria Colonna." In *Oxford Bibliographies in Renaissance and Reformation*, edited by Margaret King. New York: Oxford University Press, 2013.

Bufalini, Maria. "Sulla canzone del Petrarca, *Chiare fresche e dolci acque*." *Giornale Dantesco* 7 (1899): 385–401.

"Canzoniere 199." *Petrarchreadinggroupoxford*. https://petrarchreadinggroupoxford.wordpress.com.

Casella, Mario. "Studi sul testo della *Divina Commedia*." *Studi danteschi* 8 (1924): 5–85.

Cavalcanti, Guido. *Rime*. Edited by Roberto Rea and Giorgio Inglese. Rome: Carocci, 2011.

Clarke, K.P. "Humility and the (P)arts of Art." In *Vertical Readings in Dante's Comedy*, vol. 1, edited by George Corbett and Heather Webb, 209–27. Cambridge: Open Book Publishers, 2015.

Clitheroe, Terry. *The Poets Garret*. Accessed 11 January 2020. http://www.thepoetsgarret.com/2005/050115.html.

A Companion to Vittoria Colonna. Edited by Abigail Brundin, Tatiana Crivelli, and Maria Serena Sapegno. Leiden, Netherlands: Brill, 2016.

Cornish, Alison. *Reading Dante's Stars*. New Haven, CT: Yale University Press, 2000.

The Courtesan's Arts: A Cross-Cultural Perspective. Edited by Martha Feldman and Bonnie Gordon. Oxford: Oxford University Press, 2006.

Cox, Virginia. *Lyric Poetry by Women of the Italian Renaissance*. Baltimore, MD: Johns Hopkins University Press, 2013.

– *Women's Writing in Italy, 1400–1650*. Baltimore, MD: Johns Hopkins University Press, 2008.

Crivelli, Tatiana. "'A un luogo stesso per molte vie vassi': Note sul sistema petrarchista di Veronica Franco." In *"L'una et l'altra chiave": Figure e momenti del Petrarchismo femminile europeo*, edited by Tatiana Crivelli, Giovanni Nicoli, and Mara Santi, 79–102. Rome: Salerno Editrice, 2005.

Croce, Benedetto. "Veronica Franco." In Veronica Franco, *Lettere, dall'unica edizione del MDLXXX*, edited by Benedetto Croce, ix–xxxii. Naples: Ricciardi, 1949.

CURSUS: An Online Resource of Medieval Liturgical Texts. http://www.cursus.org.uk.

Curtin, Michael. "A Question of Manners: Status and Gender in Etiquette and Courtesy Author(s)." *Journal of Modern History* 57, no. 3 (1985): 395–423.

Dante Alighieri. *Dante's Lyric Poetry*. Edited and translated by Kenelm Foster and Patrick Boyde. 2 vols. Oxford: Clarendon Press, 1967.

– *Dante's Vita Nuova, New Edition: A Translation and an Essay*. Translated by Mark Musa. Bloomington: Indiana University Press, 1973.

– *De vulgari eloquentia*. Edited and translated by Steven Botterill. Cambridge: Cambridge University Press, 1996.

– *Inferno*. Edited by Anna Maria Chiavacci Leonardi. 7th ed. Milan: Mondadori, 2004.

– *Paradiso*. Edited by Anna Maria Chiavacci Leonardi. 6th ed. Milan: Mondadori, 2004.

– *Paradiso*. Translated by Robert and Jean Hollander. New York: Doubleday, 2007.

– *Purgatorio*. Edited by Anna Maria Chiavacci Leonardi. 5th ed. Milan: Mondadori, 2004.

– *Vita nova*. Edited by Guglielmo Gorni. In *Opere*, vol. 1, edited by Marco Santagata, 745–1063. 2nd ed. Milan: Mondadori, 2015.

Della Casa, Giovanni. *Galateo*. Edited by Stefano Prandi. New rev. ed. Turin: Einaudi, 2000.

– *Galateo*. Translated by Konrad Eisenbichler and Kenneth R. Bartlett. Toronto: Centre for Reformation and Renaissance Studies, 1986.

Dolce, Ludovico. *Le Trasformationi di m. Ludovico Dolce: In questa quarta impressione da lui in molti luoghi ricorrette*. Venice: Gabriel Giolito de' Ferrari, 1557.

Dunant, Sarah. "Who Was Vittoria Colonna? Just One of Italy's Great Poets …" *New York Times*, 1 June 2018, online. Also under "Free Verse," book review, *New York Times*, 3 June 2018, 53.

Eibenstein-Alvisi, Irene. "Dialoguing with the Past: Veronica Franco and Her Modern Readers." In "The Dialogic Construction of Woman in the Italian Renaissance," PhD diss., Cornell University, August 2003.

Falkeid, Unn, and Aileen A. Feng. Introduction to *Rethinking Gaspara Stampa in the Canon of Renaissance Poetry*, edited by Unn Falkeid and Aileen A. Feng, 1–12. Farnham, UK: Ashgate, 2015.

Feng, Aileen A. *Writing Beloveds: Humanist Petrarchism and the Politics of Gender*. Toronto: University of Toronto Press, 2017.

Ferrante, Joan M. "Canto XXIV: Thieves and Metamorphoses." In *Lectura Dantis – Inferno: A Canto-by-Canto Commentary*, edited by Allen Mandelbaum, Anthony Oldcorn, and Charles Ross, 316–27. Berkeley: University of California Press, 1999.

– "Good Thieves and Bad Thieves: A Reading of *Inferno* XXIV." *Dante Studies* 104 (1986): 83–98.

– "A Poetics of Chaos and Harmony." In *The Cambridge Companion to Dante*, edited by Rachel Jacoff, 153–71. Cambridge: Cambridge University Press, 1993.

Finotti, Fabio. "Il teatro cortigiano di Veronica Franco." In *Studi di letteratura italiana per Vitilio Masiello*, edited by Pasquale Guaragnella and Marco Santagata, 519–33. Rome and Bari: Laterza, 2006.

I fioretti di san Francesco. Edited by Guido Davico Bonino. Turin: Einaudi, 1998.

Fiori di rimatrici italiane dal secolo XIV al XVII. Trieste: Lloyd Austriaco, 1857.

Forni, Pier Massimo. *Choosing Civility: The 25 Rules of Considerate* Conduct. New York: St Martin's Press, 2002.

Foster, Kenelm, O.P. "Beatrice or Medusa: The Penitential Element in Petrarch's *Canzoniere*." In *Italian Studies Presented to E.R. Vincent*, edited by Charles Peter Brand, Kenelm Foster, and Uberto Limentani, 41–56. Cambridge: Heffer, 1962.

Franco, Veronica. *Lettere*. Edited by Stefano Bianchi. Rome: Salerno, 1998.

– *Lettere familiari a diversi*. S.n.t. [Venezia], 1580.

– *Poems and Selected Letters*. Edited and translated by Ann Rosalind Jones and Margaret F. Rosenthal. Chicago: University of Chicago Press, 1998.

– *Rime*. Edited by Stefano Bianchi. Milan: Mursia, 1995.

– *Terze rime al Serenissimo Signor Duca di Mantova et di Monferrato*. S.n.t. [Venezia], 1575.

Fulkerson, Laurel. "The *Heroides*: Female Elegy?" In *A Companion to Ovid*, edited by Peter E. Knox, 78–89. Malden, MA: Wiley-Blackwell, 2009.

Graf, Arturo. *Attraverso il Cinquecento*. Turin: Loescher, 1888.

Grande dizionario della lingua italiana. Edited by Salvatore Battaglia. Turin: UTET, 1961–.

Grandgent, C.H. "Confessio Dantis." *Revue Philosophique de Louvain* 11 (1926): 303–23.

Harris, Oliver. *Lacan's Return to Antiquity: Between Nature and the Gods*. London: Routledge, 2017.

Herskovitz, Marshall, dir. *Dangerous Beauty*. New Regency Pictures, Bedford Falls Productions, 1998.

Howe, Nancy. "Laura in the Grass, Alas? (Canzoniere 126)." *Romance Notes* 7, no. 2 (1966): 193–7.

Jacobson, Howard. *Ovid's Heroidos*. Princeton, NJ: Princeton University Press, 2015. First published 1974.

Jaffe, Irma B., with Gernando Colombardo. *Shining Eyes, Cruel Fortune: The Lives and Loves of Italian Renaissance Women Poets*. New York: Fordham University Press, 2002.

– "Veronica Franca (1546–1591): The Unhappy Courtesan." In *Shining Eyes, Cruel Fortune: The Lives and Loves of Italian Renaissance Women Poets*, 339–85. New York: Fordham University Press, 2002.

Johnson, Barbara. "Teaching Deconstructively." In *Reading and Writing Differently: Deconstruction and the Teaching of Composition and Literature*, edited by G. Douglas Atkins and Michael L. Johnson, 140–8. Lawrence: University Press of Kansas, 1985.

Jones, Ann Rosalind. "City Women and Their Audiences: Louise Labé and Veronica Franco." In *Rewriting the Renaissance: The Discourses of Sexual Difference in Early Modern Europe*, edited by Margaret W. Ferguson, Maureen Quilligan, and Nancy J. Vickers, 299–314. Chicago: University of Chicago Press, 1986.

– *"The Currency of Eros: Women's Love Lyric in Europe, 1540–1620.* Bloomington: Indiana University Press, 1990.

– "Designing Women: The Self as Spectacle in Mary Wroth and Veronica Franco." In *Reading Mary Wroth: Representing Alternatives in Early Modern England*, edited by Naomi J. Miller and Gary Waller, 135–53. Knoxville: University of Tennessee Press, 1991.

– "Eros Equalized: Literary Cross-Dressing and the Defense of Women in Louise Labé and Veronica Franco." In *The Currency of Eros: Women's Love Lyric in Europe, 1540–1620*. 155–200. Bloomington: Indiana University Press, 1990.

Jones, Ann Rosalind, and Margaret F. Rosenthal. "Introduction: The Honored Courtesan." In Veronica Franco, *Poems and Selected Letters*, edited and translated by Ann Rosalind Jones and Margaret F. Rosenthal, 1–22. Chicago: University of Chicago Press, 1998.

King, Margaret L. *Women of the Renaissance*. Chicago: University of Chicago Press, 1992.

Lindheim, Sara H. *Mail and Female: Epistolary Narrative and Desire in Ovid's Heroides*. Madison: University of Wisconsin Press, 2003.

Liriche del Cinquecento. Edited by Monica Farnetti and Laura Fortini. Rome: Iacobelli Editore, 2014.

Lirici del Cinquecento. Edited by Luigi Baldacci. Milan: Longanesi, 1975.

Lollini, Massimo. "Reading, Rewriting, and Encoding Petrarch's *Rerum vulgarium fragmenta* as Hypertext." *NEMLA Italian Studies* 39 (2017): 100–24.

Machiavelli, Niccolò. *Machiavelli's The Prince: A Bilingual Edition*. Translated and edited by Mark Musa. New York: St Martin's Press, 1964.

Maraini, Dacia. *Veronica, meretrice e scrittora*. Milan: Bompiani, 1992.

– *Veronica Franco: Courtesan and Poet*. Translated by J. Douglas Campbell and Leonard G. Sbrocchi. Ottawa, ON: Legas, 2001.

Marino, Giambattista. "L'amore incostante." Translated by Joseph Tusiani. *Journal of Italian Translation* 5, no. 1 (2010): 152–9.

Migiel, Marilyn. "Gender Studies and the Italian Renaissance." In *Interpreting the Italian Renaissance: Literary Perspectives*, edited by Antonio Toscano, 29–41. Stony Brook, NY: Forum Italicum, 1991.

– "The Untidy Business of Gender Studies: Or, Why It's Almost Useless to Ask If the *Decameron* Is Feminist." In *Boccaccio and Feminist Criticism*, edited by Thomas C. Stillinger and F. Regina Psaki, 217–33. Chapel Hill, NC: Annali d'Italianistica, 2006.

– "Veronica Franco (1546–1591)." In *Italian Women Writers: A Bio-Bibliographical Source Book*, edited by Rinaldina Russell, 138–44. Westport, CT: Greenwood Press, 1994.

Mirollo, James V. "In Praise of *La bella mano*: Aspects of Late Renaissance Lyricism." *Comparative Literature Studies* 9 (1972): 31–43.

Il nuovo La scrittura e l'interpretazione. Edited by Romano Luperini, Pietro Cataldi, Lidia Marchiani, and Franco Marchese. Palermo: Palumbo, 2011.

The Oregon Petrarch Open Book. https://petrarch.uoregon.edu.

Ovid. *Heroides and Amores*. Translated by Grant Showerman. Cambridge, MA: Harvard University Press, 1963. First published 1921 by Loeb Classical Library.

– *Metamorphoses, Volume 1: Books 1–8*. Translated by Frank Justus Miller. 3rd ed. Revised by G.P. Goold. Cambridge, MA: Harvard University Press, 1984. First published 1977 by Loeb Classical Library.

– *Metamorphoses, Volume 2: Books 9–15*. Translated by Frank Justus Miller. 2rd ed. Revised by G.P. Goold. Cambridge, MA: Harvard University Press, 1984. First published 1977 by Loeb Classical Library.

Petrarca, Francesco. *The Complete Canzoniere*. Translated by A.S. Kline. *Poetry in Translation: A.S. Kline's Open Access Poetry Archive*. http://poetryintranslation.com.

– *Petrarch: The Canzoniere, or Rerum Vulgarium Fragmenta*. Translated by Mark Musa. Bloomington: Indiana University Press, 1999.

– *Petrarch's Lyric Poems: The "Rime sparse" and Other Lyrics*. Translated and edited by Robert M. Durling. Cambridge, MA: Harvard University Press, 1976.

– *Le rime di Francesco Petrarca, s'aggiungono le Considerazioni rivedute e ampliate d'Alessandro Tassoni, le Annotazoni di Girolamo Muzio, e le Osservazioni di Lodovico Antonio Muratori*. Modena: Soliani, 1711.

– *Le rime di Francesco Petrarca di su gli originali*. With commentary by Giosuè Carducci and Severino Ferrari. Florence: Sansoni, 1899.

Phillippy, Patricia. "*Altera Dido*: The Model of Ovid's *Heroides* in the Poems of Gaspara Stampa and Veronica Franco." *Italica* 69 (1992): 1–18.

Poesia italiana: Il Cinquecento. Edited by Giulio Ferroni. Milan: Garzanti, 1978.

Quaintance, Courtney K. "Poems in Terza Rima by Veronica Franco." Encyclopedia.com. https://www.encyclopedia.com.

– *Textual Masculinity and the Exchange of Women in Renaissance Venice*. Toronto: University of Toronto Press, 2015.

– "Women Writers Between Men: Gaspara Stampa and Veronica Franco." In *Textual Masculinity and the Exchange of Women in Renaissance Venice*, 134–68. Toronto: University of Toronto Press, 2015.

Ray, Meredith K. "The Courtesan's Voice: Veronica Franco's *Lettere familiari*." In *Writing Gender in Women's Letter Collections of the Italian Renaissance*, 123–55. Toronto: University of Toronto Press, 2009.

Regn, Gerhard. "Eros and Eschatology: Phantasms of Postmortal Love in Petrarch." In *Love after Death: Concepts of Posthumous Love in Medieval and Early Modern Europe*, edited by Bernhard Jussen and Ramie Targoff, 97–110. Boston: De Gruyter, 2014.

Le rime di Francesco Petrarca, s'aggiungono le Considerazioni rivedute e ampliate d'Alessandro Tassoni, le Annotazoni di Girolamo Muzio, e le Osservazioni di Lodovico Antonio Muratori. Modena: Soliani, 1711.

Rethinking Gaspara Stampa in the Canon of Renaissance Poetry. Edited by Unn Falkeid and Aileen A. Feng. Farnham, UK: Ashgate, 2015.

Robey, David. "Terza rima." In *The Dante Encyclopedia*, edited by Richard Lansing, 808–10. London: Routledge, 2010.

Robin, Diana. "Courtesans, Celebrity, and Print Culture in Renaissance Venice: Tullia d'Aragona, Gaspara Stampa, and Veronica Franco." In *Italian Women and the City: Essays*, edited by Janet Levarie Smarr and Daria Valentini, 35–59. Madison, NJ: Fairleigh Dickinson University Press, 2003.

Rogers, Mary. "Fashioning Identities for Venetian Courtesans." In *Fashioning Identities in Renaissance Art*, edited by Mary Rogers, 91–105. Aldershot, UK: Ashgate, 2000.

Rosenthal, Margaret F. *The Honest Courtesan: Veronica Franco, Citizen and Writer in Sixteenth-Century Venice*. Chicago: University of Chicago Press, 1992.

– "Veronica Franco's *Terze Rime*: The Venetian Courtesan's Defense." *Renaissance Quarterly* 42, no. 2 (1989): 227–57.

Sloan, Wendy. "Veronica Franco." The Mezzo Cammin Women Poets Timeline Project. http://www.mezzocammin.com.

Stampa, Gaspara. *The Complete Poems*. Edited by Troy Tower and Jane Tylus. Translated with an introduction by Jane Tylus. Chicago: University of Chicago Press, 2010.

Stampa, Gaspara, and Veronica Franco. *Rime*. Edited by Abdelkader Salza. Bari: Laterza, 1913.

Sturm-Maddox, Sara. *Petrarch's Laurels*. University Park: Pennsylvania State University Press, 1992.

Targoff, Ramie. *Renaissance Woman: The Life of Vittoria Colonna*. New York: Farrar, Straus & Giroux, 2018.

Tassoni, Alessandro. *Considerazioni sopra le rime del Petrarca d'Alessandro Tassoni*. Modena: Giulian Cassiani, 1611.

Tassoni, Luigi. "*Aequivocatio* e statuto del senso in Dante." *Verbum* 3, no. 1 (2001): 131–41.

Thomas Aquinas. *The Summa Theologiæ of St. Thomas Aquinas*. Translated by Fathers of the English Dominican Province. 2nd rev. ed. 1920. Online edition 2017. www.newadvent.org.

Vellutello, Alessandro. *Il Petrarca con l'espositione d'Alessandro Vellutello*. Venice: Giovanni Antonio Bertano, 1584.

"Veronica Franco: Poems and Letters." In *Veronica Franco Project*, directed by Margaret Rosenthal. https://dornsife.usc.edu.

Wend, Petra. *The Female Voice: Lyrical Expression in the Writings of Five Italian Renaissance Poets*. New York: Peter Lang, 1995.

Wojciehowski, Dolora [now Hannah] Chapelle. "Veronica Franco vs. Maffio Venier: Sex, Death, and Poetry in Cinquecento Venice." *Italica* 83, nos. 3–4 (2006): 367–90.

Zehn italienische Lyrikerinnen der Renaissance / Dieci poetesse italiane del Cinquecento. Edited by Emanuela Scarpa. Tübingen, Germany: Gunter Narr Verlag, 1997.

Zorzi, Alvise. *Cortigiana veneziana: Veronica Franco e i suoi poeti*. Milan: Camunia, 1986.

Index

Works by writers other than Franco are indexed under the writer's name.

www.ingramcontent.com/pod-product-compliance
Lightning Source LLC
Chambersburg PA
CBHW030534310726
48979CB00010B/1899/J

9781487542580